INSIGHT

INSIGHT

Encouraging Aha! Moments for Organizational Success

Nancy K. Napier

 PRAEGER

AN IMPRINT OF ABC-CLIO, LLC
Santa Barbara, California • Denver, Colorado • Oxford, England

Library of Congress Cataloging-in-Publication Data

Napier, Nancy K., 1952–
    Insight : encouraging Aha! moments for organizational success /
    Nancy K. Napier.
        p. cm.
    Includes bibliographical references and index.
    ISBN 978–0–313–36643–7 (hard copy : alk. paper) — ISBN 978–0–313–36644–4
    (ebook)
1. Organizational change. 2. Creative ability. I. Title.
HD58.8.N364   2010
658.3´14—dc22   2010000478

ISBN: 978–0–313–36643–7
EISBN: 978–0–313–36644–4

14 13 12 11 10   1 2 3 4 5

This book is also available on the World Wide Web as an eBook.
Visit www.abc-clio.com for details.

Praeger
An Imprint of ABC-CLIO, LLC

ABC-CLIO, LLC
130 Cremona Drive, P.O. Box 1911
Santa Barbara, California 93116-1911

This book is printed on acid-free paper ∞

Manufactured in the United States of America

To The Gang
For all the mischief you started

Contents

Acknowledgments

Projects like these happen because people graciously give me their time and ideas. More than 100 individuals were kind enough to answer questions and tell stories about their own aha journeys. Thanks especially to several remarkable organizations and their members, who have open doors and open minds: the Ada County Sheriff's Office, Balihoo, Drake Cooper, Healthwise, Microsoft, the Idaho Shakespeare Festival, the Trey McIntyre Project, WhiteCloud Analytics, and the Boise State University football program.

My terrific research assistants, Larissa Lee, Ryan Cooper, and Betsy Venard, helped on various phases of this project, from interviewing to analyzing data and more. Thanks also to Stephanie Chism for her constant questions!

Colleagues in Idaho and beyond helped me sort, spark, and check the many insight flashes I had along the way. In particular, Hildy Ayer, Caroline Blakeslee, Cheryl Larabee, Mark Rivers, Kirk Smith, Sully Taylor, and Angeli Weller each gave me ideas that helped shape this into a better outcome. Throughout this and other projects, Jeff Olson, former editor at Praeger/Greenwood/ABC-CLIO, always seems to know what to say at just the right time. Thanks much, Jeff.

I have been studying creativity and innovation with some extraordinary organizations and people for the past several years. For this project, Bob Lokken and Chris Petersen, in particular, generated some of the key leaps of imagination that moved the project along. Over the years, each time I have talked with them, I sat up straighter, my brain moved in new ways, and only later did I realize the punch of a comment that became a crucial transformation moment. Thanks, gentlemen.

Thanks always to Tony, who has inspired aha moments and more for three decades.

The best insight thinker I know is my father, who should be glad that I am finally "starting to get it."

Nancy Napier
McCall, Idaho
February 2010

Introduction: On the Road to *Aha Moments*

> I was sitting in a chair in the patent office at Bern when *all of a sudden* a thought occurred to me: "If a person falls freely, he will not feel his own weight." *I was startled*. This simple thought made a deep impression on me. This *led me to the theory of gravity*. [Italics added]
> —Albert Einstein, Kyoto Address, 1922[1]

Albert Einstein won the Nobel Prize but missed the award ceremony. He knew he would win it someday, and even promised the $32,000 prize money to his ex-wife.[2] But when the honor came, he was already committed to visit Japan. So in December 1922, he was in Kyoto, not Stockholm. But his talk in Japan may have been better for the rest of us in terms of learning about his aha experience, or as the Germans say, "Aha Erlebnis," that forever changed scientists' understanding of the universe.

The man who changed our views so dramatically and became the equivalent of a rock star was certainly on no top-40 or any other lists in the spring of 1905. According to biographer Walter Isaacson, Einstein had so alienated his university professors that he failed to receive a doctorate, could not get a position at a university, and ended up as a "third-class examiner at the Swiss patent office in Bern."[3] So who would have expected the discovery that was about to burst onto the physics scene?

From the mid-1890s, Einstein had been learning about several bodies of knowledge that triggered his curiosity on the concept of the "invariance" (relativity) of the velocity of light and energy.

He reached a point in 1904 where he could not reconcile two long-held assumptions about "the invariance of the velocity of light" and "the rule of velocities used in mechanics,"[4] and he spent a year trying to resolve the dilemma.

A close friend and colleague of Einstein's, Michele Besso, walked with him in the early Bern mornings on their way to work. Besso had a curly head of dark hair and a bushy beard. As an older man, that bushy beard turned stark white, giving him a look of a filled-out Abraham Lincoln, with his beard hanging along the base of his jaw. I can imagine two European men strolling together, hands behind their backs, eyes on the gravel path before them, tilting forward and backward like waddling ducks. In his Kyoto talk, Einstein recalled that he approached Besso one day with his challenge of reconciling the theories he had studied.

> It was a beautiful day when I visited him with this problem. I [said to Besso] ... "Today I come here to battle against that problem with you." We discussed every aspect of this problem. Then *suddenly* I understood where the key to this problem lay. Next day I came back to him again and said to him, without even saying hello, "Thank you. I've *completely solved the problem*."

Einstein told Besso that the solution lay with an analysis of "time" and its relationship to velocity. As he said triumphantly, "With this new concept, I could resolve *all the difficulties completely* for the first time."[5] He wrote and completed his first paper about the special theory of relativity five weeks later. He published it and three more during his "Miracle Year" of 1905 in the *Annalen der Physik* (Annals of Physics).[6]

Einstein's next creative aha moment, however, took longer. He became dissatisfied with the special theory in 1907 and began thinking of a general theory that would include acceleration and gravity, which led to his ideas of curved space. Again, according to his account in the 1922 speech in Kyoto, Einstein's key breakthrough on this problem came while "sitting on a chair in the patent office in Bern."[7] That flash of insight, helpful as it was, required more development. Einstein said that he could not solve the problem "completely" at that time but needed another eight years to find a "complete solution,"[8] which became the "general theory" of relativity.

Following his development of the general theory, Einstein once again took on another problem, one that would occupy his mind for the next 30 years: developing a so-called "unified theory" that would integrate relativity and quantum theories. Unfortunately, the singular BIG aha moment in that journey never came and physicists have continued to pursue the problem since.[9]

ALIGNMENT OF THE STARS

Harlan Hale looks nothing like Albert Einstein. He could be an assistant store manager at a large grocery chain with his wide and very white-toothed smile and a faint rose-blond buzz haircut. He is intelligent, often witty, and sports a tattoo necklace, with what looks like a large black bat at his throat, wings stretching from mid–collar bone on each side of his shoulders. On one Web site, he wrote:

> I'm very open-minded and enjoy life, even in this environment. I used to enjoy hiking and mountain biking. I like all kinds of music, especially country. I like it 'cause it's positive.[10]

Hale made a name for himself, and changed the course of an organization, on June 18, 2005. That day, two jail deputies escorted Harlan Hale, who was called the most dangerous inmate in a western U.S. county jail with 1,132 inmates, outside for his hour of sunlight. After an hour, the deputies ushered Hale back to his solitary confinement cell. Hale shuffled back, no longer the unpredictable disruptive inmate he had been when arrested in March 2005. In the process of returning to his cell, an "alignment of the stars" happened and Hale escaped.[11]

Ada County, Idaho, is not Los Angeles. The city of Boise feels like a small town despite a population that nudges 200,000 in a county of about 400,000. The growth in population has been nearly 10 percent since 2000, as people migrate from the West Coast on a steady basis to get away from the crowds, pollution, and crime more common in urban parts of California or Washington or Oregon.[12] It is the sort of city where, after a few months, the ladies at Baird's Dry Cleaners see your car and have your clothes at the front desk by the time you enter. People brag about not locking their cars or houses, and then feel affronted if someone breaks in.

Having an inmate escape, particularly one who was known to be dangerous, was a shock, not only to the citizens, but especially to the sheriff's office employees. The jail had almost none of the problems common to others its size, with minimal gang or racial tension, and very few incidents of suicide.[13] Inmates do not usually escape. And certainly, never before had such a violent offender escaped from the county jail.

Hale was first arrested in Boise for several felonies, including attempted murder of a police officer and a wild car chase with police. He had been a long-term methamphetamine user, but was described as "intelligent and cunning" when he was clean. And the day he escaped, he was clean.

A basic rule in jails is that only one door is opened at a time. When an inmate moves from one area to another, a deputy opens one door, the inmate and guards step through, and the deputy closes and locks the first door behind them. Once that happens, they open the next door. In Hale's case, deputies left doors open as the guards moved him from the outer to the inner hallways. As they put Hale into his cell, the deputies also removed leg and belly chains before closing his cell door. The belly chains circle an inmate's midriff, keeping his hands in cuffs in front of him. Those three mistakes meant Hale's legs and arms were free, and his cell door and outer doors were open. He sprinted. Hale ran out of the jail building, broke a hasp on a locked chain link fence gate, climbed over razor wire and onto a roof, leapt into an exercise yard, and climbed over a final fence.

Three days later, he was still on the run. At a press conference on June 21, 2005, the Ada County sheriff took responsibility for the escape and asked the community for help in finding Hale.[14] As the sheriff said later, if any one of the three security breaches had not happened, the escape would never have been possible. But doors, belly chain, and leg restraints were all unlocked.

Over the next ten days, Hale ran up several more felonies on his way to Uinta, Wyoming, where he was taken into custody. When police tried to pull him over, he gave chase, eventually leaving his truck and running on foot. He then stole another pickup truck at gunpoint and fled, before he was caught. Hale is serving a life sentence in Idaho, and spends some time on the Web, seeking out pen pals.

I'm Harlan from San Diego, California. I came up here to Idaho in '01 to get away from the three strikes law in California. Didn't work out so good for me, ha, ha. I ended up getting a life sentence here instead of back home. This place is really awful.[15]

Hale is eligible for parole in 2030.

* * *

Ada County Sheriff Gary Raney in a suit and tie has a likeness to Bill Bradley, the former basketball player and U.S. Senator. Over six feet tall, broad in chest and shoulders, he is solid in body and sharp in mind. Raney teaches periodically at Northwestern University's leadership program in law enforcement. He comes across, not as a lawyer or banker, but more as a senior manager trying to turn a traditional manufacturing firm from being stodgy to solid using best business practices and forward thinking. His face is open, his smile is wide, and you would never know he is a police officer. Indeed, when Raney wears his sheriff's uniform, it seems nearly out of place, like he is stepping from another world.

When the escape happened, Sheriff Raney had been in office barely six months. Such a problem would unnerve any sheriff, but here was Raney just six months into the job, elected when the former sheriff retired after 20 years in office. It was not a great way to start a job.

In the days and months following the escape, people within the Ada County Sheriff's Office replayed the escape every possible way. Beyond frustration with the deputies, people acknowledged that a review of security was in order, an expected outcome from such a shattering experience for a new sheriff.

But months later, when he summed up the period following the escape, Raney said, "it was the worst thing that ever happened in our office . . . , but it was the best thing that happened."

Was it the "best thing that happened"?

The Cancer of Complacency

Most people assumed the escape meant the security system and procedures were at fault and that a good review, and maybe some tweaking, would solve it. After all, for a decade the jail had been well run, with suicides and lawsuits below the national average. But Raney saw the escape as an opportunity, a trigger to slow down and take a more systematic review of the system. He collected and sorted through information about the jail and its security procedures to be sure, but much more. He questioned his direct reports, invited an outside consultant to review the situation, and made his own analysis to find what really mattered. In the process, he experienced an aha moment regarding the organization as a whole. He uncovered a deeper, systemic, and potentially much more dangerous flaw than a security breach. Instead, Raney discovered that the jail, in particular, suffered what he called "the cancer of complacency." And that could prevent the rest of the organization from possible future aha moments and innovative change. As he said,

> You won't have aha moments so long as you are complacent about the way things should be. I think you have aha moments when you recognize the change that needs to come.

The sheriff's office had done a good job over the years, but Raney realized that deeper challenges existed, and ultimately, he saw the escape as a catalyst for change. He used the insight he had gained through looking at the situation in new ways to come up with ideas. He asked his Police Services Director at the time, Major Ron Freeman, to spearhead an effort in the jail to reassess its mission and purpose in a very fundamental way. Freeman asked the jail employees a simple question: "Why do we exist?" Several employees mentioned later that Freeman's initial question forced them to step back and really think about, for the first time, what the purpose of the jail should be. That 18-month-long process eventually led to what Raney and others called a "collective aha" for the nearly 300 employees who worked in the sheriff's office jail. It resulted from Raney's willingness to question what existed and then reshape the way people viewed the problem, from a question of security to something much more profound, with much greater long-lasting implications.

"SNAP YOUR HELMET"

A third example of the aha journey comes from a young student and football player who experienced several flashes of insight—some from good triggers, some from not so good.

"I think his hair is straight up and leaning to the side today," says Vicki Sullivan, the administrative assistant who sits at the front desk of Boise State University's football complex. "You can't miss him—tall guy, tall hair." On the day we met, 6-foot 3-inch George Iloka's hair stood up about 1.5 inches, tilting sideways from his head. His hair may be a trademark, but he is much more interesting for his grit and aha moments. During our interview, he gave several examples of flashes of insight that have led him to a spot where several of his coaches say "he's got it, faster than a lot of other players."

Iloka's case illustrates the key characteristics in a person but also of an organization that supports and encourages aha moments. He experienced his own aha moments, but also his coaches knew how to encourage aha moments in others.

Iloka took an unusual route when he completed and left high school a semester early to join Boise State in January 2008. More surprising was that the Boise State University coaches offered him a scholarship without ever seeing him in a varsity game at Kempner High School (Sugar Land, Texas). In the spring of his junior year, he had just moved to safety, the position he was to play in Boise. He said, after the fact, if the coaches had that much confidence in him, he wanted to be part of the team. He joined Boise State University, despite later offers from better known schools, like Rice University.

But life was not always that easy nor would it be at Boise State. When he was in high school, Iloka wanted to play receiver, since "offense is where the glory is." And as a freshman, he thought he was one of the best candidates to play during his sophomore year. Then he had a shock. The coach called all of the receivers together and turned to one player and said, "You're the best receiver, by far." Iloka could handle the thought that there would always be someone better than he, but he was completely taken aback at the thought that a coach, "somebody with authority," said someone else is not just better than you are but "better by far."

Aha moment #1: Iloka realized that he could take charge of his future. He started "training hard, waking up on my own at five in the morning. I walked to school and lifted weights right when the janitors got in." But he did not make the varsity team in his sophomore year. He had counted on a scholarship to go to college so his family invested in summer football camps, where he hoped college recruiters would notice him. He learned later that no one with serious chances paid to go to the camps; they received scholarships because colleges wanted to pluck them.

So going into his junior year, Iloka started to panic. As he said, "by the end of junior year, you should know if colleges are looking at you. . . . I didn't hear from any colleges . . . I went into desperation mode."

More bad luck came when a new high school coach arrived. Iloka's reaction: "BAM. It can't get any worse, because usually new coaches don't want seniors playing . . . they want to get the young guys playing," since they'll be coaching them for several years. Then more bad news: The coach moved him to safety, a position on the defensive side of the scrimmage line. Iloka admits he first "wanted to get mad," but he kept his mind open. He began progressing, then suddenly, a week after moving to safety in spring training, "colleges started flocking . . . it was just ridiculous." His confidence exploded when Boise State coaches made an offer before he had even played a varsity game as safety. He took it during the spring of his junior year. He finished high school a semester early and moved from warm humid Texas to dry cold Idaho in the middle of winter.

But just because Iloka showed up did not ensure he would play. Starting off on the second string, he did not perform well during summer practice, so the coaches moved him to the third string, with the other freshmen, destined for redshirting.

Aha moment #2: College ball demands a different type of effort than high school. He decided to "give it my all," and a week before the first game, the coaches moved him back to second string. Suddenly, Iloka needed to "catch up" from when he had closed his mind down thinking he was redshirting. He knew that he was not a starter, just second string, but still expected to have a chance to play. But even that did not work out as expected. When the team played a much poorer team and Boise State was "blowing them out, [the coaches] put me in for just the last five minutes . . . I just barely got to play, with a not so good team that we were blowing out . . . what does that mean for the rest of the season?"

Once again, Iloka's motivation and desire to do well led to aha moment #3: time to change his mind-set and "think like a player." His confidence that he *would* play made him think like a player, even when he stood on the sidelines, not knowing if he would have the chance to play. But he assumed he would and was always ready, just in case.

> I felt like . . . you don't snap your helmet assuming you won't play . . . I put my helmet on, snapped it.

The coaches saw something in him and he has played a lot. During his first season, as a freshman, he ended up making news for his repeated pass breakups, interceptions, and tackles. After the season, his coaches pushed him to aha moment #4:

> One coach said, "You aren't a freshman anymore. I want you to become more mature . . . don't crack as many jokes, it's a serious situation. Try to be more vocal and be someone that people . . . could look up to." Now they have different plans for me. I'm a sophomore who wants to stand out and make plays.

And he has stood out in the second season as well.

Iloka says confidence from "opposite directions" was key to his aha moments. In high school, the coach had said one player was better than all of the others, including Iloka. That shattered his confidence in a "negative" way, but helped him reach an aha of understanding that he needed to do something to regain his confidence. Confidence came into play in a positive way when Boise State coaches "believed in him," both when they offered him a chance to join the program and in his freshman year, when his confidence was down and they boosted it by telling him "we think you're ready to go."

Defensive Coordinator Pete Kwiatkowski agrees with Iloka's assessment. He thinks that Iloka "saw the carrot," that he could do well and be a better player than some of the others around him, if he worked at it. As Kwiatkowski said, "I think that was his aha moment, that it was attainable" if he listened to his coaches, became more consistent, and studied what he needed to learn.

Iloka exemplifies characteristics that individuals talk about when they repeatedly experience aha moments. He had enough experience playing (and not playing) football in high school and college to know that he badly wanted to have the chance to play, giving him motivation to improve. As he said, he wanted to "get mad" but kept his mind open to learning and changing. He was humble enough also to realize that he had a lot to learn—about the true reason behind the football camps, about ways to train, and about ways to become a leader. His confidence exploded when he saw that he could learn and improve. Having the experience of multiple aha moments, he now knows his confidence will help him generate more. But Iloka's example also illustrates the importance of the "bigger box," the organization in which he landed. The program and coaches also had the experience, openness, and habit of trying to encourage insight that allowed players to take risks, learn from them, and make those leaps.

COMMON THREADS?

Albert Einstein, Gary Raney, and George Iloka capture much of the traditional and emotional ways we talk about "aha moments": sudden, emotionally powerful, a moment that helps clarify understanding or definition of a vexing issue or problem. For Einstein, it was how to view time, light, and ultimately gravity. Their insight flashes came dramatically, often when they appeared not to be directly pondering their problems. Einstein was at his patent clerk job in Bern, Switzerland, when his sudden thought came as a picture—a person falling. It was a simple idea, obvious to him, once he had it (but apparently not before), and it had clear implications, in terms of propelling him toward development of a "theory of gravitation."

Young football player George Iloka too had dramatic moments he could recall, including where he was, who said something to him, and how he felt. He realized that he was not as good as he had thought and that his future did not lie "in the glory" of the one position he had hoped for. Yet, when he decided to push himself, work hard, and play "his game," that boosted his confidence and those leaps of insight happened.

Sheriff Gary Raney, on the other hand, describes his experience less dramatically, although its impact has been far reaching. His aha journey developed like a collection of mini-aha moments, sort of "a slow door opening" before he realized the obvious security problem was just a symptom, not the more fundamental one of complacency, that was a jolt of recognition when he saw it. Sometimes, such innovative thinking emerges from the accumulation of several smaller aha moments, part of a series of smaller leaps or jumps along the way.[16]

Einstein, Raney, and Iloka all had aha moments that helped them understand something they did not understand beforehand: Einstein understood a new way to view time, Raney realized that the escape was not the core problem, and Iloka discovered how he could influence his own path. Einstein and Raney then also came up with aha moments that generated new ways of looking at problems: Einstein's ability to mesh time with light and Raney's approach to complacency. But all three used similar approaches to reach their moments of insight: They worked hard sifting through information, looking at a situation differently than they had before, and seeing things that others had missed. For them, their common experiences with insight led to positive and long-lasting outcomes, some more abstract and others more practical: understanding the universe, playing a game better than before, and revamping an organization that is responsible for community security. Their journeys took them from gathering and sorting through information to triggers that sparked insight, to validating their new thinking and creating value from their aha experiences.

As Einstein made clear, after his walk with Besso, he had clarity about the problem and that allowed him to write his famous

Miracle Year papers. Raney, once he stepped back from the jail escape, saw with clarity that the challenge facing his organization was deeper and broader than security. Likewise, for Iloka, when he stopped to assess his situation (in high school and college), the clarity of his aha moments were triggers for determining "what to do next." They may not have known what the "next steps" would be, but they clearly understood the problem that needed to be solved. On the other hand, when Einstein's next big aha moment came regarding gravity (i.e., "If a person falls freely, he will not feel his own weight"), he "was startled." The idea made a big impression on him and led him to develop, over the coming eight years, the general theory of gravity.[17] The aha moments for each person seemed universal and perhaps have common themes.

CONNECTING THE DOTS FROM FOOTBALL TO JAILS TO SOFTWARE: WHY THIS BOOK THIS WAY?

After regularly "commuting" to a work site 36 hours away from my home, I completed a nine-year Swedish and USAID funded aid project in Hanoi, Vietnam (from which many aha moment examples have come and will follow). When I finished, I wrote a book about management in transition economies with a colleague and then sought a new research topic that I could do in my own backyard.

By happenstance and then by design, I began working with a cadre of high-performing (measured objectively), highly creative (and recognized by others), diverse organizations that happen to be based in Boise, Idaho, consistently ranked over the past decade among one of the "best cities" in the United States on a variety of measures (e.g., "place to start a business," "quality of life," "cycling," "to be an entrepreneur").[18] To find such creative organizations in America's "most remote city" (five hours by car from the nearest metropolitan area), in a state that has fewer than 2 million people and is geographically slightly smaller than Great Britain, was a surprise. But then—like all good aha moments—"it was so obvious, after the fact."

Indeed, size and place matter, but not the way many people expect. Rather than "big cities" being the major or only magnets for creative people and organizations, I am coming to realize how a strong entrepreneurial spirit can develop, in out-of-the-way, unexpected places. Lacking the resources of larger cities, smaller communities are forced to find their own ways, and as a result they may be more fertile ground for creative ventures and people. This project about encouraging aha moments, and a previous one about creativity and innovation in organizations, draws some of its ideas from a diverse group of smaller organizations that have consistently sparked creativity and aha moments. That the organizational leaders so enthusiastically interact with and learn from one another across discipline lines has been part of the unexpected joy of working with them.

The community and the organizations are in a sense "test tubes" for what does or could happen elsewhere. In a community that is relatively small, those leaders see how "connecting the dots" among organizations can help build a stronger whole, a community that boldly makes its own future.

The original "Gang of Four" organizations were cases that a colleague and I studied for a previous book on organizational creativity.[19] They included for-profit and nonprofit organizations, such as software engineering, theater, education/sports, and a provider of medical information. The group included the Idaho Shakespeare Festival, which has been the focus of a Yale Drama School case study; ProClarity, a global business intelligence analytics firm that built such a successful business and market share that Microsoft bought it in 2006; the Boise State University football program, which has been consistently ranked in the top 25 U.S. programs, despite its often much lower level of financial resources than competitor schools; and Healthwise, a health information provider that has led the industry in helping people take responsibility for their own health decisions and was one of the 15 *Wall Street Journal* small enterprises of the year in 2007.

The Gang continues to grow as I find more organizations that meet the criteria of being high performers, highly creative, and Idaho based. The Gang now includes even more diverse organizations: law enforcement, dance, and marketing/advertising. The Ada County sheriff teaches in Northwestern University's leadership program, and his organization is developing new approaches to problems like inmate housing. The Trey McIntyre Project is a full-time dance company that settled far outside the normal dance hot spots, yet still spends half the year touring worldwide and receives rave reviews in such publications as *The Washington Post* and *The New York Times.* Drake Cooper, winner of regional and national advertising awards, has built a powerhouse of creative output for a range of clients. Finally, a founder of ProClarity has started a new company—WhiteCloud Analytics—which brings

The Gang to eight. Each of these organizations epitomizes qualities of outstanding creative organizations: never-ending curiosity, openness about examining their successes and mistakes, relentless attention to building and preserving strong cultures, and a disciplined approach to creativity and innovation. Encouraging aha moments is part of that process.

To have access to such acknowledged highly creative high performing organizations and to bring them together to learn from one another has been magical. The chance for coaches, dancers, law enforcement managers, engineers, and actors to interact has been valuable for me as a researcher, but also for them, as participants. Many books focus on a specific industry sector or on business organizations generally; this one looks across disciplines and sectors for similarities and lessons that are useful beyond a single one. Hence, many of the examples in this book will draw upon these remarkable organizations and what they can teach us.

As Mikael Nilsson and I did in the last book on creativity, this project also sought to understand whether similar patterns hold in the ways that successful organizations and individuals approach the aha journey—would people from different organizations and backgrounds have similar experiences? What could we learn from them and what could they learn from each other? In addition to lessons from The Gang, of course, many others came from individuals and other organizations outside of the Boise community. That breadth of industry sectors and diversity of people I interviewed are two of the reasons the ideas in this book make sense. They have been generated and tested across a wide range of skeptics.[20]

In sum, while many examples from fields like medicine, the military, and sports are sprinkled throughout, quite a few examples draw upon the interviews of The Gang because their stories illustrate the universal experiences of insight thinking.

BOOK LAYOUT

The book follows the structure of a trip, or "aha journey." Chapter 1 offers an overview and lays out the key phases of the journey. Chapters 2 and 3 provide the initial lay of the land—identifying problems and sorting through information. Chapters 4-8 offer tools to help spark aha moments and nudge the process along, including "stepping aside" or taking a break from the journey, the rest or pause before the flash insight. Each of these chapters also includes some "tips" on how to practice the various techniques to help encourage aha moments.

Chapter 9 focuses on the flash or snap or "aha moment" itself, particularly in terms of what is happening in our brains. Chapter 10 moves the aha experience to the "check it" phase, in which we seek to test out what we have understood or solved to see if it works beyond a single case. Chapter 11 talks about how to make aha moments standard operating procedure for individuals and organizations—what characteristics are useful for both to make the aha experience more embedded and part of normal routine. The book closes with Chapter 12, a summary of key points and implications of the aha experience.

NOTES

1. In December 1922, Albert Einstein gave a talk at Kyoto University, without notes, to students and faculty. He spoke in German; translation during the talk was done by a Japanese colleague and former student, J. Ishiwara, who published his notes in Japanese in 1923. In 1982, a translation to English from Japanese was published. This quotation and the opening comments about Einstein's insight come from the publication of the talk that Einstein gave. See Albert Einstein. 1982. How I created the Theory of Relativity, translated by Yoshimasa A. Ono, *Physics Today*, 35 (8): 45–47. This quote comes from page 47.

2. Denis Brian. 1996. *Einstein: A Life*. New York City: John Wiley & Sons, Inc.: 146.

3. Walter Isaacson. 2007. *Einstein*. New York: Simon & Schuster. Much of this section comes from Isaacson's book, as well as the Kyoto talk.

4. Yoshimasa A. Ono. 1982. How I created the Theory of Relativity, *Physics Today*, 35 (8): 46.

5. Yoshimasa A. Ono. 1982. How I created the Theory of Relativity, *Physics Today*, 35 (8): 46.

6. Albert Einstein. 1905. On a heuristic point of view concerning the production and transformation of light, *Annalen der Physik*, 17: 132–148; Albert Einstein. 1905. On the movement of small particles suspended in stationary liquids required by the molecular-kinetic theory of heat, *Annalen der Physik*, 17: 549–560; Albert Einstein. 1905. Does the inertia of a body depend upon its energy content?, *Annalen der Physik*, 18: 639–641; and Albert Einstein. 1905. On the electrodynamics of moving bodies, *Annalen der Physik*, 17: 891–921.

7. Yoshimasa A. Ono. 1982. How I created the Theory of Relativity, *Physics Today*, 35 (8): 47.

8. Albert Einstein. 1916. The foundation of the general theory of relativity, *Annalen der Physik*, 49: 769–822.

9. Brian Greene. 2003. *The Elegant Universe: Superstrings, Hidden Dimensions, and the Quest for the Ultimate Theory*. New York City: W. W. Norton & Company.

"For three decades, Einstein sought a unified theory of physics, one that would interweave all of nature's forces and material constituents within a single theoretical tapestry. He failed. Now, at the dawn of the new millennium, proponents of string theory claim that the threads of this elusive unified tapestry finally have been revealed." (pp. 4–5)

"Intense research over the past decade by physicists and mathematicians around the world has revealed that this new approach to describing matter at its most fundamental level resolves the tension between general relativity and quantum mechanics. In fact, superstring theory shows more: Within this new framework, general relativity and quantum mechanics *require one another* for the theory to make sense. According to superstring theory, the marriage of the laws of the large and the small is not only happy but inevitable." (p. 4)

10. From the Web site Writeaprisoner.com—Harlan Hale's profile.

11. Term coined by Sheriff Gary Raney, in his article about the turnaround of the jail, triggered by the escape. See Gary Raney and Jeffrey A. Schwartz. 2008. "Turnaround" in a good jail, *American Jails*, 21 (6): 61–65.

12. U.S. Census Bureau. 2009. State & County QuickFacts (http://quickfacts.census.gov/gfd/states/16/1608830.html); Boise Idaho Real Estate. 2009. Boise Population Growth (http://www.boiserealestateplus.com/boise-population-growth-2-23-2009).

13. Gary Raney and Jeffrey A. Schwartz. 2008. "Turnaround" in a good jail, *American Jails*, 21 (6): 61–65.

14. Gary Raney. 2005. Information release: Recap of today's press conference, June 20 (http://www.adasheriff.org/Press/2005/062005HaleUpdate.pdf, last accessed on July 27, 2009).

15. From the Web site Writeaprisoner.com—Harlan Hale's profile.

16. Scott Berkun. 2007. *The Myths of Innovation*. Sebastopol, CA: O'Reilly.

17. See Albert Einstein. 1982. How I created the Theory of Relativity, translated by Yoshimasa A. Ono, *Physics Today* (August): 45–47. This quote comes from page 47.

18. Examples: #2 Best place to live, *U.S. News*, 2009; #19 Best place to live and launch (a new business), CNNMoney.com, 2008; #4 Best City to Live, Work and Play: *Kiplinger Personal Finance*, May 2008; #7 Best Minor Pro-Sports Market, *Street and Smith's Sports Business Journal*, August 2007; #3 Best Place for Business and Careers, *Forbes*, April 2007; #6 Best City for Environmental Quality, Earth Day Network, February 2007; #10 out of 400: Bert Sperling and Peter J. Sander. 2007. *Cites Ranked and Rated*. Hoboken, NJ: Wiley; Best City for Mid-Level Professionals, Kiplinger.com, May 2007; #8 Best place to live, CNNMoney, 2006; #1 Best Place to Live and Play, *National Geographic Adventure*, 2006; #7 Best Place for Business, *Forbes*, 2004; #8 Best Place to Live, *Money Magazine*, July 2006.

19. Nancy K. Napier and Mikael Nilsson. 2008. *The Creative Discipline: Mastering the Art and Science of Innovation*. Westport, CT: Greenwood Press.

20. The 1–1.5 hour long semistructured interviews were mostly recorded, and often another interviewer joined me. We analyzed the interviews using a content analysis software program in addition to three interviewers' assessments of themes and concepts.

Chapter 1

Insight: The Universal Experience

> While pondering this dilemma ... I had an "aha" insight, one of those *emotional* powerful moments when suddenly what was a tangle of *confusion becomes clear* and *understood*. All I did was ask what would happen if .... [Italics added]
> —Jeff Hawkins, *On Intelligence*[1]

> The *instant* I saw the picture my mouth fell open and *my pulse began to race.* [Italics added]
> —James Watson, *The Double Helix*[2]

The aha moment appears to be a universal human experience, although we express it differently. Germans will say, "oh, you mean AH-ha experiences." Then they will claim that the whole idea of "AH-ha Erlebnisse" (AH-ha experiences) comes from Germany, not from the United States.[3] Indians will nod their heads sideways, ears leaning toward their shoulders, like they are athletes stretching their necks, and say, "OH-ho" as they realize what I'm saying. And in Vietnam, people sit back and say, "*AHH! Day Roi!*" (AHH, "Got it!") to describe *Giay Phut Xuat Than,* the "lightning moment."

Think of a memorable lightning moment. Perhaps you were trying to understand something complex or find a solution to a problem. Or you were looking for a new idea or innovative way to manage. You gathered information, drew on whatever experience and knowledge you had, and tried to think logically. You looked at the problem from many different angles. You found a possible solution, checked it out but it didn't work; you tried other approaches, but nothing seemed quite right. You nearly gave up. Then, when you least expected it, BOOM. Things clicked. You experienced the sudden, complete clarity common to the aha experience.

English speakers use similar ways to talk about aha moments or the insight that comes suddenly. We say, "he connected the dots," "the pieces just fell into place," "she finally saw the big picture," or "he gets it." Some professions have their own lingo. A former air traffic controller turned professional air photographer says in the aviation world controllers talk of "getting the flick," or getting the whole sense of what is going on around them.

Others use analogies to describe the feeling. Chad Sarmento, jail sergeant, thinks of the insight flash as finding clear vision with new glasses:

> You've been trying to read a book with glasses that aren't right and it's all blurry and eventually gives you a headache. So now you get a nice pair of glasses you say, Yes! Now I can get something done.

Then there's the feeling right after the flash, once a person "gets it," that (now) the whole solution seems so obvious.

> Sometimes, I'll wake up in the middle of the night and [think] "oh, THIS is how that fits." And it's completely logical, and [I wonder] why ... didn't I see that before? It's so obvious, why didn't I see that?
>   Jaimie Barker, crime scene investigator

As Hawkins and Watson reported, the aha experience for most of us tends to be "one of those *emotional* powerful moments when suddenly what was a tangle of *confusion becomes clear ...* " (Hawkins) and we feel "a racing pulse" (Watson). That sense of excitement and thrill, and sometimes relief, comes with the territory and affects many of our senses, even in those people whose senses may be harder to stimulate.

On March 3, 1887, Annie Sullivan met seven-year-old Helen Keller. She became Keller's teacher and companion for 49 years, until Sullivan's death.[4] When they first met, Sullivan spelled out, in Helen's hand, the words for "doll" (a gift she had brought) and "cake." Keller did not seem to grasp it. Many years later, though, Keller recalled that one month later, on April 5, 1887, Sullivan helped create an aha moment that affected Keller's remarkable life story:

We walked down the path to the well-house, attracted by the fragrance of the honey-suckle with which it was covered. Someone was drawing water and my teacher placed my hand under the spout. As the cool stream gushed over one hand, she spelled into the other the word "water," first slowly, then rapidly. I stood still, my whole attention fixed upon the motions of her fingers. *Suddenly* I felt a misty consciousness as of something forgotten, a thrill of returning thought, and somehow the mystery of language was revealed to me.[5]

Within the following hour, Keller learned how to spell 30 words and continually pestered Sullivan to teach her more. Keller eventually graduated from Radcliffe and became a well-regarded speaker and activist for causes ranging from politics to people with disabilities.

The power of insight: Previously unconnected pieces of a puzzle or problem suddenly fall into place. Ideas fuse together in unexpected ways that make sense, once they do. And that feeling—relief, exhilaration, and euphoria. Oh, if it were only that easy.

WHY AHA MOMENTS NOW?

You can't use the same thinking to solve a problem that you used to get into it.

—Attributed to Albert Einstein

Ask managers at just about any level in any organization, from software firms to grocery chains, how they spend their time. Most will say, "solving problems," messy ones that some people call "wicked." John Camillus, in the *Harvard Business Review,* points to the lack of approaches for helping managers solve such wicked problems. In fact, CEOs find they face issues "that cannot be resolved merely by gathering additional data, defining issues more clearly, or breaking them down into smaller problems. . . . "[6]

Messy problems may have no clear precedent, cause, or right answer. They demand, as Einstein said, different ways of thinking from that which got us into these messes. That means finding creative and new solutions for organizations and countries. If they are what we are more likely to face, as seems probable when we look at events in the past few years, then we need new and better ways of understanding and solving problems. Managers eventually admit, after prodding, that they often draw upon "gut feel," not only analytical approaches, for decision making.[7] Several management experts have also called for multiple ways to view problems, beyond straight analytical approaches.[8]

Ultimately, we need some balance of logic and insight to improve and speed up decision making and action. With analytical thinking alone, we may not achieve the synthesis of information and recognition of patterns that are critical to resolve messy problems. With insight thinking alone, we may miss some key points that would emerge during logical evaluation. So with both logic and insight, the chance for better decisions should be greater. Finally, if we can make insight thinking a habit or a way of thinking as a matter of course, can we perhaps speed up the process of learning and understanding or solving messy problems?

Historically, insight was generally accepted as part of the journey of significant advances in knowledge. Mathematician Henri Poincaré talked of "characteristics of conciseness, suddenness and immediate certainty"[9] when he experienced insight thinking. Alfred Russel Wallace, Charles Darwin's closest competitor in the 20-year "race" to understand evolution, walked as he thought about evolution and noted that he "experienced joy . . . almost equal to those raptures which I afterwards felt at every capture of new butterflies on the Amazon."[10] From Copernicus to Apple's Steve Jobs, individuals have followed a journey to achieve aha moments that have had impact.[11] So what do we know about insight thinking, then?

WHAT WE TALK ABOUT WHEN WE TALK ABOUT AHA MOMENTS

Raymond Carver's well-known short story "What We Talk about When We Talk about Love"[12] takes place over a kitchen table during an increasingly woozy evening as two couples pass a gin bottle and try to define "love." It becomes clear to us, even as their minds and words become slurred, that each person defines and experiences "love" in dramatically different ways, because they feel they have experienced it. In the end, they really cannot articulate what they mean by "love." For many people, the aha experience is similar—it is unclear, it is hard to articulate, and like love, it "just happens." And like Carver's characters, we think we know all about it because aha experiences are universal.

When I tell people I'm studying ways to encourage aha moments, most are unfailingly polite and do not voice what they are very likely thinking:

I have those moments all the time. But what a weird topic to write about. Aha moments just happen all of a sudden, when the pieces to a puzzle fall into place. They come from out of the blue, when I'm not thinking about my problem. Since they're not logical, I can't control them, and certainly can't force them. So what could you talk about when you talk about aha moments?

When pressed, they try to articulate what they think and boil it down to several assumptions. In essence, aha moments:

1. come out of nowhere.
2. are single moments, sudden flashes of insight.
3. generate complete clarity.
4. are unpredictable, so I cannot encourage them.
5. are personal, so I cannot help encourage them in anyone else.
6. are isolated events, independent of place, since they "just happen."

This book will argue that each of those assumptions is misleading or outright wrong. We will look at each in turn here, and in more depth in future chapters.

Aha Moments Come Out of Nowhere

Many of us experience aha moments that seem to come from "out of the blue"—while walking with a friend or sitting in a chair in the office, or quite often while in the shower. But, in fact, those moments come after much work.[13] We may not think of it as work, but we have to put in time and effort for aha moments to happen "spontaneously."

Flashes of insight may feel like they come from nowhere, but, in fact, they do not happen without preparation and knowledge or information related to what we are trying to resolve or learn. According to Graham Wallas, one of the earliest scientists to try and understand insight, four stages are necessary for insight to occur and be useful: preparation, incubation, illumination, and verification.

Preparation involves gathering information and sorting through it, trying to make sense of the information and the problem in as many ways as we can.[14] Next comes a period of incubation or simmering. New information percolates, the problem festers, but eventually we need to step away from it. We take a break, change activities, and do not "consciously think about" the problem. Often this is when "everything falls into place," and a "snap" comes from what we think is "nowhere." In the past decade, neuroscientists have found that neurons continue to make connections in the brain, or "unseen mind," even as we move away from directly thinking about a problem.[15] This state of being relaxed, whether talking to someone else, walking, or playing music, has benefits. So, we are more open to unexpected encounters, observations, or events that may trigger connections and flashes that "seem" to come from nowhere but do not.

Aha Moments Are Single Moments, Sudden Flashes of Insight

We normally think about aha moments as a "flash of insight," a "click," or "BOOM" when the right "dots connect." One former Microsoft executive calls it "juice," the buzz that comes with innovation, while still others talk of strategic intuition, elements that combine in a flash of insight to direct a person in what to do next, usually involving knowledge from the past to generate steps for the future.[16] Often these tend to be the "big" moments, a sense of major accomplishment.

But some people report smaller "snaps" and seem almost embarrassed not to have experienced a huge insight flash that changes the direction of their organization or the world. For this project, I interviewed over 100 people, from different genders, jobs, ages, and countries. I talked to senior managers and students, nurses and entrepreneurs, dancers and detectives, and people from 18 to over 80 years old. About 40 percent talked about the insight experience not as a single big "flash" but as several smaller aha moments that built up to a clear resolution or understanding. They made comments like "it was lots of mini-aha moments that finally gelled," or "it was a slow door opening" with smaller jumps along the way. In all cases, though, they realized that their willingness to be open and cognizant of what happened to them made many of their experiences memorable.

Alain de Botton, in his book *The Art of Travel*, characterizes the traveling mind-set as being receptive to new places, approaching them with humility and no rigid ideas or expectations about what will come.[17] That is one reason the "aha journey" may be a better description than a single aha "moment." Certainly people experience a flash of insight, but it comes after much work, time, and effort—in learning, sorting information, and thinking or wrestling with a problem. Then, once the aha moment happens, it becomes a catalyst for more work to be fully realized and valuable.

Aha Moments Generate Complete Clarity

Insight is commonly defined as sudden, complete clarity in understanding or in solving a problem. While clarity is a critical feature, some people describe it as happening in stages, which ties back to the notion of several mini-aha moments that build into a bigger one. One entrepreneur likens the experience to the development of a photograph, in the days when film, not digital photos, dominated. When he wrestles with a problem, he goes through a period of great fuzziness, uncertain how to make sense of incoming information. At that stage, his "photo" is grey and black and white, with no clear edges or defined shapes. But slowly the "photo in his mind" becomes sharper, gaining clearer edges and tones of blacks and white; this is the stage when he is beginning to see patterns and connections of pieces within the photo. Still further into the process, after he has experienced an aha moment or two or twenty, the "photo in his mind" is even clearer. During this stage he is able to put clarity to the problem or solution, he sees more implications, and thus the "photo" becomes more defined, has color, and shows clear images. So for him, and others, clarity happens in mini-insight flashes and then builds to completeness as the process continues.

The questions raised about these three assumptions—that aha moments come out of nowhere, are "single moments," and bring total clarity—suggest that insight thinking is an experience, which may vary across people, but which ultimately does lead to clearer understanding or problem solving. The next three assumptions relate more to the idea of encouraging aha moments.

Aha Moments Are Unpredictable, so I Cannot Encourage Them

Aha experiences feel like they come from nowhere, when we least expect them. As a result, most people assume they are unpredictable. Yet, neuroscience research and anecdotal comments suggest that, indeed, we may be able to nudge them. And as we learn more from research on the brain, we should be better able to speed up the process, perhaps even increasing our ability to generate insight "on demand."

Our brain's hemispheres play different roles in problem solving, with the "left side" using more analytical or linear approaches to problem solving. This means we seek more readily accessible solutions, called "strong associations," drawing from solutions or ideas that we have used before or found helpful in solving a similar problem. But when this approach fails, our brains shift to more "right side" thinking, which looks for what neuroscientists call "weak associations," or less familiar or commonly used ideas and solutions. A flash or click appears as a culmination of our brains connecting less familiar ideas or associations. Since the nonlinear thinking is more apt to lead to aha moments, the sooner and more effectively we can employ "right side thinking," the more likely we will be to experience insight.

Part of the preparation and work to generate insight includes several phases and techniques to nudge our thinking in directions that we might not normally pursue. Given the brain's natural tendency to seek familiar ideas or strong associations in problem solving, one of the goals of this book is to offer ways to encourage us to reach for weaker associations and use more insight thinking tools that shift us from strictly logical, linear approaches.

We typically use insight thinking less frequently because it is less comfortable for most of us. As a result, it's easy to be out of practice or simply unfamiliar with how to spur such thinking. Perhaps the more we can understand (logically) and use techniques to encourage insight thinking, the easier it will be to create "muscle memory" for aha or nonlinear insight thinking. That, then, may improve our chances for making leaps of understanding and problem solving.

Finally, creating the aha experience may be partly a numbers game of making corrections. Our brains have 100 billion neurons. As we struggle with a problem or learn a new field or skill, neurons make new connections, although the "right ones" may not always connect as quickly as we would like. But the more practice we have at finding new connections and pathways, the greater the possibility of generating connections may improve.

Aha Moments Are Personal, so I Cannot Help Encourage Them in Anyone Else

Most writing and research about insight thinking focuses on how a single individual experiences aha moments, emotionally and physiologically. But during interviews for this book, I soon heard talk about "generating aha experiences in others" in all directions. Many of us help peers experience aha moments. But also common are "downward" aha moments, when a manager or coach helps someone less experienced reach a flash of insight by suggesting another way to look at a problem or an additional piece of information that "makes all the difference." "Upward" aha moments happen when someone in a position that is lower in the organization or with presumably less experience makes just the right contribution at the right time to help a superior "get it." Finally, several people mentioned the notion of a "collective aha experience," when a group of people reaches an aha moment—perhaps not all at the same exact moment, although that happens periodically, but over the course of time. So, it does appear that we can nudge others to help generate aha moments.

Aha Moments Are Isolated Events, Independent of Place, Since They "Just Happen"

If an aha moment happens in the desert, does it count?

Insight thinking helps us reach understanding of a knotty concept or find a creative solution for a messy problem. But if we are in organizations that do not support a creative culture, will they matter, let alone happen? In other words, if we operate in an organizational desert, with no nurturing or support for the dangerous and risky process of coming up with creative insights, will they be valuable?

A number of interviewees commented that they were able to be creative and experience aha moments because their organizations' cultures allowed and encouraged them. The organization valued the process and the outcome of insight thinking. But the organization is only part of the equation—individuals need certain characteristics as well. Five common attributes emerged for both individuals and organization. First, the individual and an organization (through the collection of people working for it) need "enough" experience to appreciate the need for or acknowledgement of insight, when it happens. Next, motivation is critical—as one manager said, "you have to answer the 'what's in it for me?' question." Why would people be interested in using insight in trying to learn or solve a problem? Openness on the part of individuals and organizations' cultures supports risk taking, a key element of insight because it means looking at an issue in ways that one has not done before. Individuals need confidence, instilled by the organization, that they will be able to solve or learn and, in the process, experience aha moments. This type of confidence seems to build rapidly: Once people experience the euphoria of an aha moment more than once, they come to think it is possible to have the experience again. By learning techniques to enhance insight thinking, the chance for aha moments jumps. Finally, once these characteristics become embedded and easily called up, insight thinking can become habit.

BAD NEWS, GOOD NEWS

By challenging the assumptions about what we think we know about aha moments, we come to very different types of assumptions:

- Aha moments do not come out of nowhere, but rather out of hard work and effort spent trying to learn a new concept or wrestling with a problem.
- Aha moments are not only single moments, sudden flashes of insight, but may be a series of smaller "clicks" that build upon one another. Also, as they happen, more work is necessary to create value from aha moments.
- A single aha moment may not generate complete clarity about a problem, but adds to prior ones, building toward full and complete clarity over time.
- Aha moments may be unpredictable in the exact time they arrive, but they can be encouraged through different ways and techniques of thinking.
- Aha moments are not only for us as individuals, but can be encouraged in others—up, down, sideways, and even in groups.
- Aha moments are more likely to happen in environments—organizational and individual—that have common characteristics—experience, motivation, openness, confidence, and habit.

Those new assumptions mean bad news and good news for both individuals and the organizations they work in. Bad news first: If insight flashes do *not* just happen, that puts some of the responsibility for having them onto us. We cannot just wait, hope, and wish for them to come. Instead, high-quality aha journeys appear to take work, need time, and force thinking in ways that do not come naturally to many of us. Also, when an aha moment happens, even more work has to take place to make use of it. The last piece of bad news is that if organizations are serious about sparking aha moments, creativity, and innovation, then the environment and culture become critical, and building a supportive culture takes effort as well.

But with the bad comes good news: If insight does not "just happen," then perhaps we can learn techniques to encourage it, just as we can with creativity in organizations. Neither creativity nor innovation "just happens," and much research suggests that organizations that have various types of discipline can encourage them. So, if we learn to encourage insight, could we then speed up the process of learning and understanding or problem solving?[18]

Some research suggests that the networks that connect neurons in our brains can be "trained," so to speak, to be more or less efficient. Utrecht University (The Netherlands) medical researcher Martijn van den Heuvel says that the number of connections among neurons is less important than the *efficiency* with which networks can send information from one region of the brain to another. Further, he claims that the "speed" of information transfer among network regions helps explain intelligence. So if we can learn to speed information transfer, and perhaps the frequency and predictability of aha moments, perhaps we can speed learning and problem solving as well. Finally, if we can indeed encourage aha moments in other people, could we perhaps make members of organizations more successful at generating new ways of thinking in the longer term?

TWO TYPES OF AHAS

When I first started interviewing people about insight and aha moments, I used the phrase "to get it" to explain what I meant. And people did "get it." But early on, one person asked if I meant "getting it" by understanding something or "getting it" by coming up with a creative approach or way of thinking about something. It became clear that two types of "aha moments" are common.

Interestingly, the two types of aha experiences—understanding and creative—follow similar paths but sometimes have different levels of emphasis on how to reach the aha moment. When we try to learn or understand (e.g., a new language, organization politics, or how to play the guitar), we may not need as many techniques to spark flashes of insight. When we face a tough problem, though, we may need to use several different approaches to spark insight. Either way, the general stages in the process seem to be common. But before we come to the aha journey phases, let's explore the two types of aha experiences.

The Understanding Aha—I Get It!

The initial idea for this book came when Chris Petersen, head football coach at Boise State University, made what seemed like an offhand comment several years ago:

> We get football players for four years, on average. And it takes some of them two or two and a half years to "get it." Just imagine how much better it would be for the players and the coaches if we could speed that process up to help them "get it," understand the system, how they fit in it, what they're doing at the university. . . .

This "understanding aha" experience is common for most of us. We suddenly feel we have understood something that had eluded us. Think about learning to read—the thrill of recognizing a new cluster of letters or sounding out a word that previously made no sense. Or remember the feeling of a solid golf swing or moving from just plucking strings to "playing" the guitar. When we fit together existing pieces, we understand the "whole," and the task "makes sense." When graduate student Brent Quam and his team discovered through a consulting project with founders and owners of several start-up firms (1–2 years old) and small companies (3–5 years old) that the firms were *not* separate groups, but rather firms on the same trajectory, it seemed obvious after the fact (as insight experiences do). The students realized that start-up founders do not think of themselves as future "small business owners," even though they will be if they remain viable long enough. This revelation meant that the students—and the firms—could predict what sort of problems start-up firm managers would likely face as they moved to the stage of being "small business owners."

Likewise, when a teenager "gets it" that the world does not revolve around her, when a hard-driving baby boomer understands that work is not all there is to life, when the parent of a child who dies early accepts that accidents "happen," these are aha moments where people are likely to say, "I get it now," "it makes sense," and "why didn't I see that before?" And it can happen to 80-year-olds as well as 20-somethings. This type of comprehension aha occurs when we *understand something that others before us already do*—rather than creating new information, we take existing knowledge and put it together in a way that helps us see "a bigger picture."

Even "old dogs" can experience ahas of understanding. After 24 years in the U.S. Senate, George McGovern retired in 1981, lectured worldwide, made money, and pursued a longtime dream. He purchased a well-run 43-year-old business venture, The Stratford Inn—a hotel, restaurant, and conference facility in Connecticut. Three years later, it was bankrupt.[19]

In editorial opinion page pieces a decade later, McGovern revealed his own aha moment. He realized long after he left the Senate that many policies and laws he supported were partly to blame for his failure as a businessman. Many "federal, state, and local rules that were passed with the objective of helping employees, protecting the environment, raising tax dollars for schools, protecting our customers from fire hazard" were red-tape requirements detrimental to small business firms. As he said,

> I wish that during the years I was in public office, I had had this firsthand experience about the difficulties business people face every day. That knowledge would have made me a better U.S. senator and a more understanding presidential contender.

This was an aha of understanding: McGovern had realized something that others had known, but he had not.

Such "aha moments of understanding" are quite common, such as when a teenager realizes the differences between rights and privileges, when a young manager understands that her authoritative style may not work with professional employees, or when newspaper publishers understand the dramatic impact of declining readership among people under 40. Essentially, this type of insight flash happens when someone or members of an organization have all the information they need and suddenly "see" or understand it fully for the first time.

The Creative Aha—Eureka![20]

A second type of insight flash is the "creative aha moment." In this type of aha moment, people look at an existing body of knowledge and try to understand what is missing, or what information could be rearranged, or how the information might be viewed from a very different perspective, or what could be done within serious constraints. Putting together new or previously unconnected information often generates new products or services and ways of thinking or solving problems. Less frequent than the aha moment of understanding, this creative aha moment will likely be increasingly important as our problems become messier.

Numerous examples of creative aha experiences exist in history as well as among some of the people I interviewed. Historical examples include Archimedes realizing the relationship between volume and weight (Eureka!) in a new way. Copernicus shattered the prevailing view of the relationship between the earth and sun (that the earth revolves around the sun), not by creating new information but by reshuffling existing information to explain discrepancies in observations.

Entrepreneurs are classic pursuers of creative aha moments. They "see" an opportunity in the marketplace that others do not, they put odd pieces of information together to form something that others have never conceived, and they look at the same information in different ways than most of us. They use constraints—being small, unknown, with limited resources—as a nudge to chase alternative ideas.

As Steve Jobs mentioned in his commencement speech at Stanford University in 2005,[21] three unconnected experiences influenced the direction of his life. First, he dropped out of college but took a class in calligraphy the next semester, "because [he] was interested." By later integrating two odd "dots"—principles of calligraphy (i.e., the pictographs and icons) and computers, he created the icons that have driven the computer industry's user interface approach for almost three decades. Second, he was publicly fired from Apple, the company he had founded. But that allowed him freedom from any constraints so he could pursue his next (NeXt) venture. And finally, he was diagnosed with pancreatic cancer, one of the most serious types, which jolted him to focus on what most mattered to him. His subsequent winners—the iPod, iPhone, and more—were creative ahas that have had major impact in the consumer products and technology world.

Jobs and others who have had a creative aha moment found new information or put existing information together in ways that others have not. It goes beyond understanding a concept that others already do, to creating something—product, service, process—of value. So how do we achieve either type of aha moment?

THE AHA EXPERIENCE AS A JOURNEY

Both types of aha experience—understanding and creative—seem to use a similar path to reach a moment of insight. People often describe their aha experiences as a journey or process with several stages. Many see it graphically, like an S curve. They struggle at the beginning of the journey to understand or to solve a problem, with little progress. Eventually they experience the sudden burst of clarity that is an aha moment, but the journey still continues while they find ways to create value from the experience. Figure 1-1 shows the simple insight S curve, with the sharp upward slope and the point where a flash of insight—"Aha!"—occurs.

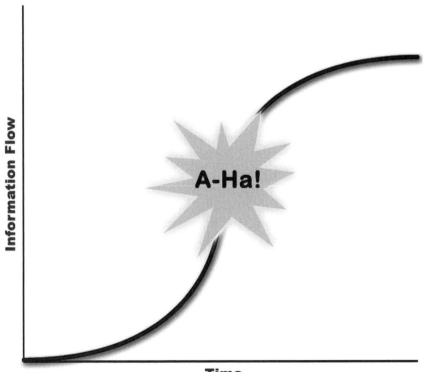

FIGURE 1-1   The Insight S Curve

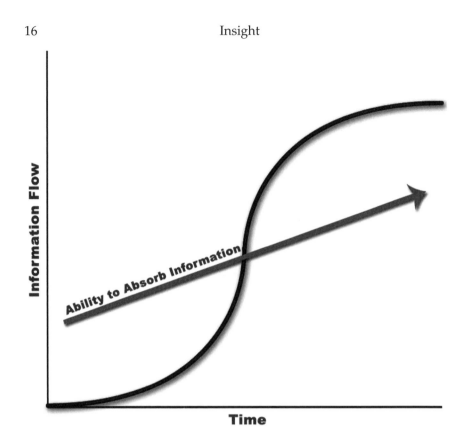

FIGURE 1-2 Information Absorption

But the insight curve happens in relation to information that we absorb (or try to) during the process where we are trying to learn a new skill (e.g., language, dance step, functional area in business).

The straight line in Figure 1-2 represents our rate of information absorption. Early in the aha journey, at the bottom of the curve, we receive overwhelming amounts of information and can make little sense of it. But some people absorb information and process it more quickly than others, moving them more quickly up the insight curve toward an aha moment. Figure 1-2 shows the insight and information curves, as well as their intersection, which is the area (or range) where we achieve insight.

With the flood of information, we go through a period of much confusion. We try and fail to make sense of the information pouring in before we finally reach an aha moment. Once we reach an insight flash, the "puzzle pieces" fall into place and we integrate the information; then we use that experience as a catalyst to think or act differently. We seek value from it by applying the synergy

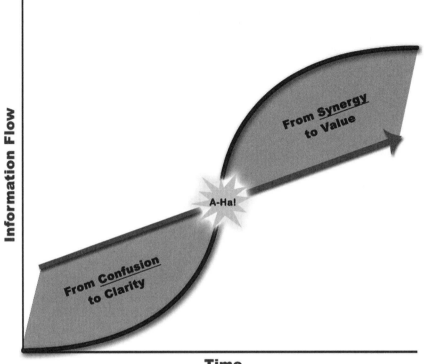

FIGURE 1-3 From Confusion to Value

gained from the insight flash to other situations (Figure 1-3). When a dancer finally "clicks" with the moves and their purposes, then his performance takes a large leap, metaphorically; when a manager is able to help an employee recognize that her sales efforts affect the region's goals, not only her own individual pay, the salesperson can achieve more value from understanding her role in a bigger context.

We go through several stages to reach that point of synergy and creating value from insight. At least three very broad phases seem common for many people: sorting information, sparking insight, and checking its validity (Figure 1-4).

Sort

While we are in the early stage of confusion, we try to identify the correct problem and sort information by gathering, organizing, and processing it. Typically, the amount of information we receive

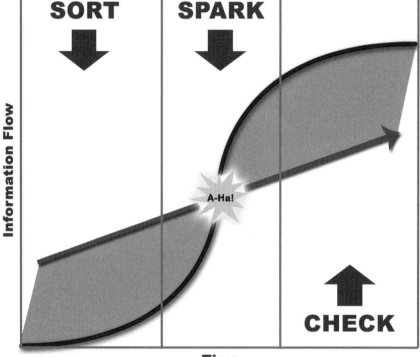

FIGURE 1-4   The Aha Journey

in this early stage is overwhelming, like standing in front of an open fire hydrant. It is diverse and unconnected and feels chaotic. Even sophisticated engineers have talked of feeling lost, with no systematic way to make sense of information they have never encountered before. But slowly, we organize it in ways that work for our own ways of thinking and understanding—we classify or "chunk" it in simpler clusters and identify factors that are most important. Finally, we begin to process the information—we try it out, use it, and reshuffle it to see if putting it into different categories helps clarify it. We let it simmer and begin to build fuzzy frameworks or patterns of information that we can use. These activities tend to be mostly left-hemisphere-driven, but sometimes our brains shift and we use less linear thinking. If that happens an aha moment may burst through and we feel we have correctly framed or solved a problem, or we understood a situation that was new to us. But very often, we still need to nudge our thinking, and thus move to a spark phase.

Spark

The spark stage shifts our thinking more formally to insight thinking, with what neuroscientists would tell us is a focus on right-hemisphere brain activity. In this stage, people more consciously seek techniques that will encourage aha moments. Looking at how odd pieces of information might connect, considering a problem from a completely different perspective, and looking for what might be missing are techniques that help encourage aha moments.

Also in the spark phase we might hit obstacles or walls. Rather than being stumbling points, they can also nudge us to think differently. If we hit a wall, that will force us to look for ways through or around it or ways to use it. But, if we feel we are making no progress, sometimes we take a detour, step away from a problem, and change from directly worrying about it. This too, although we may not be aware of it, can be a way to spark aha moments.

And then BOOM! Finally, a flash of insight. The full force of the right hemisphere, lots of neurons and brain waves kick in, and we experience the *moment* of insight. At this point, all the clichés appear: We experience a sense of the moment coming from nowhere ("out of the blue"), where synergy happens ("the pieces fell into place"), and clarity ("I finally got it") appears. And when that aha experience is profound, we never forget it. We know what we feel, but neuroscientists know what goes on, which is more than we might think.

The implications can be dramatic, which lead us to a final phase.

Check It

To verify whether the aha moment makes sense and has value beyond our single case, though, we face a third stage of checking or sending the idea into a broader public. In this stage, we test out the insight to see if it makes sense and if we can replicate it. Common methods are to ask whether it stacks up against existing ways of thinking or theory, whether it makes sense to our peers and to people who are not necessarily as knowledgeable, and whether, when we look back, the insight still makes sense.

If the aha moment holds true beyond a single situation, then it can become more valuable. A football player uses his new understanding in a game and makes two crucial tackles. A patrol officer goes after the next "bad guy," and his new skill and understanding pay off.

The Big Box

Finally, the aha experience has little chance of success without a bigger box to fit into: the individual and organizational crucible that supports the process and makes it routine. Individuals need to exhibit key characteristics, ranging from basic knowledge, motivation, and confidence that they can learn or solve a problem. And organizations need to have a culture that values creativity and insight. Without that, no matter how many good ideas or aha experiences an individual may have, they will be unused and seen as wasteful in an organization.

Bending Space

In his general theory of relativity, Einstein developed an idea of "curved" space. Without becoming too far-fetched, it is important to remember that even an insight curve (Figure 1-1) may seem like "curved space." People may not march cleanly from one stage to the next; often they describe their journeys as ones of fits and starts. It may be necessary to return to the sort stage to gather more information or reshuffle it. Perhaps the spark phase includes several detours or walls or circles. Also, people who tend toward more analytical problem solving as a default approach (e.g., engineers, managers) may have a tendency to leap from the sort to the check-it stage, bypassing the spark techniques. Instead, they may need to learn to slow down and not rush to a solution too early.

Environmentalist and author Barry Lopez[22] experienced something akin to this when he used photography in his "note taking" for a story. He reached a point where he feared that the photos he took during note-taking for a project were locking his words into a pattern and "that the pattern was being determined too early." He worked best when he let a story emerge or "settle" more slowly, but a finished photographic image stopped and locked him into a way of thinking or writing. Such a leap to a pattern or problem solution may not be a problem, if a desired insight comes during the sort task. But sometimes it is worthwhile to slow down and consider what other solutions, ideas, and possibilities might emerge if we explicitly try to spark insight, moving away from strictly analytical approaches to insight thinking.

NOTES

1. Jeff Hawkins, creator of the Handspring, is a brain researcher by interest and avocation. In his book, *On Intelligence*, he considers

just what makes the brain unique and what intelligence is (ability to predict). Throughout *On Intelligence*, he reports several "aha moments," many of which come from the question "What If?" Jeff Hawkins. 2004. *On Intelligence*. New York: Times Books: 86.

2. Watson has numerous examples of "aha moments," many of them "failed" in terms of being the correct understanding or resolution but were positive in that they helped to eliminate false directions. His reports of them are often vivid, as this one, when he saw an x-ray print made by Rosalind Franklin and recognized its potential connection to explaining the structure of DNA. James D. Watson. 1968. *The Double Helix*. New York: A Mentor Book: 107.

3. German Gestalt psychologist Karl Buehler (1879–1963) apparently first coined the term.

4. Dorothy Hermann. 1998. *Helen Keller: A Life*. New York City: Alfred A. Knopf.

5. Helen Keller. 1905. *The Story of My Life*. New York City: Grosset & Dunlap Publishers: 23.

6. John C. Camillus. 2008. Strategy as a Wicked Problem, *Harvard Business Review*, 86 (5): 98–106.

7. Stephen C. Harper. 1989. Intuition: What separates executives from managers, in W. H. Agor (Ed.), *Intuition in Organizations: Leading and Managing Productively*. Newbury Park, CA: Sage Publications; Alden G. Lank and Elizabeth A. Lank. 1995. Legitimizing the gut feel: the role of intuition in business, *Journal of Managerial Psychology*, 10 (5): 18–23; John R. Patton. 2003. Intuition in Decisions, *Management Decisions*, 41 (10): 989–996; S. Sandkuehler and J. Bhattacharya. 2008. Deconstructing insight: EEG correlates of insightful problem solving, *PLoS ONE*, 23, 3 (1): e1459.

8. Henry Mintzberg. 1976. Planning on the left side and managing on the right, *Harvard Business Review*, 54 (4): 49–58; Robert J. Sternberg. 1997. Managerial Intelligence: Why IQ Isn't Enough, *Journal of Management*, 23 (3): 475–493; Naresh Khatri and H. Alvin Ng. 2000. The role of intuition in strategic decision making, *Human Relations*, 53 (1): 57–86; Jon Aarum Andersen. 2000. Intuition in managers: Are intuitive managers more effective? *Journal of Managerial Psychology*, 15 (1): 46–67; J. R. Patton. 2003. Intuition in Decisions, *Management Decision*, 41 (10): 989–996; Malcolm Gladwell. 2005. *Blink*. New York: Little Brown & Company.

9. Henri Poincaré. 1952. *Science and Method*. New York City: Dover Publications, Inc. Translated from the original: Henri Poincaré. 1908. *Science et Methode*. Paris: E. Flammarion.

10. Alfred Russel Wallace. 1906. *My Life: A Record of Events and Opinions*. New York City: Dodd, Mead & Company: 194.

11. Even celebrities are getting into the act. Oprah Winfrey began asking famous people to report their aha moments on her Web site. Their experiences tend to focus on reaching understanding about something in their lives.

12. Raymond Carver. 1981. *What We Talk about When We Talk about Love*. New York: Alfred A. Knopf.

13. Scott Berkun argues that innovation, and "big" aha moments as an ingredient of innovation, may happen slowly from a collection of smaller insights. Scott Berkun. 2007. *The Myths of Innovation*. Sebastopol, CA: O'Reilly.

14. Experts from the early part of last century now make the point that effort and work are involved to make results look "spontaneous" or easy. Graham Wallas, one of the first researchers to examine insight thinking, mentioned four stages—from preparation to incubation to illumination (the aha moment) to verification. Graham Wallas. 1926. *The Art of Thought*. New York: Harcourt, Brace and Co. Others talk of the importance of standing at the "corner" or "bend" of disciplines, where the past and future are visible for the innovative leader. See William Duggan. 2007. *Strategic Intuition*. New York: Columbia Business School. More recently, Malcolm Gladwell talks of the "10,000 hours" of purposeful practice that extremely successful people need to reach the peak of their fields and become "overnight successes." Malcolm Gladwell. 2009. *Outliers*. New York: Little Brown.

15. T. D. Wilson and Y. Bar-Anan. 2008. The Unseen Mind, *Science*, 321 (5892): 1046–1047.

16. Evan I. Schwartz. 2004. *Juice: The Creative Fuel that Drives World-Class Inventors*. Boston, MA: Harvard Business School Press; William Duggan. 2007. *Strategic Intuition*. New York: Columbia University Press: 15–16.

17. Alain de Botton. 2002. *The Art of Travel*. New York: Pantheon Books: 242.

18. Ewen Callaway. 2009. Speeding up brain networks might boost IQ, *New Scientist* (http://www.newscientist.com/article/dn17280-speeding-up-brain-networks-might-boost-iq-.html, last accessed on July 29, 2009).

19. George McGovern. 1992. A politician's dream—a businessman's nightmare, *Nation's Restaurant News*, September 21 (http://findarticles.com/p/articles/mi_m3190/is_n38_v26/ai_12685435/?tag=rbxcra.2.a.44).

20. "Eureka!" Or, translated: "I've found it! I've found it!" As Galileo showed in his tract *La Bilancetta*, or "The Little Balance," a scientist of Archimedes's stature could have achieved a far more precise result using his own law of buoyancy and an accurate scale, something far more common in the ancient world than a very precise pycnometer, which is used to measure displacement. (The surface tension of water can render the volume of a light object like a wreath unmeasurable.) "There may be some truth to it," Rorres adds. "Archimedes did measure the volume of things but the eureka moment was maybe due to his original discovery [concerning buoyance], not to sitting in the bathtub and then running through the streets of Syracuse naked." David Biello. 2006. Fact or Fiction?: Archimedes Coined the Term "Eureka!" in the Bath, *Scientific American* (http://www.scientificamerican.com/article.cfm ?id=fact-or-fiction-archimede, last accessed on July 29, 2009).

21. Steve Jobs. 2005. "You've got to find what you love," Jobs says, *Stanford University News*, June 12 (http://news-service. stanford.edu/news/2005/june15/jobs-061505.html, last accessed on July 29, 2009).

22. Barry Lopez. 1998. *About This Life*. New York: Alfred A. Knopf: 235.

Part I

Sort: Getting the Lay of the Land

There is no moment of delight in any pilgrimage like the beginning of it.
—American Essayist Charles Dudley Warner (1829–1900)

The start of a journey typically begins with sometimes giddy preparation—deciding on the destination, gathering and organizing equipment, and then, once the journey begins, processing the impressions that emerge along the way. Often the aha journey feels likewise—the thrill of starting to learn about a new concept or wrestle a challenging problem. But soon, the true challenge becomes overwhelming, and we are forced to take it in steps.

The next two chapters illustrate this early stage in the context of the aha journey: sorting out the problem and initial flood of information. Chapter 2 focuses on how to identify the "destination," or problem to be solved, examining in particular two types of problems—straightforward, clear problems and those that are "discovered," unclear ones that require more study to understand their true nature. The discovered, "messier" problems are the ones that typically need insight thinking.

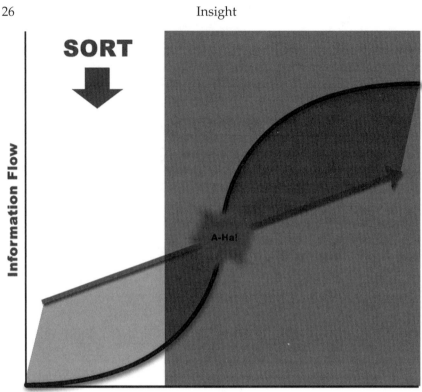

Sorting Information

Chapter 3 focuses on the sort phase: gathering, organizing, and processing information. This is a somewhat logical phase that sometimes, especially in the information processing stage, may lead to possible aha moments.

Chapter 2

Destination: What Is the Problem?

If I had one hour to save the world, I would spend fifty-five minutes defining the problem and only five minutes finding the solution.

—Attributed to Albert Einstein

You observe a lot just by watching.

—Yogi Berra[1]

Frequently, the *New York Times Magazine* has a two page mystery column—detectives encounter a case, look for evidence, form theories and test them, and try to solve the case. Something unexpected always comes up. The information is often disconnected, can be overwhelming, and leaves the detectives and victims confused.

The detectives are doctors: residents, medical students, specialists, and generalists, physicians with decades of experience. Each case is like a mini-TV drama—a crisis appears and the medical detectives investigate the problem, only to find that frequently the expected problem is not the actual problem. They struggle, try various options, and usually have an aha moment when they find a solution. In this mini-drama, they always find a solution. And when they do, being good detectives, the doctors reflect on what they can learn from their experience.

In a recent episode, a sleep detective followed Yogi Berra's advice: He was able to observe a lot just by watching. When he first met the patient, the physician saw a clue: the patient's very large hands. But since none of the other numerous specialists had mentioned the hands during years of medical scrutiny, Dr. John Helfrich set his observation aside. The 51-year-old patient's mysterious symptoms were numerous: insatiable hunger, high blood pressure despite healthy eating and exercise habits, difficulty in breathing, and inability to sleep more than 90 minutes at a stretch. He could fall asleep, anywhere, anytime—in meetings, while driving his car, and in his own bed—but he could not stay asleep longer than 90 minutes. Also, after turning 40, he developed other symptoms. He fell and discovered his bones were thin and weak, he developed acne, and he needed braces on his teeth to adjust to the shifting of his bite. Over the years, specialists from allergists to endocrinologists had tried to treat pieces of the patient's puzzle, like his blood pressure, eating and sleeping problems, but nothing worked. Because the patient's sleeping disorder became the key (or at least, the most recently noted) driving symptom, he went to Helfrich, a sleep specialist.

Once again, Dr. Helfrich did all the usual tests—took the patient's blood pressure and heart rate, ran blood tests, asked the patient scads of questions—but something just did not fit. One blood test revealed that the patient was generating high amounts of a growth hormone, suggesting the possibility of a disease called acromegaly, which leads to enlargement of hands, feet, and face. In fact, Dr. Helfrich was right: He discovered a tumor in the patient's pituitary gland, and within a month after the tumor was removed, the patient's hands, feet, and face shrank to normal size. His blood pressure dropped, his breathing became normal (since pressure on his nose tissue was gone), and his eating and sleeping patterns settled into regular patterns.

A fundamental question, then, was why dozens of specialists had not noticed and considered the enlargement of the patient's hands and face as a possible symptom of acromegaly disease? Why had no one found the correct problem, but continued to treat symptoms?

One answer is that the information and symptoms emerged in discreet pieces over time—the insomnia, the allergies, and the blood pressure, to the point where it was difficult to see the connections. As the *New York Times* article put it, "[The symptoms] developed separately, years apart, and each was addressed by a specialist. It would take an act of imagination to link these symptoms. The patient never made that leap, and neither did any of his doctors."[2]

But Helfrich followed Einstein's axiom and spent much time defining the patient's real problem rather than treating the sleeplessness symptom that would have been his obvious approach, given his specialty. In doing so, he found the pituitary gland tumor, which explained the seemingly unconnected symptoms. Once the problem was clear, the solution was simple to implement.

Helfrich was the first doctor to have that "act of imagination," starting with his willingness to slow down and really *look* at the patient. The other doctors had missed the diagnosis, although the symptoms were right in front of them, developing over the years. They were caught in "inattention blindness," missing something because they had not expected to see it.[3] Helfrich, in contrast, noticed key elements that others had missed and recognized that they were the major pieces of the puzzle and were linked. "A light went off in his head as soon as he saw the patient. Earlier in his career, he heard about a female patient who suffered for many years before anyone figured out she had acromegaly. Seeing this patient reminded him of that missed diagnosis."[4] He had the knowledge and previous experience of the earlier missed diagnosis, and he had the curiosity and the habit of slowing down to delve deeply enough to find the core problem.

WHAT IS THE PROBLEM?

The mere formulation of the problem is far more often essential than its solution, which may be merely a matter of mathematical or experiment skill.

—Albert Einstein[5]

Dr. Helfrich's story exhibits a first critical step in the process of reaching insight or aha moments: finding the correct problem. He took time to understand and read the landscape of the potential problem and identify (some) possible obstacles along the journey. His approach to problem solving demanded first a "formulation" or assessment, rather than starting with an assumption that he knew the problem. While other specialists appeared to have sought solutions from their own perspectives, Helfrich, like Einstein, was able to focus on defining the problem and stave off the inclination to jump to solutions too soon.

Helfrich took several steps that helped him reach his insight and final diagnosis. First, unlike some of the other specialists, he did not assume he had a straightforward problem (how could he, when he learned that so many specialists had tried to treat the patient's symptoms for 15 years?). Thus, he treated the patient like a fresh landscape, needing to be understood and mapped. He started by collecting information, some of which he received ready-made from previous physicians' reports and some of which he sought from the patient. It must have seemed overwhelming and fragmented, coming from years of records and comments from specialists in several different fields. Next, he needed to organize the information, classifying or "chunking" it in ways that would help make sense of it. He had some existing categories for the information, like past symptoms, but he needed to sort them and seek out patterns within and across the data. Helfrich ranked the pieces of information to determine which were most likely to explain the patient's whole illness and perhaps link all the conflicting symptoms into a comprehensive whole. For Helfrich, the large hands emerged as a critical factor, the clue that he had noticed early on and set aside but which ultimately helped him identify the underlying illness: the faulty hormone condition. Last, as Helfrich processed the information, including exploring different possibilities—a sleep disorder, blood problem, or something else—he moved from details or symptoms to "trial theories" or ways to explain what was happening to his patient.

Ultimately, he zeroed in on what others had not seen and saw how the odd symptoms connected. Helfrich's "act of imagination," or "aha moment," came when he was able to integrate the details and seemingly unrelated symptoms into a bigger picture. By putting together what seemed to be odd pieces of information and looking at them from different angles, he reached an accurate diagnosis. Realizing that the patient had a tumor in his pituitary gland explained all of the other symptoms, including the sleep dysfunction.

Helfrich succeeded, in part, by learning a lot just by observing. Rather than acting without thorough understanding, he slowed down to observe. Then, when he reached a solution, an aha moment as it were, he also recognized he still had work to do to confirm or disprove his diagnosis. When he found that the patient's symptoms disappeared a month after the tumor was removed, he validated his insight.

GIVE ME PROBLEMS, GIVE ME WORK ...

Give me problems, give me work, give me the most abstruse cryptogram or the most intricate analysis, and I am in my own

proper atmosphere. I can dispense then with artificial stimulants
. . . I crave for mental exaltation. That is why I have chosen my
own particular profession,—or rather created it, for I am the only
one in the world . . . the only unofficial consulting detective.
                    —Sherlock Holmes, "The Sign of the Four"[6]

From cave men carving better spears to babies reaching for color-
ful hanging mobile figurines, humans are curious. We need the
challenge of problems, and we seem never to lack for them.[7]

At least three types of problems seem common. Some problems
come to us as fairly straightforward ones, often readily solved by
logic. We face such problems dozens of times on a daily basis, both
small ones—a stopped-up toilet, lost mail, a child's scuffed knee—
and larger ones, like a downed power line, a bank teller who makes
repeated balancing errors, or a customer who is 30 days past due
on an account. These problems, which "come to us," are often
called "well-defined" or "presented" problems.[8]

Other problems are ones "we find." Usually, they are ill-defined
or "discovered," tough to define, and often demand insight thinking. Many times, such "discovered" problems become business
ideas or inventions, such as Edison's light bulb, Apple's iPod, or
Wizzit Bank's mobile banking service in South Africa.

A third type of problem—the hybrid—may seem straightforward and well-defined but, in fact, is a foxy "discovered" problem
wearing the sheep's clothing of a presented one. The patient who
came to Dr. Helfrich with a sleep disorder turned out to have a very
different problem, much less clear than had originally been
thought. Interestingly, we may encounter such problems that
seem well-defined but morph into something else, more often than
we realize. The teller who is frequently out of balance may not be
poor in math but distracted by personal problems, less simple to
solve.

We might view presented and hybrid/discovered problems as
two ends of a continuum of the ways that we encounter problems.[9]
Presented, well-defined problems typically have shorter time
frames, they appear unexpectedly, and they may be one of a series
of existing problems or may have the potential to occur on a
regular basis. A jail escape (or attempt) may have the potential to
happen anytime a dangerous inmate moves within the facility.
Ill-defined hybrid and discovered problems, on the other hand,
tend to take longer for us to recognize or identify, are more difficult
to resolve, and often require aha moments. While a jail escape is an

obvious presented problem, Sheriff Gary Raney really had a hybrid problem, more difficult to recognize and solve. Like Helfrich's diagnosis, discovered and hybrid problems typically demand a shift in the normal pattern of thinking about the problem.[10] The next section explores and illustrates each type in more depth.

Presented Problems—Unadorned and Straightforward

Arthur Conan Doyle's Sherlock Holmes mysteries generally present straightforward problems fit for a detective with supreme logical thinking skills. Holmes was a master at absorbing and making sense of what appear to be disparate pieces of information. A passage from "The Adventure of the Blue Carbuncle" illustrates his observational strength and the way he sorts and organizes information into a logical whole.[11] In this selection, Holmes asks his friend Dr. Watson to look at a hat and tell him all he could about its owner. Watson does so and comes up short:

> I took the tattered object in my hands and turned it over rather ruefully. It was a very ordinary black hat of the usual round shape, hard, and much the worse for wear. The lining had been of red silk, but was a good deal discoloured. There was no maker's name; but, as Holmes had remarked, the initials "H.B." were scrawled upon one side. It was pierced in the brim for a hat-securer, but the elastic was missing. For the rest, it was cracked, exceedingly dusty, and spotted in several places, although there seemed to have been some attempt to hide the discoloured patches by smearing them with ink.

Watson then comments, "I can see nothing."

Holmes replies, "On the contrary, Watson, you can see everything. You fail, however, to reason from what you see. You are too timid in drawing your inferences."

Holmes then goes step by step through his observations about the hat's owner, painting a clear portrait of a highly intellectual man, who had been well-to-do within the last three years but had fallen on hard times, and who earlier had shown foresight but now has come under evil influence (perhaps drink). Finally, said Holmes, the man's wife no longer loves him.

Like Watson, we readers are usually stunned.

Elementary, dear Watson and readers. Holmes goes on to reveal his deductive powers.

The man's intelligence is evident because the hat's size is large, fitting on the head of a man with a large brain and skull.[12] The hat is three years old (out of fashion), but of the best quality, as shown by the silk lining. If the man could afford to buy such a hat three years ago and not replace it, reasoned Holmes, he must be in difficult economic straights. Further evidence is the attempt to conceal stains on the hat with ink. The hat owner's foresight came from the existence of a little disc and loop of the hat-securer, which are not sold on hats. For the man to have gone to the effort of putting such a hat-securer on the hat, he must have had the foresight to take such a precaution. Finally, Holmes's conclusion about the wife's loss of love stemmed from the observation that the hat had not been "brushed" in weeks and no caring wife would allow her husband to leave the house without such a touch.

* * *

Many presented problems, like the mysterious hat owner, are readily solved with straightforward approaches. Traditionally, a logical problem-solving approach starts with identifying the goal or problem, which can be a challenge in itself. Next steps include gathering information about the current situation and possibilities, generating and evaluating alternatives given the resources at hand, and taking action or implementing the solution. Finally, good problem solving includes an assessment of the result or outcome. In essence, we saw the basic approach in the medical problem at the beginning of the chapter as well as Sherlock Holmes's challenge to Watson, assuming we have the "right" problem.

Holmes would likely say that any of us could solve presented problems if we had the three skills key for an "ideal detective": knowledge (of a wide range of fields), the power of observation, and the skills of deduction. For example, a challenge during long surgical operations is accurate delivery of appropriate amounts of anesthesia to patients. Gauging the correct amount of anesthesia, based upon patient age, weight, and physical condition, can vary widely during the course of an operation that may last 5 hours or 12 hours. The necessary focus, constant monitoring and adjustment, can drain a physician during the course of the operation, potentially causing mistakes. So a clear problem is how to avoid the human error or fatigue that may influence the control, monitoring, or maintenance of anesthesia at accurate levels during a long operation.[13] To solve it requires knowledge of the field of anesthesia, observation of how doctors work, and deduction to find a reliable and logical solution: Fully automated anesthesia systems, which determine the level, sequencing, and adjustments to anesthesia without constant human physician attention, have been used in about 40 operations in the United States so far.

The logical, presented, straightforward problems are ones that many people face, and solve, on a regular basis. The more challenging, and increasingly more prevalent, problems are those that are unclear, emerge more slowly, and are more likely to require us to follow the aha journey. Such problems are often "discovered."

Discovered and Hybrid Problems

To raise new questions, new possibilities, to regard old problems from a new angle requires creative imagination . . .
—Albert Einstein[14]

In contrast to straightforward or presented problems, discovered problems (and hybrids that start as straightforward ones and change to discovered problems) demand a shift from strictly logical to more insight thinking. They often require an "act of imagination," a leap from logic to a different way of thinking. Entrepreneurs provide some of the best examples.

Jayme Mullaney loves gardening and after years of working as a garden designer and in retail nurseries, she knows her plants. She knows the Latin names, the amount of sun, water, and food each plant needs, and when and how to plant—everything an expert would know and a beginner would not.

Mullaney moved from the low desert of Arizona to the high desert of the intermountain West, between the Sierra/Cascade and Rocky mountain ranges. Landing in Idaho, she began to work as a garden designer in a small nursery. The nursery owner, originally from the lush Pacific Northwest, had filled her nursery with botanicals native to her homeland. She asked Mullaney to design and pick out plants for a customer's garden, something Mullaney had done for years in her previous home. Yet, as she walked through the nursery, filled with completely different plants than she was used to, she was lost. She found that the plants seemed to have no rhyme or reason to their order because they were unfamiliar, and she thus had no idea which to recommend in a design. It took her two hours to pick out plants in the small nursery because she was so overwhelmed. Although a brilliant garden designer, who had worked for years in nurseries with thousands of plant types, she was stymied and frustrated. But in that frustration, an aha moment exploded. She suddenly realized that the feeling of "being lost" is what the customers in her nursery always felt, because the plants were unfamiliar to them.

Mullaney's inability to find plants she wanted (and those were plants she knew she wanted) led her to discover a problem that needed solving: how to help customers select plants for their gardens without personally consulting a gardening professional. She wanted to erase the mystique behind garden design so laymen could do what came naturally to her. She shifted her viewpoint and began to think like a novice gardener. By reframing her problem, she discovered a new one, which became the seed for a future business idea—a Web site to help customers design and choose plants for their gardens. By thinking in a new way, as a beginning gardener, she had different questions of how to lay out a nursery. A beginning gardener might find it helpful to locate plants "by season": which plants bloom in summer vs. which bloom in the cooler autumn temperature and fading light. Then Mullaney realized that although beginners do not know how to select specific plants, they generally know which colors they prefer, like blue and orange, or purple and gold. That helped her rethink the nursery organization yet again: to put plants of certain colors together within the season groupings. Then she sorted them by exposure and height.

Ultimately, a customer could visit the Web site and say, "I want a sunny, summer garden, with lots of purples . . . Tall, medium, short purples." The Web site then would show the customer the plants and combine them into a plan, which could be used to purchase and install a garden. Alternately, the site could be a tool for designing a garden upon entering the above parameters and dragging and selecting various plant choices. It also could include information about gardening, planting, maintenance, and design, all in a very simple, methodical way: a one-stop shop for anyone needing gardening help, specifically beginners. Mullaney realized, in that "aha moment," that the marketplace lacked any sort of Web site or information source for novice gardeners to design and choose plants for a garden.

Mullaney and her business partner, Mary Ann Newcomer, are in the process of developing that business idea into a Web site, which uses a step-by-step process for garden design. Using simple questions, the site helps both beginner and advanced gardeners plan their gardens based upon size, amount of sunlight and direction, and desired color for various seasons. In her case, the discovered problem and insight thinking came from the frustration she felt at being forced to think from a different perspective, that of a beginner.

Frustration is a common driver of discovered problems. Einstein could not reconcile ideas from two streams of research; Gary Raney could not accept that security was the sole issue leading to the jail break. And like Jayme Mullaney, entrepreneur Mario Moretti Polegato found his creative aha moment in the high desert, this time outside Reno, Nevada. In the early 1990s, Polegato attended a conference representing his family's wine company. During a jog from the center of town to the desert, all of 15 minutes, he realized quickly how hot and sweaty his feet became in the high desert heat. He cut holes in the soles of his running shoes to allow air circulation. When he returned to Italy, he refined his holey shoe idea, and he realized he needed to find a way to prevent dirt and water from entering the shoes. From one step to the next, he developed a shoe that he tried to sell to German and American shoemakers, but they turned him down. In 1995, Polegato started his own firm, GEOX, which now sells casual and dress shoes worldwide. Frustration in gardening and running in the heat—both discovered problems that led to insight moments.

THE QUESTION OF QUESTIONS

> The important thing is not to stop questioning. Curiosity has its own reason for existing. . . . It is enough if one tries to comprehend only a little of this mystery every day.
> —Albert Einstein[15]

Discovered and hybrid problems are the focus of this book, because these are the ones that most often require us to nudge aha moments and leaps of imagination that allow us to learn and solve. Einstein's quote raises a key issue, which is the importance of questions, critical in problem finding and ultimately in insight thinking.

Children ask questions to learn and do so without concern for whether the questions seem naïve or simple. Lawyers ask to learn as well, but often with a goal in mind, and sometimes they ask when they already have answers. People who value aha moments and learning also use questions. They do so because they want to understand something that seems, to them, unexpected or unusual. They question to get the information needed to solve problems. And sometimes they ask questions to help others learn or solve problems.

Attorney Patti Powell has 25 years of experience in different governmental agencies and private sector organizations, covering environmental issues to health care to law enforcement. Since she knows the law, she can apply it in different settings, without in-depth knowledge (at least at the start) about the organization's role. But she builds her own knowledge through questions and, in the process, helps existing members understand and view their own situations more fully. During discussions about a crime investigation, for example, she will force officers, detectives, and command staff to stop during a meeting and explain their points in simple language so she can understand what is going on. Often it becomes clear that some of the key players may have viewed the situation differently, so what seemed clear-cut is not really so straightforward.

Powell holds unique status in that her position as an "outsider" allows or excuses her to "play stupid," as she says. Coming from outside the operational disciplines in the organizations where she works has given her a perspective unlike what entrenched organizational members may hold. She has performed her legal counsel job well, gaining the so-called "street cred[ibility]" and status she needs to be allowed to slow down a discussion and query officers more intensely on what happened in a given crime scene, who was acting when and how. Her legal training using the Socratic Method suits the way she poses questions and provides an avenue to help others view a situation differently, which in turn may lead to insight on their part as well.

Sheriff Gary Raney's experience with the jail escape, described in the Introduction, also illustrates the power of questions. The escape, presented as a relatively neatly wrapped problem, was not. Largely because of Raney's willingness to question deeply, he discovered the more fundamental problem. Rather than assuming the security of the jail was the problem (it was, in part), rather than assuming some jail deputies had become complacent (some had), rather than assuming that fixing the problem was "just a matter of tweaking" (it was not), Raney asked questions that cut to the fundamentals of what and how the jail operated.

When Major Ron Freeman pushed jail employees to identify their unit's reason for being, he used what appeared to be very simple questions, but which were really very difficult to answer: "What is this jail for? What are the three most important things we should be doing here?" One sergeant commented that when

Freeman posed those core questions, it was jolting. The questions forced employees to go "back to the basics" and explain "why we exist, why we do things like this, and what are the most important parts of this job?" Few people could remember having thought or explicitly talked about those issues. The jail identified three "pillars" or basic values that drive every decision employees make, every day: safety of staff, security of the facilities, and well-being of inmates. All are easy to remember and clear, but are absolutely critical and integrated into every action employees take. The process thus shook up, ultimately in a good way, the mind-set and behavior of participating employees. The leadership made the act of raising questions part of the culture. The outcome—the key pillars—set the tone for the rest of the organization, which is using a similar process in each of the other key units.

Being open to questioning processes and ways of operating has trickled throughout the jail in several ways. One manager builds "asking questions" into his expectations for new hires, especially in their first days and weeks at the jail. He tells new people that their "newness" gives them liberty to ask lots of questions. He does not expect them to know the routines and practices of the office, so he wants to tap their fresh eyes to find better ways to carry out tasks. He encourages them to ask why the unit does something as it does and what the purpose of certain forms or policies might be, as well as to identify practices that make no sense. He estimates that within a few months of joining the organization, that advantage of newness will wear off, so he purposefully seeks ideas from newcomers.

In his book *How Doctors Think*, Jerome Groopman emphasizes that successful physicians have made and learned from mistakes

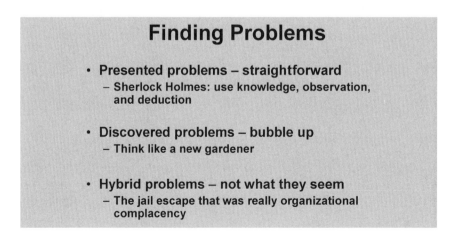

Finding Problems

- **Presented problems – straightforward**
  - Sherlock Holmes: use knowledge, observation, and deduction

- **Discovered problems – bubble up**
  - Think like a new gardener

- **Hybrid problems – not what they seem**
  - The jail escape that was really organizational complacency

and become incessant question askers. Often doctor and patient together search for clues to solve the patient's problem, sparked by a simple request from the physician: "Tell me the story again, as if I'd never heard it—what you felt, how it happened, when it happened."[16]

Whether medicine, law enforcement, or management, the critical first question—What *is* the problem?—can be one of the more difficult ones. And although it typically demands logical thinking, sometimes that is exactly where an important flash of insight can come—in defining the problem itself. But as that happens—sometimes in conjunction with that process—we typically begin to seek information to help us in the next phase of the journey.

NOTES

1. This famous remark can be found in John Bartlett. 2002. *Bartlett's Familiar Quotations, Seventeenth Edition.* Boston: Little, Brown and Company: 14.

2. Lisa Sanders. 2009. Sleepless, *The New York Times Magazine*, May 10: 17.

3. Lisa Sanders. 2009. Sleepless, *The New York Times Magazine*, May 10: 17.

4. Lisa Sanders. 2009. Sleepless, *The New York Times Magazine*, May 10, referred to Marvin M. Chun and Rene Marois. 2002. The dark side of visual attention, *Current Opinion in Neurobiology*, 12 (2): 184–189.

5. Isaac Asimov and Jason Shulman (Eds.). 1988. *Isaac Asimov's Book of Science and Nature Quotations.* New York: Weidenfeld & Nicolson: 95.

6. Several of the Sherlock Holmes's stories include a discussion of deduction. This one comes from Sir Arthur Conan Doyle. 1930. The Sign of the Four: The Science of Deduction, in *The Complete Sherlock Holmes.* Garden City, NY: Doubleday & Company, Inc.: 89–90.

7. Alain de Botton. 2009. *The Pleasures and Sorrows of Work.* New York City: Pantheon Books: 324–326.

8. Robert W. Weisberg. 2006. *Creativity: Understanding Innovation in Problem Solving, Science, Invention, and the Arts.* Hoboken, NJ: John Wiley and Sons: 138–140.

9. M. Csikszentmihalyi and K. Sawyer. 1995. Creative insight: The social dimension of a solitary moment, in R. J. Steinberg and

J. E. Davidson (Eds.), *The Nature of Insight*. Cambridge, MA: MIT Press: 329–361.

10. Robert W. Weisberg. 2006. *Creativity: Understanding Innovation in Problem Solving, Science, Invention, and the Arts*. Hoboken, NJ: John Wiley and Sons: 409–410; Thomas Kuhn. 1970. *The Structure of Scientific Revolutions*. Chicago: The University of Chicago Press: 6.

11. Sir Arthur Conan Doyle. 1930. The Adventure of the Blue Carbuncle, in *The Complete Sherlock Holmes*. Garden City, NY: Doubleday & Company, Inc.: 244–257.

12. Stephen Jay Gould's book, *The Mismeasure of Man*, offers one of the best historical descriptions of the enthusiasm given to the notion that skull/brain size and intelligence were once thought to be linked. In the 1880s, when Doyle began publishing his Sherlock Holmes stories, this theory was generally accepted. Researcher Samuel Morton proposed the theory based upon a series of measurements of skull and brain size of cadavers from different races. Gould later shattered Morton's theories, which had long before lost favor, by remeasuring some of the skulls Morton used. He found inaccuracies and miscalculated numbers because of Morton's poor methods. Nevertheless, Doyle, being a doctor, used theories prevalent in the time period to support Holmes's deductive reasoning. See Stephen Jay Gould. 1996. *The Mismeasure of Man*. New York City: W. W. Norton & Co.

13. Jeffery Delviscio. 2008. Automated anesthesia, *The New York Times*, December 14: MM40.

14. Laurence Chang. 2006. *Wisdom for the Soul: Five Millennia of Prescriptions for Spiritual Healing*. Washington, DC: Gnosophia Publishers: 179.

15. Alice Calaprice (Ed.). 2000. *The Expanded Quotable Einstein*. Princeton, NJ: Princeton University: 280–281. From the memoirs of William Miler, quoted in *Life* magazine, 2 May 1955.

16. Jerome Groopman. 2007. *How Doctors Think*. New York: Houghton Mifflin: 260–261.

Chapter 3

"Whirling Vortex and a Creative Chaos..."

It was a process that began in a *whirling vortex and a creative chaos* that proceeded slowly at the expense of *infinite confusion*, toil, and error toward clarification and the articulation of an ordered and formal structure. [Italics added]
—Thomas Wolfe, writer[1]

In the spring of 1986, as I sat at my desk day after day reading scientific articles, building my history of intelligence, and watching the evolving worlds of AI [artificial intelligence] and neural networks, I found myself *drowning in details*. There was an *unending supply* of things to study and read about, but *I was not gaining any clear understanding* of how the whole brain actually worked or even what it did. This was because the field of neuroscience ... was *awash in details*. [Italics added]
—Jeff Hawkins, 2004: 33–34[2]

"Whirling vortex and a creative chaos." "Awash in details." That is what we experience when we try to understand something complex, whether a new language or the workings of an organization, but are overwhelmed with the flood of information, like standing in front of an open fire hydrant. The pieces of information seem fragmented, disparate, and unconnected. We do not know which will be helpful or which will be the most important ones. Confusion reigns.

But then, as Thomas Wolfe describes, we move away from "infinite confusion ... toward clarification." We find ways to organize the flood of information, make sense of it, and find some structure.

In this chapter, we will talk about this early stage of the insight curve, where we are sorting information that bombards us at a powerful rate. First, we will talk about gathering information, the "travel gear" we need for the journey. We can either seek information ourselves, as Jeff Hawkins did when he sought to understand the way intelligence works, or, if we are helping others on the aha journey, we may transfer information to them. In both cases, the whirling vortex and creative chaos is daunting.

Next, we begin to organize the information, sorting it into categories that help us begin to see what is more (or less) important. Again, often we must do that ourselves; sometimes others, like coaches or managers, do it with and for us. Finally, we start to process the information and move toward insight and understanding. The next three sections cover each of these phases.

THE FIRE HYDRANT OF INFORMATION

When I want to discover something, I begin by reading everything that has been done along that line in the past . . . I see what has been accomplished at great labor and expense in the past. I gather data of many thousands of experiments as a starting point, and then I make thousands more.

—Thomas Edison[3]

Collecting Information

Two issues come into play in how we collect information: the ways in which we seek it and our ability to absorb it. When you last needed to come up to speed on a topic, a problem, or a situation that was new for you, how did you get the information you needed? Your approach could well be quite different, depending upon your field, your method of learning, and your ability to absorb. Some people, like brain researcher Jeff Hawkins, take information in without knowing where it might lead, what will be most important, or how to use it. Others, like Edison, have more systematic methods to gather past knowledge and perhaps have a fuzzy idea of where it could fit even in the gathering process.

The nonprofit organization, Healthwise, is one of the largest producers of English language health information—printed and online —in the world. Senior Vice President of Consumer Experience Karen Baker was a print journalist before joining the award-winning consumer health information organization.[4] She has vast experience in seeking information from a variety of people and sources and does it efficiently and broadly. Her experience enables her to filter information that might be inaccurate or irrelevant, but she throws a wide net early in the process. Her search is methodical and includes looking "outside" of the organization and her job. For a given topic she wants to learn about or a problem she needs to solve, Baker strives first to identify the goal and then asks questions of and seeks input from colleagues, stakeholders, and other professionals, collecting both "facts" and opinions. She also researches sources such as the Internet, books, and journals. The aha moment comes after she does her research.

* * *

Crime Scene Investigator Jaimie Barker has less control over what information comes to him than Baker does. While she seeks it on her own terms, his comes to him on the crime's terms. He nonetheless looks for pieces that exist and some that may disappear. When crime scene investigators like Barker enter a homicide site, they typically ignore the dead body. They look everywhere else first. They reason that the victim will still be there in a few minutes or an hour, but other evidence may not. Melting ice in a glass may give an indication of how long the victim has been dead or when a suspect left; footprints in a streambed wash away, destroying evidence of the boots that made the prints.

Barker relies less on "words" than on physical forensic evidence. He does not talk to suspects, victims, or their families. Instead he says, "I allow the crime scene that I visit *to tell me the story.*" He is attuned, after many years of experience and floods of information, to know what to look for, depending upon the type of crime. And even as the information begins to come to him, he starts to sort and consider what it could mean. Rape requires one type of information, a homicide quite another.

* * *

John Drake, director of business development at the marketing/advertising firm Drake Cooper, uses blogs, travel, and history as starting points for finding information to help him understand or view a problem in a different light. Like Barker, he finds that sometimes information or ideas need to come to him, rather than his seeking them out. A story about the Italian painter Rafael during the Renaissance period helped him realize the value of "right timing" for information.

I was recently reading about Rafael, the painter. He traveled to Florence to become famous because that's what all the famous artists at the time were doing. They put his work against Michelangelo and other established painters of the day and I guess it wasn't standing out. So he moved to Rome, started doing his art there. Years went by and people in Florence got tired of the same art . . . and wanted something new. So they went to Rome to find new talent and discovered Rafael. Sometimes you need to get away and let that person or subject find you.

Finally, while the methods we use to learn are important in information gathering, age and expertise may also influence retention of and ability to process information. When researchers have compared the ability of medical students (early and later in their studies) with practicing physicians, the older, more experienced doctors perform better in certain aspects.[5] A project looked at the ability to recall, explain, and diagnose signs and symptoms in four medical cases across three groups—medical students in their second and sixth years, and practicing neurologists. The sixth-year students had better recall about the cases and could explain them better than second-year students, but the practicing physicians were better at diagnosing than either of the other two groups. Basically, this means that to absorb complex information, we need some level of knowledge about a field. But even more striking is that the ability to process information is even higher once we add experience and practice to that knowledge.

Giving Information

In teaching the treatment of disease and accident, all careful teachers have first to show the student how to recognize accurately the case. The recognition depends in great measure on the accurate and rapid appreciation of *small* points in which the diseased differs from the healthy state. In fact, the student must be taught to observe. To interest him in this kind of work, we teachers find it useful to show the student how much a trained use of the observation can discover in ordinary matters such as the previous history, nationality, and occupation of a patient.

—Dr. Joseph Bell,
University of Edinburgh medical school professor[6]

Dr. Joseph Bell (1837–1911), who became Sir Arthur Conan Doyle's model for his character Sherlock Holmes, must have been a master teacher. Bell was one of Doyle's medical school professors and among the first to apply forensic methods and careful observation to solve crimes. His lectures and mentoring of Doyle followed similar systematic thoroughness. Bell was organized, was precise, and had high expectations for solving a problem.

Trey McIntyre is a choreographer and co-founder of the Trey McIntyre Project, a full-time dance company and one of the few arts organizations to remain financially viable in tough economic times. He has set the dance world on fire for over two decades, creating several dozen commissioned works, with performances across the United States and in more than a dozen countries. His work has been acknowledged in *The New York Times* and *The Boston Globe*, and the company was featured in a cover story in the leading dance magazine, *Pointe*.[7]

But McIntyre's approach to delivering information to his dancers may be as far from Dr. Joseph Bell's as salsa dancing is from physics. He has tried to explain how he "gives information" to his dancers in a one- to two-week frenzy of choreographing. It is unfair, in one sense, to ask a man who creates kinesthetic art to describe how he does it in words, but he is a good sport and tries. From one verbal description, though, it is hard to imagine how it works:

> I'm trying to tell them everything: your arms here, lean into this for this part of your body, think of this image while you're doing it, because it needs to convey this sort of idea. I'm trying to give them all that information and in the early stage... They're really taking in, taking in, taking in... I'm trying to get it out so I can see all the connections and all the dots are clear to me.... [The dancers] have to be on the edge of their seats taking that information in, internally notating all the details as much as they can, and then once that's out there, then I can step away, relax, look at it as an outsider, and then help them digest all that information that I threw at them so quickly.

The contrast between the organized, deliberate description of how Bell delivered information and McIntyre's gushing flood of ideas could not be more striking. Yet each is able to convey a lot of complex information to the right group, medical students and dancers, in ways that seem to make sense to the recipients. John Michael Schert is executive director of the company and a dancer who is on the receiving end as the choreography takes place. He claims that during the creative process, McIntyre focuses on the big picture. Dancers are trying to gather as much as they can from his comments, acting almost as "tools" for his imagination. After the two-week frenzy of choreography occurs, the dancers then have 11 months to take the flood of information they have received, "go back to do the detail work," and fill out the dance to shape it as their own.

These cases are perhaps extremes—highly methodical and highly free-form—that work in their contexts. Each individual and organization needs to find that "just right" approach to collecting or receiving information. A group of coaches has done a remarkable job at finding a "balance" that works for them and their students.

As a fellow teacher, I marvel at the Boise State University football coaches' ability to judge and understand how to give players the fire hydrant of information they need during the course of training and practice and do it so players absorb and use it effectively. These instructors fall somewhere between Bell and McIntyre in their approaches of complete order and structure to creative chaos, and they do so by tailoring their fire hydrant flood of information to the individual players. They use a system they call "whole-part-whole," learning a flood of information, then breaking it down into parts, and then helping players build it back to a larger picture. In the process, the coaches hope that the players will eventually, if they work at it, reach "aha experiences" in their play and lives as students.

Former defensive coordinator Justin Wilcox says his approach is not uniform, because of the wide variation in the ways his student players learn. Some learn visually, others physically, still others orally, and at least when they start as young players, they may not know which way they learn. So the coaches use all three.

To ensure that each type of learner gets what works for him, Wilcox and fellow coaches give them some of each style. The football players hear their coaches talk about plays and training, they watch film of games, and they practice on the field. The result is that all players have exposure to the different forms of information delivery, and each one "finds" his own best way to learn. Defensive Co-ordinator Pete Kwiatkowski wrestles as well with how much and how to deliver the information:

When we're teaching players . . . how to perform in a game sit-uation, you want to give [them] as much as they can handle . . .

so it's up to the position coaches to know what your group can handle [physically] and mentally. And then, we [coaches] get together and build the game plan. [If the players can't execute a play,] we've got to figure out a different way to teach it.

The approach permeates the full group of coaches and other players. Defensive second coach Marcel Yates stresses the role of older, more experienced players in the learning process; they help guide the younger players, "translating" what the coaches might say in a meeting so the newer players understand expectations. With that range of input and learning, the coaches say that aha moments often come to players during practice, even before the players quite understand intellectually or conceptually what they are doing. The repetition of practice builds "muscle memory" and ultimately the players find ways to understand and use what they are doing in a more integrated way. In the process, the younger players come to realize (like the older ones who have "got it") that their specific positions and movements belong to a larger whole—the game itself.

Dance is likewise grounded in learning physical movements on the road to gaining insight. Dancers claim that practicing a step or movement until it becomes their "own" is critical and often a precursor to a flash of insight. John Michael Schert of the Trey McIntyre Project describes the process as one where dancers move from learning a physical movement to making it "something bigger" than what the choreographer "gave" to the dancer. Dancers, like jail deputies or software engineers or football players, take information and connect it with their experiences and past knowledge to put it in a larger context. But to get there requires similar repetition to the point where they do not think about the specific movement but rather how it can fit into something larger.

Good learning practices, adapted for the learner (whether we are orchestrating our own learning or someone else is guiding), help to begin to put order onto the information flood and move us toward the next phase of making sense of it.

FINDING PATTERNS: ORGANIZING INFORMATION

In the process of moving toward insight thinking, receiving information—lots of it—is often the starting point. But to make progress, the information needs to be organized. Many people mention two basic steps: putting the information into categories or chunks so that it is manageable and then deciding which critical pieces of the information are most important for understanding or solving a problem.

Chunking Information

When my children were very young, we lived for several months in Belgium, where they were in kindergarten and first grade. As we prepared to travel, they felt overwhelmed with the task of packing. So we developed a simple system, going from feet to head. What went on their feet—shoes, socks. What about their legs—pants, shorts, PJs. Their chests? T-Shirts, sweaters, jackets. And so on. At first, we drew a picture of a boy and all the items he needed to pack, set against his feet, head, and so forth. As they got older, they didn't need the physical drawing of the boy and his gear, but could simply go from "feet to head" in their minds, using a mental check list. Our packing system was a simple way to remember information and solve a problem.

Now imagine a typical jigsaw puzzle. Some pieces have edges, some do not; the colors and patterns on the pieces vary, and match the picture on the puzzle's box. North Americans typically approach such a puzzle by classifying or sorting the pieces into groups—edges and corners, patterns of color or image, often working from outside in or from clusters of images and then connecting them. Finally, imagine a jigsaw puzzle with no box and no picture to guide you, only pieces of the puzzle laid out on a table. What if the pieces were all one inch square, making edges and inner pieces look the same? What if there were no colors, only shades of grey and black and white? And what if you did not realize that you had only some of the pieces, not all? How would you chunk that information, which seems to have no clear pattern? Such a puzzle is more like the nature of the messy problem: no clear solution, no clear way to even begin to understand it at first.

We use classifying and chunking systems as a matter of course, often without being fully aware of it. The "what to pack" and jigsaw puzzle problems exemplify the ways we classify information. The packing example illustrates the need to chunk information to make sense of and remember it. In the first jigsaw puzzle case, we classify information by shapes and images, allowing us to recognize relationships among pieces more easily and solve the problem.[8] In the second jigsaw puzzle, however, existing methods of classifying (e.g., sorting by edges, shapes, color) failed, so we must generate new ways to organize the information, using more subtle chunks, such as shades of grey. Each problem requires different approaches to chunking.

Our ability to classify information depends on many factors, some stemming from the way our brains chunk and remember. Can you recall your Social Security number? Your father's birthday? Your spouse's work phone number? Jeff Hawkins, founder of Palm Computing and author of *On Intelligence* about the brain and how it works, says we remember spatially (as in numbers, patterns, or even sounds) as well as temporally or chronologically, and a single trigger can evoke a whole memory.[9] Seeing a child's shoe tucked under a table brings the image of the whole child; smelling a woman's perfume can bring back a summer spent with a great-aunt who wore the same scent.

Scientists have several theories about how and why we pull up images and absorb information, and they diverge quite a bit. One traditional approach is the theory of "distributed representation," which says that millions of neurons fire and cooperate to generate a whole picture or image. Another more recent and controversial theory of "gnostic neurons" (i.e., neurons that "recognize") argues that one or just a few neurons can connect to recognize an image or face.[10] The theory depends on what have been called "Bill Clinton neurons" (or more generically, "grandmother cells") because studies found that separate neurons in different parts of the brain can recognize an image of Bill Clinton, whether it is a photo, drawing, or even the back of his head. The term "grandmother cells" is the broader term, since studies found that a small group of neurons were the ones that allow us to recognize our grandmother's face in a sea of other "grandmothers' faces."

Absorbing information also relates to memory, which typically follows a three-stage process: encountering information with our senses, putting it into short-term storage, and (sometimes) moving it to longer-term memory.[11] Short-term memory is limited by our ability to absorb and retain information, and putting it into chunks helps that process. In contrast, long-term memory is more stable, which is good news for older people, who have accumulated more information over time and are better at organizing it.[12] Because of their ability to transfer information, form new "chunks," or apply information from past situations to a current one, they may also be more efficient at problem solving.

Finally, when we are overwhelmed with information, organizing it into small chunks may help us begin to make sense of it, but chunking has its limits as well. As the categories of information get bigger, our ability to hold them decreases: We can remember three bullet points in a presentation more easily than nine or eleven. Some researchers talk about the "magical number of seven": As we exceed seven chunks or pieces of information (plus or minus two), we lose our ability to differentiate and retain them. If we chunk the items into different or fewer dimensions, we can remember them more readily.[13] My children could not easily remember 23 items they needed to pack, but they could remember multiple items (not many more than seven, though!) within clear categories of the body, feet, legs, chest, and head. Hence, too, the top number limits of phone numbers (seven without area codes) and Social Security numbers (nine) make sense. Essentially, we take a complex set of information, simplify it or break it down to remember and form patterns, and then put it back together to see the relationships—insight thinking in a nutshell.

The process of "making things simpler" is important at several stages of the aha journey. A friend and colleague of Einstein's, New Zealander Ernest Rutherford, once said that any idea should be simple enough that a barmaid could understand it.[14] Simple, but not simplistic.

Football coaches have turned classifying and making ideas simpler into an art. As a freshman, former defensive back Ian Smart was inundated with information that he was unable to process. Then came abject panic as he realized he had only three weeks to learn every play (20/day) before a game. But, the coaches broke down plays by position—working with only the defensive backs at first, walking through each play until every person understood it, which took several days. Then, the coaches added in the linebackers, building more pieces to the puzzle and slowly built up to the complex full play. As Smart said, "We're able to piece ourselves into that whole puzzle. . . . by the end . . . we've come back to that whole, and you look and see exactly why we're doing all of these different things."

* * *

So how do we start chunking information? Two approaches are common: using existing categories and creating new ones.

Using Existing Categories

In his *Just So* stories, Rudyard Kipling's poem "The Elephant Child" offered us a set of categories journalists and anyone writing a high school essay knows without thinking about it.[15]

> I keep six honest serving men
> (They taught me all I knew);
> Their names are What and Why and When
> And How and Where and Who.

Those "six honest serving men" questions form the chunks for many situations—from trying to understand the current financial situation, to a political election, to an organizational challenge, to a crime scene. Within any profession or job, people use similar ways to "chunk" information and make sense of it. A person in the food service industry, for instance, can go into a restaurant he has never been to before and tell a lot about what is going on—its financial state, management, even likely customer satisfaction—by sorting information into familiar categories. A consultant described the way a former restaurant manager "walked by the kitchen and took one look at the number of orders that were up, and could tell you how many people were in the restaurant, how the wait staff was doing, how productive they were being, whether orders had been sitting or not, based on how many should be up there at the same time."

Any field is replete with existing ways to categorize factors, and interestingly most have no more than the "magical seven" chunks. Business people use analysis approaches to assess industry, company, financial, and other situations, such as four factors in SWOT (strengths, weaknesses, opportunities, and threats) analysis, five factors in Porter's industry analysis, and four elements in the Boston Consulting Group portfolio analysis. The details within a field, of course, can be daunting to the outsider even as they help the expert.

According to Microsoft General Manager Russ Whitney, the software industry uses a handful of models or "patterns" to break a very big problem down into chunks with a common nomenclature.[16] One common example pattern is the "model view controller,"[17] which allows a designer to divide the software tasks into three parts—the model, the view, and the controller. The "model" manages the application data and the semantics associated with it, the "view" displays data to a user, and the "controller" receives input from a user and translates that into action. By dividing the software into three chunks, each of which has specific responsibilities, the designer has to solve only one-third of the problem at a time, since the interaction among the three pieces is already defined. Whitney's analogy is dividing the problem of a vehicle's drive train into the engine and the transmission. Anyone who works on a car knows the role of each of these parts. In using the model of an engine/transmission, the mechanic has to determine what goes into each of these parts. The question becomes, Which engine is appropriate or should a new one be built?

While each field has its existing categories to help sort information, sometimes existing categories do not fill the need. Then, new ways to chunk or classify information emerge.

Creating New Categories

With messy problems, we need new ways of looking at and organizing information. When Apple introduced the iPhone, it developed new chunks or ways to organize mobile phone functions (from the layout of the screen to the "scrolling" voice mail). After the jail escape, Gary Raney knew that traditional ways of managing and thinking about a jail mission would no longer work. He had input and information, but created simple categories to organize it by asking a basic question, "What is our function?" The sorting and chunking of that information generated the "pillars" that defined the purpose for the jail: Short, clear, and easy to remember, the pillars provided guidelines for daily actions and decisions.

Business consultants, authors, and professors are famous for creating "new" chunks or ways to understand and decipher information. In many cases, the chunks are rearranged from existing information, but perhaps put into a set of categories that are easy to recall, such as Covey's 7 Habits and Myers-Briggs' four categories; even Jim Collins's new book, *How the Mighty Fall*,[18] has five stages firms follow as they slide from being high performers.

Ranking It: We Have the Chunks, But What Is Most Important?

It is always a bit awkward to admit to another Ohio State University graduate that I am not a fan because I have a hard time rooting for a nut (the Ohio State mascot is a buckeye or chestnut). When the football game does not go their way, Ohio State fans have been known to throw buckeyes at the other team's players. But even worse, when I heard the rumor (I hope) of diehard fans Mr. and Mrs. Grey naming their new born daughter "Scarlett Ann" to show support for the school colors (scarlet and grey), I nearly swooned.

So I feel for Vilfredo Federico Damaso Pareto (1848–1923) whose parents had similar verve but saved him in the end. Pareto's Italian father and French mother lived in Paris when he was born. They were enamored with the March 1848 German revolution that spread unrest across some 39 loosely connected states in Germany. In support of the revolution, they named their son, Fritz Wilfried Pareto. Think of it, an Italian-French child, living in France, with a German name. When the family returned to Italy in 1858, the parents changed Fritz's name to Vilfredo Federico, where we presume he avoided his classmates' taunting, at least about his name.

Pareto is famous for the "80–20 rule" that came out of research he did on income distribution in London, where he found an unusual pattern: 20 percent of the city's population held 80 percent of the city's wealth. When he investigated other regions and cities, from Prussia to Italy to Paris, he found the same pattern, which held over time. The pattern has become more pronounced in the past few decades, even more of a "social arrow" (just a few people at the very top and many poorer ones below).[19] According to the World Institute for Developmental Economics, just 1 percent of the world's population holds 40 percent of the wealth, and the richest 10 percent hold 85 percent of the total wealth.[20]

Pareto's skewed percentage principle has been applied far beyond income distribution. In business, a general rule of thumb is 20 percent of customers generate 80 percent of sales and, likewise, 20 percent of clients cause 80 percent of complaints. If we carry Pareto's principle into sorting information, we would expect that a "critical few" factors would be most important for understanding and problem solving.

So how do people identify "the" critical few factors? Again, it may vary by profession and tasks but typically involves finding ways to "simplify." For example, when caterer and chef Bill Green wants to create a subtle taste, he will "simplify, by removing ingredients," so no single flavor dominates, but rather all ingredients work together. An improv comedy team member found, "The audience just wasn't getting it. So we had to tone it down, pare it down ... it paid off ... to make it a better show, we had to lose some of its cleverness."

People who are good "rankers" of information have common approaches. First, they look for factors that have multiple impacts. When Drake Cooper's creative marketing team members sought a focal point for a jewelry firm's ad campaign, they sifted through information about the firm and industry, sorting it into broad chunks or categories of potential marketing ideas. When they hit upon the word "shine," it became the core factor for the campaign because it touched so many other aspects of the marketing plan. According to Creative Director Joe Quatrone, the word "shine" permeates the ways that jewelry can be perceived.

A piece of jewelry itself can be shiny. The person who wears it "shines" by wearing it, and the person who gives it "shines" in the eyes of the receiver. For Quatrone, the word "shine" integrated the campaign—the theme, in-store graphics, and ad campaign radio spots. The tag was "you shine, you live, you love, you shine."

A second common way to identify key factors is to ask whether addressing that factor will have implications in solving other problems. For example, as Sheriff Gary Raney gained information about his organization's strengths and weaknesses, he heard from several people that "policies were the problem." The office had policies, and managers knew how to discipline employees who may disobey them, but a more fundamental issue for him was that employees did not understand why discipline may (or may not) be needed and what its consequences would be. In fact, he realized that lack of communication was the critical factor with many implications, not "the policies." Improving communications became a key factor in solving other problems.

Finally, some organizations identify key factors by their impact on a larger goal. Don Kemper, the CEO and highly prolific creative leader at Healthwise, the nonprofit health information provider, has a goal to embed innovation throughout all units and levels of the organization. But sometimes, new ideas can choke the system. Kemper, in particular, is legendary for generating more ideas in a day than many people do in a year. Early in the organization's life, he sent the ideas down the line, overwhelming employees who were baffled about which to pursue. Productivity slowed because the organization was clogged with ideas, all of which appeared to have equal weight. Each time he might suggest a new market or product, employees began to pursue it, only to be thwarted when another new idea appeared. Since many of Kemper's ideas were ones that needed years of incubation and time before the market was ready for them, it was easy to become sidetracked.

Kemper was wise enough to realize his strength in generating ideas but his weakness in screening them for others. So, his chief operating officer (COO) at the time, Gene Drabinski, became a "ranker," of sorts, to "control the nozzle" of ideas flooding from the CEO, evaluating them on such criteria as resources needed to pursue them, long- or short-term viability, and direct support of the organization's mission and goals. The COO passed along viable ones and saved others for future possible revisiting.

Vince Martino, former chief operating officer of Balihoo, used a similar approach. At any given time, his firm had 50 ideas to consider, ranging from how to recruit new employees or manage the organization to future products or markets. Implementing 50 ideas is untenable, and many may be conflicting. So Martino evaluated the ideas' impact on the ultimate output of the company as an initial screen to identify key factors.

WHAT MAKES SENSE: PROCESSING INFORMATION

Physicist and novelist Alan Lightman's book *Einstein's Dreams*[21] is a two-month fictional journal of Einstein's thinking about the concept of time. Over the course of the book, Einstein describes time in nearly two dozen different ways. Time is circular, mechanical, or based in our bodies. Time's rate varies by geography—both height (mountains and valleys) and place (location). Time has causes and time has effects. Different time exists as a feature of the 400-year-old buildings within Einstein's Bern neighborhood. Time bounces between mirrors. There is present and continuous time, fixed future time, and discontinuous time, on and on. In reading this beautifully written book, I gleaned that Einstein processed information and thinking by trying out ideas, by reshuffling them, and by taking time to live with them before he began to form his still unclear framework that fed into his aha moment with Michele Besso.

People process information in many ways on the road to an aha moment. Sometimes during the processing, an insight flash clicks and the information does make sense: We reach clarity on understanding or solving. Other times, we need more nudging, which gets into the ways we can spark or encourage aha moments, described in the next few chapters. Three broad methods emerged from the interviews in terms of how people begin to process information:

- "Just try it"
- Give it time
- Create fuzzy frameworks

JUST TRY IT

As Lightman conveyed in his book, *Einstein's Dreams*, Einstein played with and tried out countless ideas before he found one(s) that made sense for him. We know that a large part of creativity is the "just try it" approach, illustrated four ways below: purposeful practice, accidental trying it out, reshuffling, and talking about ideas with others.

Purposeful Practice

University football coaches expect freshmen players to be overwhelmed their first semester, not only with football, but with
becoming college students—from finding classes, to learning, to
studying. But by spring term, coaches see them beginning to process the information that has come their way since the previous
summer. Former Boise State University defensive coordinator
Justin Wilcox sees it when new players start to show that they recognize "parts" of the game—their positions, the key components
of the program—as well as how to maneuver as college students.
Although they can sort information physically and mentally, they
have not yet "put all the pieces together." Wilcox described a
player who knows "the pieces . . . he knows them in the meetings,
he can tell us what they mean, and when we practice by positions . . .
he can do it to perfection. And when we ask him things about a
certain defensive call, he can tell us exactly what we want to hear."
But when it comes to a game or scrimmage, which is "putting
the pieces together" in football, and the information is no longer
"compartmentalized," the player falters. Reaching that next level,
that aha moment, according to the coaches, takes time and trying
things out.

Perhaps because of the physical element, football players and
dancers seem to learn best by doing. After hearing what to do
and seeing it on film, players practice by trying moves. Only after
it becomes part of their muscle memory, according to both players
and coaches, will a player reach an epiphany or aha moment.
When I first asked a dancer if he had aha moments, he said they
were constant. Whenever he moved his arm into a certain position
he could "feel it"—"ah! That's it! Nooo, that doesn't work, but aha!
Another one, got it"—through a constant trying out of moves
with constant adjusting to find the mini-aha of understanding
what worked. Athletes and dancers cannot "get it" in their heads.
They have got to "do it" to know when it works or does not: It must
"feel right."

One other factor comes into play in the purposeful practice process: believing in the process and the people guiding it. Coaches,
given their years of experience with many different types of players, tell each new batch to "trust us, we've been there, we've done
this before with lots of other people, we know how it works."
And the players head to the field, to the work-out room, to the film
room, and try it. Only through repetition, deliberate practice, and
trusting the coaches that it will work, do they finally "get it" when

it comes to mastering movement, learning plays, and knowing how to read the field.[22]

Managers have similar ways to encourage subordinates to "practice": shadow sales calls, perform temporary assignments, and accept increasingly more difficult project roles—all are ways that allow employees to try out new skills, see what works, and perhaps experience that flash of insight, gaining a new skill or solving a problem. Thus, practicing with purpose as a way to process information moves us up the insight curve, making sense of the information and, in some cases, allowing insight to explode.

Accidental Event to "Just Try It"

Steve Schneider, M.D., works as chief medical officer for Healthwise, an organization with a mission to help people make better health decisions. Its patient-centered focus turned the medical and health world upside down over 30 years ago by urging patients to take responsibility for their health (and illnesses), rather than rely solely on medical experts. Schneider oversees a team of physicians who review the Healthwise information that appears on health portals and health plan, hospital, and disease management company Web sites.

With bushy dark hair, Schneider smiles easily and is so fit that he puts others to shame. He is a serious mountain biker, must have a body fat ratio of about 6 percent, and for some may be a tough person to talk to about not having the motivation to exercise or eat good food.

Having worked with Healthwise for 16 years as a board member first and for the past 12 years as chief medical officer, he lives the mission statement—"helping people make better health decisions." It is so much a part of the language that leaders have regular discussions about it to be sure people do not just voice it, like the pledge of allegiance, without really thinking about it.

Schneider also understands the patient-centered philosophy of the organization, that primary caregivers and patients should work in partnership so that patients can make the best decisions for themselves. But he admitted recently that it was not until he had a direct experience with the concept of "patient-centered focus" that he truly understood it and had an aha moment about it.

Scheider had practiced medicine for 20 years, using patient-centric care as a core belief, and then joined Healthwise where he "lived and breathed" the concept. But patient-centric care truly became clear for him when he was forced to "try it" himself when he became unexpectedly ill. He became so ill (unusual for him) that he spent time in a hospital as a patient (even more unusual) and really began to understand the notion in an emotional way. As he said,

> My experience as a patient and being on the other side ... was realizing that I rationally understood and could be an expert ... but that you can never fully understand it [patient-centric care] without having a very "gut, emotional" experience. I believe that was one more extremely critical step in my evolution of trying to tie together being brought up in the medical culture but being able to see this whole medical realm from the patient side.

He lay in bed, looking up at the doctors, just as patients had done with him for years. The physicians treated him as a patient, albeit a very knowledgeable one, but as a patient nonetheless. And he did not like some of the experiences. The medical staff took from him much of the responsibility he wanted to hold onto; he felt they were making choices for him or urging him to make choices that he might not have wanted. For the first time, he had the firsthand experience of what patient-centered (or not always patient-centered) practice meant. Schneider processed information by going through an accidental "just try it" experience in a relatively short time as the patient-customer. In doing so, he had an under-standing aha moment: He "got it" and understood more fully the essence of a patient-centered philosophy.

Reshuffle

In early 2009, the Trey McIntyre Project invited 12 artists of differ-ent disciplines to make "portraits" of its nine dancers and McIntyre, the artistic director and choreographer. The portraits would be exhib-ited at a local gallery. The artists used wildly different media and approaches. A group of musicians created a "portrait song" to cap-ture the nature of each dancer; a visual artist created abstract fused glass color interpretations of each performer; a chocolate maker created three specialty chocolates representing the dancers in the current repertoire; and a sewing group made hand-embroidered pins with images of the "nine plus one" subjects.

Artist Karen Bubb, who had most recently been working as a painter, experimented in a new form for this project—printing pho-tographs on glass. She first collected information about the dancers by taking hundreds of photographs during rehearsals. She then sorted through the photographs, chose images that captured the character of the dancers and their interactions with each other, and used a process called polyester plate lithography to hand print the images directly onto art glass. When it came to processing the information, she focused in on particular images, "played" with them on the computer to adjust contrast and to experiment with combinations that would generate the look and feel she wanted. Transferring the printmaking process onto glass changed the nature of the photographic images, making them more "painterly," and brought an element of surprise to the process as they never turned out "perfect." Her overall intent was to incorporate the images of the dancers into small (1 inch by 1 inch or 2 inches by 1 inch) pendants backed with gold and silver leaf and larger but still intimate (all under 14 inches by 20 inches) stained glass artworks. The works gave sponsors and fans the chance to buy a memento of a favorite dancer to wear or give as a gift. To reach the final result, Bubb shuffled and then reshuffled images, and then made and discarded prints to see what worked. Her process was part "accidental" and part purposeful: By "playing with the images," she looked for a creative aha moment that formed a new piece of art.

Reshuffling as a way to grapple with "the whirling vortex" of information has a base assumption, which is that we start with all of (and perhaps more than) the information we want or need to solve a problem. Then we reshuffle pieces into a framework that helps us better understand or solve a problem, similar to the way an hourglass works when lots of sand moves through a smaller funnel and then settles into a different position. In a sense, the process is also similar to the whole-part-whole approach that football coaches use: bringing information about a large, complex situation together, narrowing the focus to consider parts of it, and then putting the "whole" back together in a different, reshuffled configuration as it sifts down.

Talk About It

There's definitely something to someone organizing it in their head in a way they can articulate it to somebody else.
—Craig Boobar, Principal Development Manager, Microsoft

Who has not talked about inklings of ideas as we work on problems? Collaboration by talking about ideas (or listening to others talk) is critical for many people in the process of understanding an idea or solving a problem.[23] When one high-tech manager wrestles with a problem, he eventually presents it to three or four other people, without telling them his ideas or solutions. He listens, takes their input, and combines it with his ideas. Thus, he "tries out" his ideas by *not* talking about them, but by listening to others talk.

Entrepreneur and CEO Becky Logue is convinced that talking about ideas with "the right people" who are creative and open-minded is critical for her to generate creative aha moments. Ethics director Angeli Weller finds that talking about ideas may lead to a critical piece of information that she had not thought of before and that triggers aha moments for her. In essence, by talking with others, we let them help with our "reflective reframing" as we sort through information and make sense of it.[24]

For all of the reasons people appreciate "talking out loud," it has some drawbacks. Talking about ideas and solutions early in the aha journey may lock us in to a particular solution to a problem.[25] In discussions with some of the software engineers at Microsoft, I watched as they experienced their own aha moments when they realized that in some cases they do tend to lock in on a possible solution and try it out before moving to another, which could take more time and be less efficient.

Also, the "talk about it" approach to processing information may vary across cultures. When trying to solve a problem, European Americans and East Asian Americans use the "talk about it" approach differently. European Americans tend to solve problems more effectively when they combine talking with listening.[26] On the other hand, East Asian American groups have the opposite problem: They find it *more difficult* to solve problems when they are forced to "think out loud" rather than to be silent.

The observations certainly fit with my experience during interviews for this book. Americans tend to report that they shape their ideas (and often reach a flash of insight) as they talked through problems or questions they wrestle with. The Vietnamese managers I spoke with, on the other hand, tend to "think think think" about the problems and rarely talk with others to solve problems. While they do reach aha moments, they felt it happened less because of conversations with others. A top executive at one of Vietnam's largest investment firms rarely talks to colleagues about problems he may have with the organization—in management, in financial decisions, with clients. Instead, his approach for seeking aha moments is "deeper concentration." His comments were similar to other

Vietnamese managers who may talk with peers outside of their organizations, but almost never within. The Confucian-based cultural norms may be part of the cause. In a country where hierarchy is strict, the notion of talking about challenges to anyone above might suggest weakness; to discuss challenges with subordinates below shows lack of knowledge. A possible lesson for global managers: Processing information on the road to insight may vary dramatically across cultures, meaning the aha journey stages may also vary.

GIVE IT TIME

Solving complex problems or reaching an understanding of complicated issues simply takes time for most people, and yet too often we feel we lack the time to let ideas "simmer." Engineers like to "get things done," so they often move quickly from identifying a problem to finding a solution and verifying it; if that solution fails, they return to the initial information gathering and sorting phase. But during the course of interviews, some realized that perhaps if they slow down and generate several possible solutions first, they may end up with more and better solutions in the long run. Three examples illustrate the importance of time in processing information: (1) by slowing the process, (2) by allowing others to set the pace of processing, and (3) by taking time to let the simmering happen, especially with groups.

Slow It Down

Chad Sarmento might make a great TV anchor because he sits so still when he talks, barely moving his head or hands. His calmness is something that he has always had, and it serves him well in many ways but sometimes frustrates his work colleagues. When he moved to the Ada County Sheriff's Office from another county law enforcement agency, he took a large decrease in pay and position. Moving from a supervisory job to a deputy position in a jail cut his family's income substantially, but he said it was worth it. He was able to work in an environment that appreciated his skills and had a culture he believed in.

Sarmento did not stay in the deputy slot for long. In 10 months, he was promoted to sergeant, supervising a team of 27 jail deputies working four 12-hour days a week. His team makes "hundreds of decisions every 12.1 hours," and he worries that some will be done too rapidly. So Sarmento slows things down.

When I asked where the idea of slowing down comes from, Sarmento referred me to one of his favorite books. *On Combat*[27] reports that most law-enforcement officers experience slow-motion times during a crisis, particularly during a gunfight. Remember the fight scenes in *The Matrix* and you will have an idea of what he means. But for Sarmento, it is not just what happens during a crisis situation. He slows down as a matter of course in his work. And in some cases, he is able to help others reach an aha experience in the process.

One man, well-known and highly regarded in his community, was incarcerated for the first time following a breakdown. According to Sarmento, when the man was brought into custody, he battered two officers, one quite severely. He resisted talking to anyone, including a therapist, would not listen to instructions, and refused to cooperate when asked. Over the course of several days, Sarmento spent hours sitting with, and eventually talking to, the inmate. He did it in steps, as he said, returning many times to visit the man, spending three to four hours on each visit.

Then, Sarmento claims the inmate moved toward an aha moment of understanding when he began "to see his situation clearly and that he had an option to change it." Something clicked when Sarmento said that the guards could treat the inmate "like a prisoner" but that he (Sarmento) "didn't want that and the inmate probably didn't want that either."

> [The inmate] sat there and . . . he cried just a touch. And he says "maybe I've just hit the bottom now and I can start turning around." And I said "you've already turned around. You don't realize it but you've already turned around."

Sarmento walked the man to a therapist and went home at the end of the day feeling he had made progress. In this case, the inmate had to "hit bottom" to trigger an insight that helped him understand his situation and start to make progress. And he did so thanks in part to Sarmento's ability to slow things down.

Slowing down works, as it did for Sarmento, to give a person time to adjust and recognize the need for an "aha moment." Another type of "slowing down" happens when the work of processing information has happened and the flash of insight arrives. Football players and their coaches talk of how "things slow down" when the players come to a new level of understanding. According to former Boise State coach Justin Wilcox, during the first semester new players feel "it's going 90 mph, everything is just so fast, their heads are on a swivel . . . ." It takes effort and persistence on their part (and their coaches) for the players to reach a state of being comfortable with their ability to perform. If the player is lucky, flashes of insight start to appear, sometimes during the spring semester, but more often during the following year. When they "get it," the game "slows down." They understand what is happening around them, they are able to carry out their own movements easily, and each play feels like it moves in slow motion.

Put the Pencil in the Other Hand

In football, the coaches set the pace for players and try to help players reach aha moments of understanding more quickly. That desire to speed up the process of "getting it" exists for many people, from bank branch managers to theater directors, construction project coordinators to consultants. In each case one person is trying to convey information to help another learn. And understanding how people learn may eventually lead to that transfer of knowledge and the reaching of an understanding aha.

Few professors, let alone bank managers or education administrators, have studied how to spur insight as much as Henry Gurr, retired physics professor from the University of South Carolina (Aiken).[28] For years, Gurr watched how his students did—or did not—achieve aha moments of understanding as they tried to learn physics. He found that one-on-one tutor sessions with students were a way to encourage and generate aha moments, and at its core was a practice he calls "putting the pencil in the student's hand."[29]

After class, when students come for tutorials, Gurr sits at a desk with a pad of paper between himself and the student. Then he hands the student a pencil and asks her to show how she generated a graph or an equation. According to Gurr, this act helps begin the journey toward insight for two reasons. First, it puts the focus on the problem, not on the interaction between student and professor. For students intimidated by a professor, focusing on a pad of paper avoids the need for eye contact (similar to the advice that parents of teenagers pass along to one another—riding in a car, where parent and child both look forward, allows for some good conversation— because there is no eye contact). So in a sense, it relaxes the student, allowing more openness and potential for aha moments.

Second, by "putting the pencil in the student's hand," Gurr gives the student control of the conversation, both topic and pace.

The student's questions drive what the two of them talk about, removing control from the professor and his desire to "cover material." Too often in a classroom, as well as in some business meetings, some audience members show they are not understanding— furrowed eyebrows, cocked heads, straight lips, glazed eyes. So what does the typical presenter do? He talks faster, offering *more* information, silently hoping that surely audience members will hear *something* that makes sense. The gush of the fire hydrant syndrome then sometimes completely confuses the audience rather than helps it.

But by putting the pencil in the student's hand, Gurr allows the student to direct the discussion, set the pace that fits her level of information absorption, and feel in control. That allows the student to process information at her speed, in her own way, so that Gurr in a sense guides her toward insight.

The 18-Month Rule

A final example of using time to process information comes from experience I had working in Hanoi, Vietnam. From 1994 to 2003, I managed my university's involvement in a Swedish- and U.S.-funded aid project to establish Vietnam's first international standard business school, essentially a new venture start-up within an existing university. We "trained-the-trainers" (lecturers working at the university who would become the faculty members within the business school) and advised on academic curriculum and financial, library, and technology infrastructure. We co-taught with faculty members to introduce "new" methods of teaching, like case study discussions and group projects. In the final two years, we also tried to instill a professional research culture among the faculty members and administrators so the faculty could conduct research and publish it in journals outside of Vietnam.

International standard universities argue that the goal of research is to add to a body of knowledge that will move a field forward, no matter what field, whether nanotechnology, anthropology, or meteorology. The process typically involves testing existing theory or, in some cases, developing new frameworks or theories. Then, researchers write up and submit the manuscript to a scientific journal, where two to three peers or experts in the field review the submitted paper. The review is "blind," meaning the name of the manuscript submitter is unknown to the reviewers. If the paper is deemed publishable, with valid approaches and interesting results, it appears in the journal for other scientific peers to read.

Besides the somewhat idealistic and altruistic role of research—to add to the body of knowledge in a field—universities benefit in other ways when faculty members publish research that is recognized in a wider context: It helps them recruit good faculty members and students, and it brings in money from grants or private contracts. In addition, and most important for administrators, the research "rankings" become critical for accreditation of universities within a country as well as outside. In fact, some universities have begun inviting highly prolific publishers to spend part of the year with them so they can legitimately claim the researcher is from their university, and thus receive the recognition that comes with it. Thus being well-known as a researcher and a university can have multiple payoffs.

When I first raised the question of doing international research, the vice rector said the university already was a leader in research. Then he described the process: A Vietnamese government ministry comes up with a question, like how many farmers produce rice in the Red River Valley, which runs from China through Vietnam to Hai Phong Harbor. The ministry appoints a university to conduct the research. Within the university, the senior administrators assign a senior professor to oversee the project and two or three junior lecturers/teachers to carry out the research. When completed, the research report lists the senior faculty member's name first and, if they were lucky to be listed at all, the junior lecturers' names come after. The report goes to the ministry and a version appears in the university's own academic journal, distributed to other Vietnamese universities. There is no peer review and no exposure beyond the university and governmental communities: This is not international standard research as the rest of the world views it.

The existing process meant faculty members could not choose their own research topics or partners, or publish outside of Vietnam. In fact, in the 1990s, if a Vietnamese faculty member did want to publish internationally, the government had to review the manuscript (which took up to a year) before it could be submitted to a journal outside of the country. Finally, the university administration had difficulty understanding why a faculty member would want to publish outside the country. If that happened, it meant "fame" to the individual (also to the university, although they did not see it that way) and standing out as an individual faculty member was not widely acceptable in the egalitarian communist framework of large public universities.

"We already do research," said the vice rector. He felt there was no need to change. Yet others disagreed. The project funders and the Vietnamese faculty members who had done their Ph.D.s in universities outside of Vietnam understood international standard research and wanted to pursue it. If the business school's goal was to train Vietnamese managers for future regional and global business opportunities, then new knowledge was critical. Did existing models about doing business globally work for Vietnam? What could new theories from emerging countries like Vietnam offer to the rest of the scholarly world? Counting farmers in the Red River Valley was unlikely to put the university on the international scholarship map. My view was that they at least needed to understand what others were doing, and then decide if it was something they wanted.

So I began planting seeds. When the senior administrators visited my university on a fact finding/study tour, they met with the director of Research Administration, the provost, and researchers, and all presented a consistent message. Faculty members in "international standard universities" choose their own research topics and co-researchers, conduct research using accepted research methods, decide tasks and order of names on a manuscript, and submit manuscripts for blind review. When the senior Vietnamese administrators visited a British university for management training, they heard the same. When foreign visiting professors came to Vietnam, I made sure that they casually mentioned to the administrators that they would welcome a continuing research relationship with faculty members but wanted to publish in international journals.

Eighteen months after I first raised the notion of research to the vice rector, he proposed an idea: What if the university had a process to encourage faculty members to choose topics, research them with foreign colleagues, and publish the results outside of Vietnam? Aha! I said. Brilliant! So glad you thought of that.

When I compared notes with other foreigners working in Vietnam, the 18-month rule appeared common for collective aha experiences to happen. It also seems to hold in other diverse settings. Boise State football coaches (now) say the average time for players to "get it" and reach an aha moment of understanding is also about 18 months, from the time they join the program as freshmen or as transfer students. Also, Major Ron Freeman who oversaw the development of the jail pillars likewise found it took about 18 months for the new culture to take hold within the organization. During that time, some people retired or left, and the rest picked up on the key values, understanding the changes and reasons behind them.

Time—slowing it down, allowing others to set the pace, and simply giving it to people—appears to be critical in processing information, especially as we move toward aha moments. Our brains process it, and during that time we often start to form theories and frameworks of what makes sense.

CREATING FUZZY FRAMEWORKS

The fatal mistake which the ordinary policeman makes is this, that he gets his theory first, and then makes the facts fit it, instead of getting his facts first and making all his little observations and deductions until he is driven irresistibly by them into an elucidation in a direction he may never have originally contemplated.[30]

—Said about Dr. Joseph Bell,
Arthur Conan Doyle's model for Sherlock Holmes

Finally, as people classify information and try to make sense of it, some talk about forming tentative or fuzzy frameworks or theories about what they are seeing. They shape the frameworks more fully later but often feel an inkling of explanation starts to happen as they process and look for patterns in the information.[31] Sleep expert turned acromegaly expert, Dr. Helfrich (Chapter 2) noticed symptoms that made no sense, until he began to see patterns that stemmed from the pituitary gland tumor.

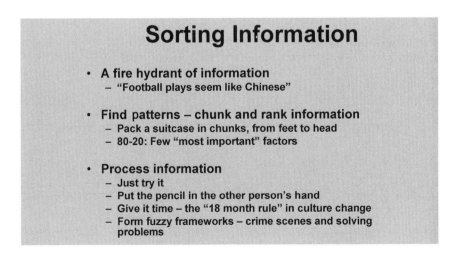

Sorting Information

- **A fire hydrant of information**
  - "Football plays seem like Chinese"

- **Find patterns – chunk and rank information**
  - Pack a suitcase in chunks, from feet to head
  - 80-20: Few "most important" factors

- **Process information**
  - Just try it
  - Put the pencil in the other person's hand
  - Give it time – the "18 month rule" in culture change
  - Form fuzzy frameworks – crime scenes and solving problems

Crime investigators are pros at beginning to form fuzzy theories about what might have happened early in the information collection and organizing process. As we saw with Crime Scene Investigator Jaimie Barker, he began to very gently start creating a "how did it happen" idea even as he was still collecting information, even before he knew which pieces of evidence would be most important. He started to form very tentative, fuzzy ideas of what might have happened. He classifies a violent crime as a homicide or suicide; that then leads him down another path where he may look for other types of information. So even as he is collecting and organizing information, he begins to structure the problem; no solutions are evident, but framing what might have happened is in process.

During the sorting stage, some people do achieve aha moments. But many, especially if they hope to have alternative possible explanations or solutions for a problem, push on, seeking to nudge an insight flash into being, which is the focus of Part II.

NOTES

1. Thomas Wolfe. 1936. *The Story of a Novel*. New York: Charles Scribner's Sons: 36.

2. Jeff Hawkins and Sandra Blakeslee. 2004. *On Intelligence*. New York City: Times Books: 33–34.

3. Rex Beasley. 1964. *Edison*. Philadelphia: Chilton Books: 39.

4. Healthwise was one of the *Wall Street Journal*'s Best Small Organizations of the Year in 2007. Top small workplaces award, Winning Workplaces (http://www.winningworkplaces.org/topsmallbiz/2007winners/index.php, last accessed August 5, 2009).

5. Remy M. J. P. Rikers, Henk G. Schmidt, and Henny P. A. Boshuizen. 2000. Knowledge encapsulation and the intermediate effect, *Contemporary Educational Psychology*, 25: 150–166.

6. Ely Liebow. 2007. *Dr. Joe Bell: Model for Sherlock Holmes*. Madison, WI: Popular Press: 176; The Chronicles of Sir Arthur Conan Doyle, http://www.siracd.com/work_bell.shtml; The Joseph Bell Centre for Forensic Statistics and Legal Reasoning, http://www.cfslr.ed.ac.uk/about/josephbell.htm.

7. Claudia La Rocco. 2008. A choreographer gives his dream an Idaho address, *The New York Times*, September 12: AR 31; Janine Parker. 2008. New company soars in debut at Jacob's Pillow, *The Boston Globe*, August 22; Lisa Traiger. 2008. Basking in a Western exposure, *The Washington Post*, October 31; Tresca Weinstein. 2009.

A new beginning: Choreographer Trey McIntyre takes his company full-time, *Pointe Magazine*, February/March: 25–26; Speakeasy with John Michael Schert, *Creative Loafing* (http://atlanta.creativeloafing.com/gyrobase/john_michael_schert/Content?oid=736111, last accessed July 22, 2009).

8. Several researchers have used jigsaw puzzles as a way to examine how we recognize patterns. See, for example, Feng-Hui Yao and Gui-Feng Shao. 2003. A shape and image merging technique to solve jigsaw puzzles, *Pattern Recognition Letters*, 24 (12) August: 1819–1835; Robert Tybon. 2004. Generating Solutions to the Jigsaw Puzzle Problem, Dissertation, Griffith University, Queensland, Australia.

9. Jeff Hawkins and Sandra Blakeslee. 2004. *On Intelligence*. New York City: Times Books: 71–73; Dorothy Leonard-Barton and Walter Swap. 2005. *Deep Smarts: How to Cultivate and Transfer Enduring Business Wisdom*. Boston, MA: Harvard Business School Press.

10. Katja Gaschler. 2006. One person, one neuron? *Scientific American*, February, http://www.scientificamerican.com/article.cfm?id=one-person-one-neuron&page=3.

11. Ellen Pastorino and Susann Doyle-Portillo. 2009. *What Is Psychology?* Belmont, CA: Thomson Wadsworth: 246–255.

12. Sara Reistead-Long. 2008. Older brain really may be a wiser brain, *The New York Times*, May 20: D5; Steven Laureys, Association for the Scientific Study of Consciousness Meeting. 2005. *The Boundaries of Consciousness: Neurobiology and Neuropathology*, Progress in Brain Research, v. 150. Amsterdam: Elsevier.

13. George Miller. 1994. The magical number seven, plus or minus two: Some limits on our capacity for processing information, *Psychological Review*, 101 (2): 343–352.

14. W. Bennett Lewis. 1972. Some recollections and reflections on Rutherford, *Notes and Records of the Royal Society of London*, 27 (1), August: 61; G. J. Whitrow. 1973. *Einstein: The Man and His Achievement*. New York City: Dover: 42.

15. Rudyard Kipling. 1907. *Just So Stories*. Garden City, NY: Doubleday: 85.

16. There are also so-called "anti-patterns," or models that are easy to fall into that will cause problems in software design.

17. Model-view-controller, Wikipedia (http://en.wikipedia.org/wiki/Model-view-controller, last accessed July 27, 2009).

18. James C. Collins. 2009. *How the Mighty Fall: And Why Some Companies Never Give In*. New York City: Collins Business.

The five stages include:

Stage 1: Hubris Born of Success

Stage 2: Undisciplined Pursuit of More

Stage 3: Denial of Risk and Peril

Stage 4: Grasping for Salvation

Stage 5: Capitulation to Irrelevance or Death

19. Benoit B. Mandelbrot and Richard L. Hudson. 2004. *The (Mis) Behavior of Markets: A Fractal View of Risk, Ruin, and Reward.* New York City: Basic Books: 152–155.

20. Aaron Glantz. 2006. Richest 2 percent own half the world's wealth," *Common Dreams,* http://www.commondreams.org/headlines06/1222-04.htm.

21. Alan Lightman. 1993. *Einstein's Dreams.* New York: Vintage Contemporaries.

22. Geoffrey Colvin. 2008. *Talent Is Overrated: What Really Separated World-Class Performers from Everybody Else.* New York City: Portfolio.

23. C. J. Price, R. J. S. Wise, E. A. Warburton, C. J. Moore, D. Howard, K. Patterson, R. S. J. Frackowiak, and K. J. Friston. 1996. Hearing and saying: The functional neuro-anatomy of auditory word processing, *Brain,* 119 (3): 919–931; Howard J. Rosen, Jeffrey G. Ojemann, John M. Ollinger, and Steve E. Petersen. 2000. Comparison of brain activation during word retrieval done silently and aloud using fMRI, *Brain and Cognition* 42 (Part 2): 201–217; Heejung S. Kim. 2002. We talk, therefore we think? A cultural analysis of the effect of talking on thinking, *Journal of Personality and Social Psychology* 83 (4): 828–842.

24. Andrew B. Hargadon and Beth A. Bechky. 2006. When collections of creatives becomes creative collectives: A field study of problem solving at work, *Organization Science,* 17 (4) July–August: 484–500.

25. E. M. Bowden and M. Jung-Beeman. 2003. Aha! Insight experience correlates with solution activation in the right hemisphere. *Psychonomic Bulletin & Review* 10 (3): 730–737.

26. Heejung S. Kim. 2002. We talk, therefore we think? A cultural analysis of the effect of talking on thinking, *Journal of Personality and Social Psychology* 83 (4): 828–842; Torkil Clemmensen, Morten Hertzum, Kasper Hornæk, Qingxin Shi, and Pradeep Yammiyavar. 2009. Cultural cognition in usability evaluation, *Interacting with Computers,* 21 (3): 212–220.

27. Dave Grossman and Loren W. Christensen. 2007. *On Combat: The Psychology and Physiology of Deadly Conflict in War and in Peace.* Millstadt, IL: Warrior Science Publications.

28. Gurr has several papers and discussions on the Web. See, for example, Henry S. Gurr. 1999. The flash of insight in teaching and tutoring ... AHA, Eureka, It dawned on me, light bulb, bolt of lightning, Zeus, epiphany. Paper presented at the American Physical Society, 66th Annual Meeting of the Southeastern Section of the American Physical Society, November 7–9, Chapel Hill, NC.

29. Henry S. Gurr. 2005. The AHA in teaching and tutoring: The flash of insight, resolving student conceptual confusion, and one-on-one help session tutoring, Working paper, November 8 (www.usca .edu/math/~mathdept/hsg/TeachingTutoring+Pix.html).

30. Jessie M. E. Saxby. 1913. *Joseph Bell: An Appreciation by an Old Friend.* Edinburgh: Oliphant, Anderson & Ferrier: 23.

31. Evan I. Schwartz. 2004. *Juice: The Creative Fuel that Drives World-Class Inventors.* Boston, MA: Harvard Business School Press.

Part II

Moving Toward the Peak: Finding Ways to Spark Aha Moments

Russ Whitney, general manager for Microsoft, is a highly competent, very smart software designer and manager of research. He is tall and lanky, has a constant half-smile, and has floppy hair that falls on his forehead and makes him look younger than he may be. He opens his eyes wide when he makes a point or realizes something he had not a moment before.

While I was reviewing ideas in this book with him, Whitney said that the sorting and final verifying stages make logical sense to him, like a mini-scientific method. He was less convinced of a spark phase to encourage aha moments. But as we talked more, he experienced his own aha moment. He realized that he might be missing better ideas or ways to frame a problem because he moves so quickly from the sort to the verifying phase. At that point in our conversation, he tilted back his chair and folded his hands on his stomach and his eyes got wide. He said he needed to learn to "unsnap" his thinking, slow down, and give more effort to coming up with more ahas before settling on a problem solution. Then he said, "I need to spend more time coming up with lots of mini-ahas and then do a triage on them, rather than testing them sequentially and then returning to the sort phase." Part II is a way to help Whitney and others kick-start that process.

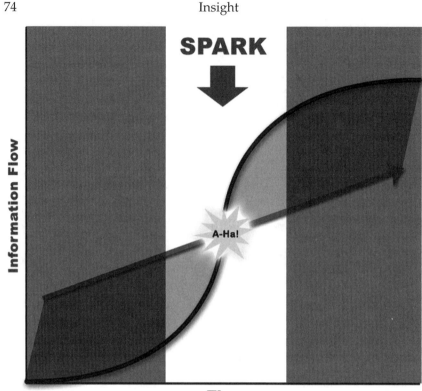

Sparking an Insight

Part II makes up the crux of this book, focusing on ways to spark aha moments (see figure "Sparking an Insight" above), techniques to shift our thinking, and ways to use walls or obstacles to nudge insight. Chapter 4 argues for the benefit of putting odd pieces of information together. Often, when we reach outside of our own disciplines, we find ideas that can help solve a problem or explain a confusing situation. The upsurge in interest in cross-disciplinary research in science and management attests to the growing recognition of the value of standing at "intersections" to look for ideas that can be used in multiple places. Chapter 5 continues the journey of looking at an issue from different perspectives by using what I call "reverse thinking" or "upside-down thinking," which is thinking in ways that seem opposite and perhaps intuitively wrong at first. Chapter 6 considers how to "see what's not there." Asking "what am I missing?" may spark insight and fill in gaps in our thinking.

Memorable trips often include disasters—planes missed, luggage lost, passports stolen. They may not make for comfortable experiences, but certainly we learn from them. We understand how to overcome obstacles, how to roll with changes of plans, and how to appreciate reaching the final destination. On the aha journey, we also can face walls and make detours on the way to the flash of insight that helps us understand or solve some problem. Chapters 7 and 8 cover what happens when the journey hits bumps. Often we feel that we have hit a wall and are stymied: We cannot figure out a problem, do not know how to make a jump in comprehension, or just feel stuck. Most of us would rather avoid such walls, but actors who specialize in improvisation offer a way to see "walls" as opportunities for making progress and, in Chapter 7, we will learn some of their techniques. Chapter 8 focuses on what most people think about when they talk about an aha moment: the period when they were not thinking about a problem and then, BOOM, the solution came to them. That detour, or incubation, when we do activities that appear unrelated to our problem, are in fact critical for the journey for some people. While we assume that a break from the problem—whether standing in the shower, taking a hike, or playing music—is really stepping away from it, our brains keep on working. Chapter 8 talks about what people do in those breaks and why they seem to work.

Finally, Chapter 9 describes the classic experience that many of us call the aha moment. At last, the snap or click occurs when pieces of information come together and we "see the light." We see a problem or solve it in a new way.

Chapter 4

"Join-Ventures" and "Deathlines": When Putting Odd Ideas Together Sparks Insight

Creativity is just connecting things.
—Steve Jobs, Apple CEO

If ever we worry that our high-tech world will overpower our high-touch needs, we should remember that in Vietnam, electronic mail is "two computers massaging each other."

During the 1990s, Vietnamese who were learning English had a lively approach for a language that I too much take for granted. Although I have some language skills—I speak German, can keep up somewhat in French, studied (and have forgotten) Japanese—Vietnamese is beyond me. When I reached the lesson where I learned that "bo" can mean "church" or "brothel" depending upon tone, I gave up. Just how would it look to some Vietnamese early on a Sunday morning if a straight-looking American female professor asked for a house of ill repute.

So it is with awe and amazement when I interact with Vietnamese learning to speak English. Some of the phrases that emerge put odd ideas or phrases together that sometimes make better sense and are more vivid than what we native speakers use daily, especially when it comes to business lingo. In Vietnam, the "regal framework" describes the business structure, which may come closer to how some regulations and legalities seem "imperial."

When the "regal structure" sets up "join-ventures," that may better capture the intended nature of joint ventures, offering a more collaborative image. Firms' managers then decide upon internal structures, with options of being "flattering" or "tall and fat," which about sums up many approaches to hierarchy. Instead of a human resource department, why not a "human rescue department," which "deeply interviews" applicants and then puts together activities where employees learn new skills and knowledge through a "training bowl."

Indeed, English from the mouths of new learners can bring a smile to any jaded manager or weary professor. Certainly when I have an upcoming "deathline" to meet, I sit up a bit straighter. And, how can I not want to be in a place where "management from the seat of my bicycle" dominates, where "gold opportunities" come from the external environment, and where a firm has "decided to delight any customer?"

LINKING ZOOLOGY AND BANKING?

Putting odd pieces of information together—whether accidental or purposeful—can be a valuable way to trigger insight. The unexpected pairing of words or ideas, especially with a small twist of humor, can force us to consider a different perspective, which may in turn spark new ways of thinking, new ideas, and aha moments. Increasingly, people in business and beyond are looking for ways to explain and solve problems and are seeking odd connections in the process.

In May 2009, *The Financial Times* reported on two reports, from people in two completely different disciplines, who reached similar conclusions about the way zoology/ecology and financial systems may be linked. Lord Robert May, a preeminent zoologist at Oxford University, commented on the "common ground" in analysis of financial systems and ecosystems to explain how easily they can move from stable to unstable, "less happy" systems. Coming from the opposite angle, Andrew Haldane, executive director of financial stability for the Bank of England, argued that the global financial network is both "robust and fragile . . . a property exhibited by other complex adaptive networks, like tropical rainforests."[1]

Looking for connections among unlikely factors often generates flashes of insight in explaining the unexplainable and in developing creative solutions to problems, which often also means new products or services. In this chapter, we will look at examples of how "odd pieces" can help explain or create.

EXPLAINING THE UNEXPLAINABLE: MAKING ODD CONNECTIONS

Putting together odd pieces of information to explain even odder situations has a healthy history and likely long future. Three examples here show the ways individuals and groups have made connections that reveal "what really is happening."

Suicide: Intent or Something Else?

The rate of suicides in the United States in 2008 was the same as that in 1965, 11 per 100,000 inhabitants. And 90 percent of suicide "completers" had some sort of mental disorder before they killed themselves. But given the major advancements in treating mental disorders since 1965, why are there still so many suicides in the United States? Have the treatments not helped quell the problems? If so, shouldn't people with better mental health treatment be less likely to attempt (and complete) suicides? Part of the answer to this paradox came from far away, both geographically and in time.

Throughout the 1950s in the United Kingdom, 2,500 people annually, almost half of all suicides in the country, committed suicide by "sticking one's head in the oven." Sylvia Plath and Anne Sexton were two well-known writers who took advantage of the oven technique. But by the early 1970s, the number of suicides in the United Kingdom had dropped by 30 percent, and of the completers, none used ovens. Why?

The way that researchers and medical experts view suicide today is based to some extent on how they connected odd pieces of information about the suicide puzzle in Britain, now referred to as the British coal-gas story.[2] For years, the British used coal-derived gas for heating and cooking. Cheap and available, it also generated dangerous levels of carbon monoxide. A leak or putting "one's head in the oven" led to death by asphyxiation almost immediately. As safer natural gas ovens replaced the coal-gas ones after the 1950s, the suicide rate dropped. Simply having access to a method of suicide increases the chance that the participant will carry out her action. As New York Times reporter Scott Anderson said, "If the impulsive suicide attempter tends to reach for whatever means are easy or quick, is it possible that the availability of means can actually spur the act?"

Such connections have replaced the old theory of suicide with a dramatically different new one. Whereas the earlier theory was that "mental health problems + intent = completed suicide," the new one says that "impulse + availability of means = greater chance of a completed suicide." As a result, professionals now understand that to reduce the extent of completed suicides elsewhere, a focus on reducing available means to do it becomes critical.

Culture and (Sub)Culture

Sometimes the "odd pieces" are just hints that do not quite fit the expected outcomes. The nonprofit organization Healthwise produces consumer health content for many health portals and health plan provider Web sites. It is known not only for its quality health information but for its strong culture and values. The mission of "helping people make better health decisions" comes up regularly in conversation, and the values are posted in conference rooms, offices, and the hallway. It is hard not to be confronted with both.

The organization's founder and senior managers are so fervent about ensuring that employees understand and live by the culture and values that a senior vice president holds periodic "culture check-ins" with groups of employees to monitor how well people understand the core values. "Culture check-in" discussions and semiannual employee satisfaction surveys help the leadership team assess understanding and application of culture and values. Recently, results from one of the surveys piqued the interest of CEO Don Kemper: Some employees commented that "the culture is unevenly distributed at Healthwise. Some teams follow it more than others ... or were more culturally focused."

In analyzing the comment, Kemper said it would be quite easy to pass over it and chalk it up to growth in the organization, which has nearly doubled in size in three years. But given the time and effort Healthwise managers put into maintaining the strong and distinctive culture, Kemper said the comment stood out—it was a signal, an odd piece of information in a way, given the organization's emphasis on consistency. And then, as he said, "I came to a potential aha moment ... that the impact on people's daily life is much more associated with their team and their workgroups than with the overall organization." Increasingly, employees identify with smaller subgroups or subcultures than with the organization as a whole. Most managers have long put effort into building and maintaining the overall Healthwise culture, but have not encouraged (or even recognized) that smaller teams are developing their own culture or their subcultures.

Now, as Kemper says, this understanding aha will simmer, until the managers decide what to do about it. Like others who experience aha moments, Kemper noted that his was "pretty intuitively obvious" once he recognized it, but helped explain the emerging culture shift within his organization.

Women Who Fail

A final example of the seemingly unexplainable is why women in power often never break into the top ranks of corporations. Over the decades, numerous theories have emerged to explain what many call the "glass ceiling."[3] A recent proposal is that women are simply set up to fail, are essentially put onto a "glass cliff," because they are appointed to positions where no one, including capable men, could succeed.[4] Two researchers reviewed historical data from 100 of Britain's largest firms and found a form of "invisible prejudice" when women take positions that have a big chance of failure. In other words, if there is need for a scapegoat, women more often get the job, step onto a "glass cliff," and fail, fulfilling the "proof" that women cannot succeed in business.

Some might claim the "glass cliff" explains why Hillary Clinton and Barack Obama made it as far as they did in the 2008 U.S. elections: Only in very hard times would Americans put forward candidates who are likely to fail, thus "proving" that women or minorities are less capable.[5]

Looking Beyond a Discipline

The suicide example of connecting odd pieces clarifies the importance of reaching outside of a discipline to understand or solve a problem. Mental health, law enforcement, and other groups had not fully seen the interaction of various factors until they reviewed the trends in British suicides and looked for what other variables had changed during that time. Such searching for odd connections is a sort of *Freakonomics* effect,[6] in which economists make interesting connections among variables that seem on the surface to have little link, such as decrease in crime rates and lower birth rates 15–20 years earlier in certain neighborhoods. Likewise, such odd connections may help stimulate unexpected aha moments, both to understand a given situation and perhaps to come up with solutions to messy problems. The Healthwise culture and "glass cliff" examples are more subtle. One helps explain the stages that one growing organization experienced but few, other than the CEO, might have picked up on; the other example considers possible "invisible prejudice" that might explain a continuing lack of strong success in women CEOs.

In each case, to understand the situation, it was critical to consider trends over time—in suicides and available means, the culture of a growing organization or patterns of employment within a group of people. In each example, connecting odd pieces of information helped provide explanations to unclear situations. Most people fail to make those connections, a process psychologists call "selective encoding":[7] a person or group may absorb information or data but not realize (at least initially) that it has a connection to other information. The value of the information may be unclear until examined more closely, such as the correlation between intent and availability of a means to commit suicide. Thus, honing our skills of looking for odd connections may help generate understanding aha moments.

CREATING NEW PRODUCTS BY BRINGING ODD PIECES TOGETHER

Identifying connections for explanation is one benefit of linking odd pieces. Another is generating creative insight for solving problems or coming up with new products or services. Think of the numerous combinations of separate products that, once "connected," are commonplace today, such as phone + computer + video player + music player . . . .[8]

This section includes two examples of odd pieces coming together to form products that may become just as commonplace in the future.

When Fruit Flies Help Quarterbacks

Several years ago a retired film producer moved to Iowa and bought a farm. An Iowa farm in summer, like the rest of the

Midwest, has its share of fruit flies and other insects.[9] After spending time swatting with little success at killing, the movie expert turned farmer wondered why flies avoid swatters so well.

As the producer investigated, he learned that the fruit fly's compound eye is far more sophisticated than that of other insects. In fact, the *Drosophila melanogaster* uses about two-thirds of its brain to process what it sees, so vision is very important. You've seen pictures of those fly eyes—they look like clusters of bee hives, which in fact are hundreds of "unit eyes," each seeing bits of the world around them. One unit, called an "ommatidium," comprises groups of photoreceptor cells, each of which brings in images. The eyes can process color and have what is called temporal resolution that is ten times better than human eyes. This means that light travels much faster to those unit eyes in a fly than in a human. If I understand it correctly, the fly eye receives news about a swatter (change in light) faster than the human arm can reach the insect. In other words, the fly can "read" the light around it, and hence its environment, and react to it, faster than we can influence his world.

The farmer was intrigued not only with the ability to absorb and interpret light changes around the eye, but also with the idea of the multiple eye units. Multiple units could also allow a wide range of images to come into the brain for processing.

And here is where the film maker made the aha moment leap: What if a movie camera replicated the eye of a fly? What if it had "multiple units" capable of reading a wide field? In other words, could it help to expand peripheral and field vision for people in sports?

Football coaches talk about the ability of quarterbacks to learn to "read" a field. The term sounds straightforward, in terms of being able to see where receivers are or will likely be and, now and then, to take advantage of some unexpected opportunities. Much easier said than done. Often it takes a college quarterback several years and games to reach that point. Some never do. But if quarterbacks could learn that skill sooner, just think of the possibilities.

Using his knowledge about fly eyes and film cameras, the film producer–farmer created a projector/camera that he placed into goggles. The goggles looked something like those in the first *Matrix* movie, and were intended to help quarterbacks learn to "read" a field faster so they would see more than other players and know better where and how to look on the field. His combination of existing knowledge—of film, farming, and sports—made obvious sense to him, but others had trouble "getting it."

The inventor peddled his idea to numerous sports teams, primarily football. No interest. He even visited former Boise State University football Coach Dan Hawkins (now at the University of Colorado), who was known for his willingness to consider "wacky ideas" that might improve training methods. Although he was excited about the idea, Hawkins did not pursue it at the time. Maybe he should have. In the past two years, several similar products have become available, and some college teams, including Georgia Tech, have adopted goggles to help quarterbacks better learn to read the football field.[10]

Biomimicry: From Animals to Fighter Planes

When airplanes age, their "skin" starts to stress, and holes, scratches, and cracks can emerge, similar to our own skin.[11] Some researchers, including Dr. Ian Bond, who is the lead aerospace engineer on a project at the Engineering and Sciences Research Council, are mixing odd pieces of information to see if they can generate "self-healing" airplane skin, like our skin works when we scrape our elbows. The researchers are developing materials that "bleed" a resin and create a "scab" on the plane's outer skin, healing a crack or hole. Just as a human with a cut generates sticky platelet cells to stop the blood flowing out, so too does the new aerospace composite material under development. The material contains a resin that is made from fibers that spread over a hole and provide 80–90 percent of the material's strength prior to the damage. The self-healing buys the pilot time to get the plane to a base for repair.

The fly eye goggle inventor and the self-healing plane skin developers brought odd pieces of information together to form new products, some of which are still in development. The key is that in both cases the inventors used "selective comparison":[12] they transferred knowledge from one discipline to another field— in one case fly eyes, film, and sports, and in the other biology, aerospace, and blood clotting—to create products that may in the future become commonplace.

Of course, we can push connections and selective comparison too far. As the 2008–2009 financial crisis swept around the world, economists and business historians desperately tried to understand it and reached for comparisons and lessons from the Great Depression, the downturns of the mid-1970s, mid-1980s, and even early 1990s. None match completely (hence, "selective" comparison), yet many seek some understanding in the present by looking for insights into the past. By the same token, some experts argue that the financial network–ecology connections mentioned at the beginning of the chapter are a stretch. Nevertheless, connecting odd pieces can be useful at times to generate insights.

SOLVING PROBLEMS BY COMBINING ODD PIECES

Finally, putting odd pieces of information together can also solve existing problems. The next example did so and also led to a new product idea.

Follow the Brain

Bob Lokken has a solid wrestler's body but a mind like a gazelle. His ice-blue eyes drill into whomever happens to be the focus of his attention, wanted or not. He is the guy you hate (or love) to have in meetings: He will find the fatal flaw in an argument and ask the questions no one wants to answer. He likes to argue ideas, but is ankle deep in the ground when it comes to solid approaches to business. And he is a wizard at connecting odd elements to solve problems or come up with business ideas.

Along with three partners, Lokken launched ProClarity, a business intelligence software company, in 1999. Over the next seven years, the company racked up numerous software industry awards, competed successfully against much larger global firms in Israel, France, the United States, and Canada, and grew to 150 employees. Then, one of its main competitors (Microsoft) became a suitor and bought the firm in 2006.

When I asked him whether he had an aha moment for ProClarity, when he "knew" it was a good idea, he responded immediately, perhaps because it was so vivid for him. His tipping point for ProClarity came when he watched people use a Web browser for the first time. When people use a browser, they enter the topic they want to learn about, click on a hyperlink and pursue that path for a while. If they do not find what they want, they type in a new topic or "back up" to follow another pathway. Information links draw them to other ideas and sources, allowing the users to pull out information in "digestible chunks" and formats that they can absorb.

But the key for Lokken, whose eyebrows rise as he remembers the moment, was realizing two key aspects of Internet browser use. First, no one needed training to use the browser. As he said, when you ask a room of people how many need training on how to use new software, 80 percent raise their hands. When you ask the same group how many need training to use Google, no hands go up. Using the Internet is relatively intuitive.

Second, and even more critical, Lokken realized that the browser does not force people to follow a certain sequence in finding information. On an Internet browser, the user decides which hyperlinks to follow when they appear on a given page. The user determines the sequence, skipping what she knows already and moving to unfamiliar areas with a click or two. Our brains do the same: follow different pathways, shift course, return to a previous thought, and we do it nonsequentially. Lokken realized then that the information search process on the Internet is more similar to the way the brain works, not how any other software worked at the time. That sudden clarity of understanding—how people interact with the Internet—blended with his extensive knowledge of decision support systems and sparked the creative "aha moment" that generated the core of ProClarity's strength. Lokken wanted to create software to help people analyze their business data in the same way they would search the Internet. He envisioned the analysis process as exploration, as on the Internet. If a manager saw a particular number, he should be able "to click on it and do a root-cause analysis" immediately rather than running another report and waiting for its results to understand what was behind the number or deal with unwieldy databases and fields. Rather, the manager should "just be able to interact" with the information as easily as using a search browser.

Lokken put odd pieces together—Internet browsing, brain function, and business data analysis—to look at an issue in a way others had not and, in the process, created a new format for managers to analyze data. ProClarity was the first business data analysis product that had a forward and a back button, allowing a user to go back and choose a different analysis direction or pathway. As Lokken said, we "back up" on the Web all the time, but in the late 1990s, no analysis product worked that way. His flash of insight was to see that ProClarity could create a new way to use and consume information.

Like Einstein, Hawkins, and Watson, Lokken also recognizes the hard work of the aha journey—gathering and sorting information and then continuing to push for an aha moment. When the last "puzzle piece" falls into place, many more connections become clear.[13] Although many people had used or watched others using Internet browsers, Lokken saw the value of finding a way to create software that could emulate how the brain works and how intuitively people used the Internet.

Lokken's skill comes from relating seemingly odd factors together where others do not. He has conscientiously worked to develop that skill of putting odd pieces together, and he has used it in the creation of yet another start-up firm. He says he has learned to look for odd pieces and connections as a routine for thinking through problems or coming up with new ideas. When such skill becomes routine (see Chapter 11), the aha journey can pay off in earnest—as a catalyst for future action.

WHEN THINGS GO WRONG

Connecting odd pieces of information is difficult to do in the best of circumstances, and other factors can affect whether it works. Two factors are timing and common sense.

When the Timing Isn't Right

Creativity is a new idea that fits its context and has value. Timing is part of that context. Today, we think of Leonardo da Vinci as inarguably one of the most intelligent and wide-ranging thinkers ever. He explained the relationships between anatomy and body shape, he painted, and he was the designer of many remarkable inventions. But he also had some whopping failures, ideas that simply were not ripe for the times: His parachute idea from around 1480 used a linen cloth and a pyramid of wooden sticks to hold it open; the flying machine, forerunner of a helicopter, is dated 1505 in the Codex on the Flight of Birds. These new ideas were formed too early for anyone to know how to work with them, so they were of little value.

It is hard to imagine a life before mobile phones or interactive television. But they first appeared nearly 40 years ago—far before anyone was ready. The birth of mobile phones came on April 3, 1973, when a Motorola employee in New York City used a portable phone for the first time. The phone was the size of 1.5 bricks and probably weighed as much. The first handheld phone in the United States was approved in 1983 and was marketed by Motorola a decade later. Similarly, the first commercial interactive television service, QUBE, was test marketed in Columbus, Ohio, on December 1, 1977, with 30 channels. Customers could pay for movies, rate performers on a talent show, answer questions on a children's show—many features that today are accepted but then were completely novel. Users loved it, but QUBE could not make a go financially; not until the 1990s did interactive commercials and eventually television become financially viable.

So making odd connections is useful, but timing can make or break some successes.

Common Sense

Finally, as any student of basic statistics and correlation will report, odd pieces placed together may generate odd outcomes or wrong conclusions. Such outcomes often happen when people from one culture try to explain behaviors or outcomes in another. That's how I learned why Americans are "so aggressive."

During the Vietnam project I worked on in the 1990s, more than 80 Vietnamese faculty members and managers participated in Boise State University's MBA program. Each of three cohort groups spent at least six weeks in the United States doing internships at local organizations—from the newspaper, to the YMCA, to retail stores, to small business consulting firms. One Vietnamese faculty member worked at a 20-person software firm in an office building downtown. He frequently had revelations about business practices that he had never encountered in Vietnam: The company president offered to pour coffee during meetings; everyone in the firm used first names; and the top managers asked for, and used, ideas from people at every level of the firm. But when my Vietnamese colleague told me that he now understood why Americans are so aggressive, I had to take the bait.

"Because of the doors. That explains it all."

"Doors?" I asked.

"Whenever I go out of the office building, or into the company, I have to push really hard on the doors. They are very heavy. That's why you Americans are so aggressive—you have to be, just to open your doors."

Odd pieces coming together in this case just did not quite make the cut.

* * *

The skill and value of learning to put odd pieces of information together—or to see odd pieces that already are "together" and need interpretation is basic to encouraging insight thinking.

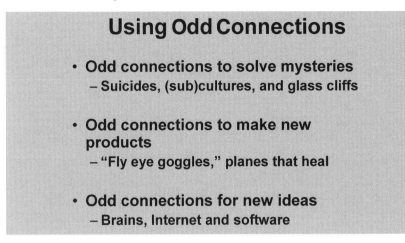

Using Odd Connections

- **Odd connections to solve mysteries**
  - Suicides, (sub)cultures, and glass cliffs

- **Odd connections to make new products**
  - "Fly eye goggles," planes that heal

- **Odd connections for new ideas**
  - Brains, Internet and software

As the range of examples suggest, any field, any type of challenge might benefit but the danger of "overdoing" also lurks. Connecting odd pieces of information also encourages new angles of thinking, explored more in the next chapter on "reverse thinking."

INSIGHT TIPS: PUTTING ODD PIECES TOGETHER

This section offers some small examples of ways to "practice" putting odd pieces together in new ways, through word puzzles, "droodles," and simple problems that can be solved by combining odd bits of information. Each of these small tips helps joggle our minds in different ways. Try the following example tests of learning to put odd pieces together to make a new idea.

Word Puzzles: What Are Each of the Following?

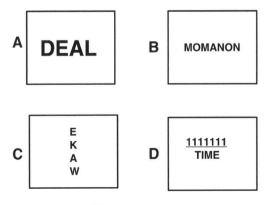

FIGURE 4-1 Word puzzles[14]

Droodles—What Do They Mean?

Putting Odd Pieces Together

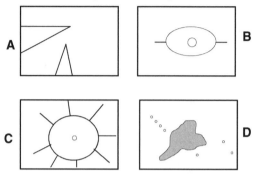

FIGURE 4-2   Droodles[15]

Problems to Solve

What connections can you make among the odd elements below? In each case, someone already has (new or improved product or service):

1. Air bags and elderly people
2. Netflix and college textbooks
3. Software and film[16]

Web Sites to Help Us Learn to Connect Odd Pieces—From Brainstorming to Jolting Your Thoughts

Random Input: http://www.mindtools.com/pages/article/ newCT_07.htm. Pick a random word (nouns are best) and then brainstorm your idea with this word in mind to see what comes up.

Provocation: http://www.mindtools.com/pages/article/ newCT_08.htm. Make a deliberately stupid statement about your problem, and then see where the new thinking pattern takes you.

Keep Alternatives: http://desktoppub.about.com/od/creati vityexercises/a/saedi_4.htm. After solving a problem, hang onto your solutions; they may apply to a new problem that pops up in the future.

NOTES

1. Gillian Tett. 2009. A timely lesson for bankers from the birds and the bees, *Financial Times*, May 2: 11; Andrew G. Haldane. 2009. Rethinking the Financial Network, Speech delivered at the Financial Student Association, Amsterdam, April 28.

2. The British coal-gas story comes from Scott Anderson's lengthy piece in the *New York Times Magazine*, The urge to end it all, *The New York Times Magazine*, July 6, 2008: 38–43.

3. Carol Hymowitz and Timothy D. Schellhardt. 1986. The corporate woman (a special report): Cover—The glass ceiling: Why women can't seem to break the invisible barrier that blocks them from the top jobs, *The Wall Street Journal*, March 24: 1; Sue Vilhauer Rosser. 2004. *The Science Glass Ceiling: Academic Women Scientists and the Struggle to Succeed*. New York City: Routledge; Linda Wirth and International Labour Office. 2001. *Breaking through the Glass Ceiling: Women in Management*. Geneva: International Labour Office.

4. Alexander S. Haslam and Michelle K. Ryan. 2008. The road to the glass cliff: Differences in the perceived suitability of men and women for leadership positions in succeeding and failing organizations, *The Leadership Quarterly* 19 (5): 530–546.

5. Clive Thompson. 2008. Women in power are set up to fail, *The New York Times*, December 14: MM80.

6. Economist Steven Levitt and journalist Stephen Dubner show unexpected and interesting correlations of seemingly unconnected variables and the impacts they may have. Classic "connecting odd pieces." Steven D. Levitt and Stephen J. Dubner. 2005. *Freakonomics: A Rogue Economist Explores the Hidden Side of Everything*. New York City: HarperCollins.

7. Robert Sternberg and Todd Lubart give good explanations of three types of insight that involve putting odd pieces together—selective encoding, selective comparison, and selective combination. See Robert J. Sternberg and Todd I. Lubart. 1995. *Defying the Crowd: Cultivating Creativity in a Culture of Conformity*. New York: The Free Press. The discussion about selective encoding is on pp. 111–114.

8. Michael Gibbert and David Mazursky. 2007. A recipe for creating new products: Take two completely separate categories. Combine, *The Wall Street Journal*, October 27: R4.

9. This story also appears in an earlier book on creativity. See reference Nancy K. Napier and Mikael Nilsson. 2008.

The Creative Discipline: The Art and Science of Innovation. Westport, CT: Praeger Press: 65–66.

10. Some teams have begun using similar high-tech goggles. See Jon Weinbach. 2007. Making the first three seconds count, *The Wall Street Journal*, August 31: W1 &W10 (http://www.vizualedge.com/publications/WSJ.com-Making-the-First-Three-Seconds-2.pdf).

11. Dave Demerjian. 2008. Airplane heal thyself? Self-repairing aircraft could improve air safety. May 20. http://blog.wired.com/cars/2008/05/airplane-heal-t.hrml.

12. Robert J. Sternberg and Todd I. Lubart. 1995. *Defying the Crowd: Cultivating Creativity in a Culture of Conformity.* New York: The Free Press.

13. Such "selective combination" happens when one piece of a puzzle helps others make sense. See Robert J. Sternberg and Todd I. Lubart. 1995. *Defying the Crowd: Cultivating Creativity in a Culture of Conformity.* New York: The Free Press.

14. Solutions:

   a. BIG deal ("deal" written in large letters)
   b. MAN in the MOON
   c. "WAKE UP"—when the letters are read vertically from the bottom, they become "wake" going "up" (ward) = WAKE UP
   d. 1s upon a time = once upon a time

15. Solutions:

   a. A ship arriving too late to save a drowning witch
   b. Man in sombrero on a bicycle
   c. Outspoken wheel
   d. Ants walking through a puddle of champagne

16. Solutions:

   • Air bags and elderly people—Wearable air bag jackets for elderly people to absorb shock if they fall. They are bulky, not as attractive as regular clothes, but may prevent broken bones.
   • Netflix and college textbooks—By fall 2009, the idea of firms "renting" textbooks to students was beginning to take hold. Chegg.com and CengageBrain.com have decided to rent texts, both hard copies and digital versions. Chegg.com will rent

books, by sending them to students, who return books in pre-paid envelops. Unlike electronic books, which cannot be easily returned or resold, this model follows the Netflix approach. In addition, Amazon is running an experiment with four universities to compare students' reactions and learning by comparing its Kindle e-book versions of textbooks with traditional hard copy books.

- Software and film—When we rent a film, we typically watch it for 10 percent of the length of the film (about 10–12 minutes) before we decide if we will invest the time to watch the whole movie.

  In considering purchasing a new piece of software, we typically give it 1–2 minutes before deciding whether to invest the time and money. One software firm looked for ideas from "grabber" films (those that grab us by the throat and keep us watching) as ways to "grab" a software user emotionally and make the potential buyer make the purchase decision.

Chapter 5

Pushing against the Rock: Going against What Makes Sense

A sudden bold and unexpected question doth many times surprise a man and lay him open.

—Sir Francis Bacon (1561–1626)

Suzie Lindberg's fingers and toes gripped a sheer granite face in the Vedauwoo climbing area in Wyoming's Laramie Mountains. A compact five-foot-tall firecracker of a rock climber, longtime marathoner and telemark skier, Lindberg was no wallflower when it came to sports and adventure.

"Just push away from the wall."

Her instructor and friend sounded like a broken record ... he had been saying "just push away" for 10 minutes.

But the thought of pushing away from the rock face far above a craggy set of rocks down below was more than she could fathom. Her friend, who was a good foot taller than she, had shimmied up the face ahead of her. He leaned over from the top to call down. She was at the "Jesus Rock," so called by climbers because it required a long and scary stretch, moving one hand from a slight indentation in the rock to the next. To remove 25 percent of her contact with the rock, reach on faith for the handhold at a two o'clock position at least two feet from her current hold seemed out of the question.

He is taller and has more reach, she thought. He has done this more than I have. But why on earth is he telling me to push *away* from the wall? All I want to do is hold on for dear life.

When Lindberg takes on a challenge, she does not back down. She runs in the Boise foothills in the dark after work or early in the morning, head lamp lit, with pepper spray just in case she surprises an unsuspecting coyote. She splashes through mud and rain for hours of a marathon, when others drop out. But one challenge that almost got the best of her unbeatable spirit was rock climbing in Wyoming's renowned Vedauwoo area, known as Joshua Tree of the north to climbers in the know.

Vedauwoo (pronounced Vee-da-voo) comes from a Native American Arapaho word: "Land of the Earthborn Spirit." It sits between Cheyenne and Laramie, in the middle of Wyoming's open range. The 1 billion-year-old granite rocks are large and rough, but lack clear hand and footholds so the idea of "pushing away from the rock," as her buddy kept saying, just did not make sense. "Put your weight on your feet and push away" sounded like giving up the protection her hand grip offered. Why go for a "two wheel drive stance" (most weight on her feet) when she had four wheels (both hands and feet)?

But nothing else worked. She became more irritated when he said "push away" yet again. But with no other obvious options, this time she tried it.

"I felt like I was standing on a table," she remembers. Putting all the weight on her toes and feet removed the weight from her hands. She felt secure, almost like she did not need her hand grip at all. She reached the "Jesus rock" with what felt like a small stretch.

Reverse thinking—pushing *away* from the rock instead of trying to pull *toward* the rock—solved the problem.

As Lindberg thought about it later, she understood why it worked.

"It made sense from a physics standpoint. Since I wasn't gripping and leaning into the rock, I was counterbalanced on my feet. Putting my weight there meant I could use my hands more freely, to balance, not to grip." But, even for a scientific quick study, she had to hear it, then try it, before she really understood and "got it." In her case, of course, she needed to "feel it." And once she did, she never forgot it.

Suzie Lindberg faced a problem, her choice of course, but a problem nonetheless. She wanted to understand how to climb better, and it took an aha experience to get her there. She also had to test out physically what she had heard and absorbed (but fought) mentally. Only after she sorted information and had some of the puzzle pieces that just did not fit, was she willing to take a leap and try something that really did not make sense. She needed a spark to reach a different level of understanding. In this situation, it was the encouragement to try some advice that seemed nonintuitive and downright life threatening: pushing *away* from a near flat vertical rock surface way above the ground.

"Push away" to do something that is the reverse of what one would normally think was the spark that shifted her action and her understanding. Once she tested it, and found success, the aha lesson was hers forever.

* * *

Reverse thinking or looking at an issue from angles that are quite different from what one normally would do works well for generating both the "understanding aha" as well as the "creative aha." The basic notion is to look at a situation in ways that go against what seems intuitive, like gripping a rock with two rather than four appendages. It requires us to consider an issue from a direction that seems opposite to what most people would do. We will talk in this chapter about several ways that reverse thinking can be useful in generating insight, finding new ideas or solutions to knotty problems, or even choosing a strategy of action. In each case, the idea of going against what "seems logical" to find answers or explanations forces us to think in different ways. This reverse thinking requires our brains to reach for "weak associations," for underused (or never used) connections, and in the process stretches us toward insight thinking. We will cover two ways reverse thinking can be useful: for explaining the "unexplainable" and in taking an action (or not).

USING REVERSE THINKING TO EXPLAIN THE UNEXPLAINABLE

In an article that rivals any Edgar Allen Poe story, Dr. Atul Gawande, an associate professor at Harvard Medical School and regular contributor to *The New Yorker*, described the horrifying experience of incessant itching.[1] A female patient, with a history of drugs, HIV, and shingles, had managed to turn her life around, only to be assailed by an unexplainable disorder. At age 38, "she got the itch." Over the next decade, she was in and out of hospitals, underwent scores of tests, tried special creams and shampoos, and went through debilitating surgery. The itching climaxed when she woke one morning to feel fluid running down her face, the result of scratching through her skull to her brain during the night.

Medical thinking about itching has long held that it is a nerve problem, which makes sense up to a point. If nerves generate an itch, anesthetic will dull nerves and quell the itching. That happened with the patient for a while. Over time, though, as the patient destroyed more nerve fibers from her relentless itching, the nerves that remained became excessively active, leading the patient to start scratching again after any sort of anesthetic wore off.

One neurologist, Anne Louise Oaklander, had an alternative theory. Since so many of the nerves were dead, she thought something in the patient's brain had misfired. Thus, while the primary theory was that the patient had a nerve problem, Oaklander thought it was a brain problem. An example of reverse thinking, or looking at a problem from a very different perspective, Oaklander's theory was hard for many neurosurgeons to accept, and thus most dismissed it. The patient, caught in the middle, followed advice—that her problem was nerve related—and pursued surgery to cut into a nerve above her right eye. The operation helped for a few weeks, but then, the itching returned with greater force. Eventually, the patient spent two years in bed in a rehabilitation hospital, wearing a foam football helmet with her hands in mitts to protect herself. At 48 years old, a decade after the itching began, she lives at home in a wheelchair, partially paralyzed from the operation, still suffering from an unending desire to scratch away her eyebrow to get into her skull and relieve the itching.

Dr. Oaklander's theory, which started from looking at a patient's problem from a very different angle, has begun to gain ground. Recent medical research suggests that even when nerves die, the brain continues to believe that they remain. This has implications for the patient who itches and also for patients with phantom limb symptoms. Oaklander's theory argues that even with dead nerves, the brain remains under the impression that they exist, which in turn allows the "itching" to continue and also the phantom limb pain that amputees experience. Apparently, the itching patient's early bout with shingles "destroyed most of the nerves in her scalp ... but her brain surmised from what little input it had that something horribly itchy was going on ... there wasn't any such thing, of course. But [the patient's] brain has received no contrary signals that would shift its assumptions. So she itches." It was a brain problem, not a nerve problem—just the reverse from what most doctors thought, but what made sense neurologically.

WHEN NO ACTION IS THE BEST ACTION

Reverse thinking—or going against the obvious—sometimes emerges in terms of an action or decisions to take. In sports and elsewhere, though, no action can be a tough choice.

Stand Still

Even Americans who understand few of the nuances of soccer— or "football" as the rest of the world terms it—know drama when they see it. The classic photo of a goalie, horizontal in the air four feet off the ground as he reaches for the ball when a penalty kick comes his way, is one of the most memorable moments in any game. But it turns out that the spectacular leap may be nothing more than show.[2]

Israeli researchers evaluated nearly 300 penalty kicks in professional soccer games and discovered that 94 percent of the time, the goalies took dives to the edge of the goal box, even though they had little chance of stopping the kick. In fact, their chances of stopping it were greater if they had not moved at all, but rather just stood in the center of the goal box. So why do goalies leap? The scientists think that goalkeepers feel compelled to dive for the ball, even when it reduces their likelihood of stopping it, because they want to look like they are "taking action." By leaping, they look decisive. Action makes the game exciting, spurs the fans, and makes the goalkeeper think he is doing something useful.

While appealing from a sports viewpoint, the implications are also interesting beyond sports. Indeed, during the past few years, how many "actions" did business and government officials take, perhaps in part to appear decisive and show they were doing something? The financial crisis offers great examples. During fall 2008, for instance, the U.S. government offered troubled assets recovery program money to the country's largest banks and the bank executives took it. Some bank executives commented privately that their banks did not "need" the money, but if the government was giving it to them, and competing banks were accepting it, so should they.[3] Six months later, however, the banks began to repay the money, in large part to avoid the potential constraints the government would impose if they kept it. Perhaps the banks should have taken the no-action route at the start, but at the time it seemed better to take action and look decisive. So going against what seems obvious—taking action—may in some cases be the correct action. Looking at a situation in "reverse," in a manner opposite to what makes sense, could generate an aha moment of understanding or problem solution.

Interestingly, in some cases, people "do nothing," which can also be a way to avoid decision and could be the wrong action. "Norm theory"[4] describes a mode of behavior in which people do nothing when they have a tough problem, rather than risk making a bad decision. The belief is that by doing nothing, maybe the problem will go away. This thinking is unlikely to succeed for goal keepers or bankers, but it does suggest that sometimes, behavior that is opposite to what many people would assume is right could, in fact, be the best course.

TAKING ACTION, BUT IN REVERSE

In other situations, doing nothing is not an option or does not solve a problem. Instead, action is necessary but it may be the reverse of what seems obvious. Many examples of this exist—from park service to business to health care.

Doing What Others Do

Who doesn't take a souvenir to remember a trip—a beautiful shell from a beach or a skipping rock from a lake shore? Ever since tourists first walked through it, Arizona's 60 million-year-old petrified wood forest has been plagued with visitors taking a souvenir "piece of the rock." Petrified Forest National Park officials estimate that visitors steal about 12–15 tons of wood yearly, decimating the park. The general thinking by tourists has been "it's ok to take a piece of rock since everyone else does." For years, park rangers urged each person entering the park not to take rock pieces, but looting continued.

Then one professor looked at the problem in reverse. Using the "what everyone else does" thinking as a focus, Arizona State professor Robert Cialdini, expert on negotiation and social influence, suggested using different signs. Rather than warning people *not* to vandalize, the park officials put up new types of requests and signs that emphasized how few people *took* pieces from the park.[5] The signs went up in 2003 and since then, looting has dropped significantly. In essence, by using reverse thinking to address a problem, Cialdini generated an aha moment of using visitors' wishes to conform to what they assumed others were doing, or not doing in this case.

Data Collection vs. Data Removal

Caroline Blakeslee, an administrator in charge of supporting the more than 400 part-time instructors at a regional university, started her job with a simple question: How many and who were the adjunct instructors "on the payroll"? Since her job was to help the instructors navigate the university system, coordinate training sessions for them, and develop other ways to integrate them into the university, she needed to know who they were. She sought basic contact data (name, phone, email) and information to help her understand their relationship with the university so she could design programs and Web sites that would address their needs. She wanted to be able to track their teaching schedules, which varied widely—some taught one course per year, others seven courses per year. Also, some of the adjunct professors taught solely within a single department, but others taught within several departments. Finally, she wished to have their history with the university—how many and which courses they had taught over recent years. Finding the information seemed straightforward, something she assumed already existed within the system.

For four months, she and the IT expert at the university looked for ways to gather the information. The existing databases had contact information for all employees, but did not identify which were current part-time instructors. During that time, she communicated with the more than 60 university departments that hired adjunct instructors and worked with the university's information technology and database experts, seeking a simple way to gather the information in a straightforward manner. Neither Blakeslee nor the IT experts could figure out a way to create a survey or data-capturing system that would automatically generate the current information. Someone would have to manually create the lists from information out of the departments.

Stymied, Blakeslee sought out the provost, the academic head of departments, to see if she could approach the academic departments to ask administrative assistants for the information.

The provost said no, fearing the cost in time and disruption to departments was more than the benefit of getting the information.

The simple, straightforward problem turned into something not so simple. Blakeslee was ready to give up. But then she turned the problem upside down, and thought "in reverse" and experienced a flash of insight.

What if, rather than a data *collection* problem, this was a data *removal* problem? In other words, perhaps the information did exist in a database but no one had recognized it because it was embedded elsewhere. If so, could she extract unnecessary data, leaving what she needed behind? Once she reframed her simple, then not so simple, problem into a once-again-simple problem, she resolved the dilemma. Indeed, the data did exist. All employees paid by the university, full and part time alike, professional, and classified, enter personal contact information in the payroll system. Generally the adjunct faculty members were hired using "Letters of Appointment," while another form, "Employee Action Forms," were used for other types of instructors and employees. No one had "seen it," including the IT database experts, until they reframed the problem. Once simply redefined, the IT experts could eliminate the unnecessary (for her) information from the database, leaving the essentials that she needed.

As Blakeslee's situation shows, even a straightforward problem may need review and consideration of whether it is "the right problem" or the one that needs to be solved. She used reverse thinking, or looking at the problem in a less obvious way, to spark an aha moment.

Treating the Sick or Learning from the Healthy

A team of knowledgeable medical experts and founders of the Positive Deviance Initiative, Jerry and Monique Sternin have worked for years to solve "intractable problems" in developing countries, ranging from female genital mutilation in Egypt to maternal health in Myanmar. Their creative solutions often involve approaches strikingly different from the normal, obvious ones, and often their unexpected solutions also find their way to the developed countries, like the United States.

Reducing the spread of infections that plague hospitals in developing countries is one of the biggest concerns in health care.[6] The Sternins visited small communities throughout Southeast Asia for years, trying to understand how infection spreads, and came up with the notion of "positive deviance." Instead of going into a community where 70 percent of inhabitants were infected and trying to find out why and how to control it, the Sternins sought to understand why the 30 percent in the community were *not* infected. They explored how that group lived and what they did to avoid the infection. Their thinking was that if they could understand what the healthy 30 percent of the group did, they could help the ill 70 percent change their behaviors.

Their positive deviance approach works in U.S. hospitals as well, by getting ideas from unexpected sources. Many good ideas for reducing hospital infection come from lower-level employees—janitors and cooks. The Sternins listened to those employees when others might not have considered them. For example, orderly Jasper Palmer developed a way to remove his infected hospital gown and place it inside his latex glove before disposing of both. Many hospitals now use the so-called "Palmer Method" and have avoided infection spread. Reverse thinking—looking where others might not—can help generate insight and solve problems.

In each of these examples, reverse thinking or doing what seemed to be the obvious of what would work turned out to help nudge aha moments and solve problems. What may seem the exact false step to take, though, helped in the end.

USING REVERSE THINKING AS A STRATEGY

At times, reverse thinking can also be a strategy to encourage aha moments in others.

Reverse Culture Training

During my time in Vietnam, I worked closely with many Vietnamese faculty colleagues. We jointly taught, conducted research, and delivered several training programs about doing business with foreigners. I often worked with one man, who had a slight stoop, as though he was deferential or lacked confidence. But when the show went on, he boosted his posture and his voice level to become a vivacious Vietnamese management guru.

When we trained Vietnamese managers, my partner often sat on the edge of the table in the front of the room. He leaned back on it, legs crossed and sticking out in front of him. Then he paced the room across the front waving his arms as he made a point, before plunging into the group, hands stuffed into his pockets, jiggling his keys. He looked at the highest and lowest ranking persons with an equally forceful stare. On those occasions, I stood in the center of the front of the room, my arms crossed in front of me, still. I was careful not to sit on the table, stroll around, lean against any walls or chairs, or put my hands on my hips. Even though my taxi-Vietnamese is useless most of the time, I could tell there was a buzz, some frustration, and eyebrows discreetly reaching toward one another on the faces of the senior managers of the group.

My partner and I had each been modeling behavior that was out of character for our own cultures. In Vietnam, to sit or lean on a desk is heresy: You are putting your backside onto a teacher's revered writing table. Showing the bottom of your feet as they stretch out toward the group is offensive. Men never stand with their hands in their pockets or on their hips because it signals aggression. I had followed correct Vietnamese cultural protocol, my partner had followed the equivalent American behavior. And we were both seen as being wrong.

When we debriefed the managers on the aspects of culture, they acted like new college students on orientation day. Direct eye contact but no comment or reaction. Finally, I asked about my presentation style.

Beautiful voice, they said. The Vietnamese say that often to native English speakers. Polite but also a cop out.

Anything else?

No, no, very nice (which comes out "nigh"). Very easy to listen to.

Then I asked what they thought of my partner's presentation. Polite as always, they said he also had a nice voice.

When we asked specifically about our actions—his offensive ones and my very Vietnamese ones—they had not noticed mine as much but were turned off by his, which was exactly what we expected and hoped for. To understand that his actions are very much what they would encounter with Americans, who had no idea how offensive such moves would be to Vietnamese counterparts, we wanted to encourage them to have an aha moment of understanding. And it worked: a collective drop of mouths and raising of eyebrows.

Ahhhhhhh.

MOVING TO THE UNLIKELY EDGE OF THE DANCE WORLD

Choreographer Trey McIntyre is what author Thomas Wolfe might call "a whirling vortex and a creative chaos" when he floods his dancers with ideas. He overwhelms them with information in a one-to two-week period—giving ideas and movements, revising them, giving out more, and expecting the dancers to remember the final versions. For several years, McIntyre worked as resident choreographer in ballet companies, including Houston and Washington, D.C., and then as a free-lance choreographer for 18 years, creating dozens of commissioned works for ballet companies around the world. For three years, he ran a summer dance touring group, with support from donors all over the country, grant money from one of the Silicon Valley's largest foundations, and performances in several top dance venues, including Jacob's Pillow in the Berkshire Mountains of Massachusetts. But when it came time to start a full-time dance company, in the middle of the 2007–2008 recession no less, he used reverse thinking and took a strategy that was the opposite of what most people would expect: He established the company in an "unlikely" site, according to *The New York Times*, far off the beaten dance path.[7]

As the group considered where to locate a full-time dance group, 25 cities were on the list, including many of the usual suspects: New York City, Washington, D.C., Houston, and San Francisco. In those cities, McIntyre and his work were well-known and the cities each had strong arts environments, so the chance for sold-out performances in town would be high. Each city overflows with creative people and opportunities for constant stimulation, and each offers a good supply of talented dancers from other companies as well as from schools and training programs. Finally, money—from donors and foundations—is typically more available in large cities.

In the end, however, the Trey McIntyre Project (TMP) settled in Boise, Idaho, known by many people outside the state only for potatoes. And now, every time the group travels for a performance—from Santa Barbara to New York City, Puerto Rico to Hungary, one of the first questions is, "Why Boise?"

McIntyre and TMP Executive Director John Michael Schert took what appeared to many to be a reverse thinking approach to their location decision, but in fact was a savvy strategy. Remoteness, in their case, had real advantages. Challenging each of the advantages most people would expect of a big city, McIntyre and Schert turned Boise's apparent disadvantages into positives. Schert says that cities like San Francisco are already "formed," that the existing arts community is less likely to change or be shaped by new companies. Far from being a long-established arts and culture community, Boise's continues to develop. The TMP group could help to shape the community and, by being a world-class dance company, could push the expectations of quality to a higher level. Likewise, as the city experiences major growth, decisions about what it wants to become are topics of discussion in all groups—from business and the arts to education and government. The TMP group saw an opportunity to be part of the "shaping" process and has consistently encountered an attitude that welcomes them and their ideas.

Next, while the stimulation of large cities is critical for many artists, McIntyre thrives creatively in quiet environments. His favorite is White Oak Plantation, Florida, a 7,400 acre woodlands site on the St. Marys River, 30 miles north of Jacksonville. Far from the stimulation of cities or noise, McIntyre takes his company there yearly for retreat, creation, and rejuvenation. Boise, even though it is a larger city (200,000), offers some of the same distance and quiet. Its geography includes a river through the center of town and foothills that lead to evergreen forests 7,000 feet above the city. Access to complete quiet is moments from almost any location in the city.

McIntyre also saw the supply of dancers in the larger cities as a potential disadvantage, rather than an advantage. In those cities, artists like dancers and actors tend to shift allegiances and companies. He saw dancers in San Francisco, New York, and Houston spend a year at one company and then, if they became bored, felt they were not moving up fast enough, or had a better offer, they "walked across the street" to another company. McIntyre's dream was to start a small full-time company, with nine dancers he could get to know well and work with over time. That would allow him, as a choreographer, to try riskier ideas and perhaps become more efficient over time because group members knew and trusted one another. So, being close to the supply source was less attractive than it might seem. In fact, McIntyre has recruited from schools like Julliard, bringing hard-core New Yorkers to the wilds of Boise. And, while other choreographers go for big name celebrities, McIntyre has gone with full-time, "star-free" dancers, but they may have the last laugh yet, as they are fast becoming local celebrities.

Finally, in addition to the idealistic reasons for a smaller city like Boise, in the end, economics must play a role. In Boise, dancers can bike to work and more easily afford food and housing. But financial sustainability for any arts organization is never assured. When the group decided to leave the Silicon Valley area, it forfeited a $1 million grant, which was tough to swallow.

And although access to money has been challenging, its wise strategy of a national board (i.e., donors in many cities, not just the home base) and frequent touring schedule has made TMP one of the few performing arts organizations in the United States that operates in the black.

Thus, reverse thinking and going against the dance world's expectation for a headquarters site has proven the right strategy for such a group. In its first year of operation, the group has become "Idaho's biggest export artistically," and it came in part because of thinking in reverse.

* * *

As the opening quote from Francis Bacon suggests, a "bold and unexpected question" is a useful way to jolt thinking and spark aha moments of understanding. Boise State University football Offensive Coordinator Brian Harsin asks his players to "self-scout," and "look at our team as if you were an opponent who knew all of our strategies and secrets. How would you play us?" That forces players to learn to shift perspectives and think in reverse. Knowing all of their own schemes and plays, they then can find the holes and weaknesses in their own—and the opponents'—games. But some unexpected questions can be even more bold and jolting, sparking creative aha moments—or depression.

When a state legislator toured a corrections facility that housed juveniles, she put a damper on the 10-year anniversary celebration. The facility administrators were proud that they had received funding for ten years and wanted to show off the facility to state politicians. But one legislator raised a question that stopped the group cold: "What would it take to put you out of business altogether? To shut this facility down?" By asking what Sir Francis Bacon called a "bold and unexpected question," she surprised the facility administrators. But such a question is just the sort of nudging that policy makers, business people, and others need to use to look for creative ideas to improve already well-run organizations or solve problems. The juvenile facility administrators, like Gary Raney's jail employees, had never questioned the reason for their existence, whether they should exist at all, and if they did, what they might do differently.

Another awkward question, and harder for even more people to understand, is, "What are we missing?" The response is "how do we know what we are missing if we are missing it?" Fair enough, but some people have learned to see what is not there. The next chapter shows us how they do it.

INSIGHT TIPS: REVERSE THINKING

Practicing the idea of looking at an issue or problem "in reverse" or from an angle that is unfamiliar can be done several ways. Below are two examples: trying to look at a situation from another person's perspective, and thinking like an architect. As you test yourself on these, try to think of other examples where you can ask yourself to "think in reverse," to challenge what you would first accept as the "right way" to operate, and to see what ways you can "push against the wall."

Whose Perspective?

How could you look at the same problem from different stakeholders' viewpoints? Could you consider how a problem might be viewed from the standpoint of a person from a different culture?

When two colleagues (a Vietnamese man and an American woman) taught together in Vietnam, their cultural clashes became legendary. One day he was speaking in front of the class, turned to his partner and asked if she could write the key points on the board while he was leading the discussion. She refused, feeling it was demeaning and sexist to ask her. He lost face in front of the students. He felt she had not understood that he needed help spelling words in English and that is why he had asked. Neither looked at the situation from the other perspective so the result was tension that never did resolve. That ability to shift viewpoints and perspectives, look

Challenging What Makes Sense

- **Reverse thinking**
  - Itching – brain problem vs nerve problem

- **No action as the best action**
  - Soccer goalies standing still

- **Take action, in reverse**
  - Learn from the healthy to treat the ill
  - Moving to the edge of the creative world

"in reverse" from another viewpoint, is handy in understanding cultural situations, to be sure, but also for problem solving.

Think Like An Architect

Practicing the "shifting" from one perspective to another is relatively straightforward in some cases. Pushing it in problem solving requires us to change angles, sometimes literally, as architects do.

When designer/architect Michael Snow works on a remodeling project for a homeowner, he sketches ideas on onion skin paper. He overlays the paper onto the house plans and then sketches in or removes walls, doors, windows, electric outlets, and stairways. If the sketches do not seem to make sense, he might turn the onion skin sheet 90 or 180 degrees, and lay it back on top of the plans. Sometimes that sparks a new way of thinking about the design. He could do the same process on the computer, but physically holding the paper, turning it around, viewing it from another angle jolts his thinking better than using a 3D computer program. If his turning the paper around still yields no good ideas for the project, Snow might turn the onion skin paper over, so that the reverse side of the sheet is up. In this process, he gives himself multiple angles and directions from which to view the sketches.

In what other sorts of ways could you "turn over" a problem or the way you are looking at it?

For instance, how would you go about demolishing a building "in reverse?" In crowded Japanese cities, where tearing down buildings by implosion can be especially dangerous, the Tokyo firm Kajima Corporation is removing buildings in an "upside down" manner—removing one layer at a time, from the bottom up.[8] The *daruma-otoshi* method ("cut and take down") uses hydraulic jacks to support the weight of the building, while workers tear out the interior of a floor and take away the interior for recycling. The jacks then lower the building down to the ground, and the process goes on again, until the entire building has been "lowered" to the ground.

Websites for More Inspiration

Reversal: http://www.mindtools.com/pages/article/newCT_01 .htm. Ask the exact opposite question of one you wish to solve, then look at the results—they may generate ideas from just the opposite of what makes sense. Can you look at it differently physically/spatially? Temporally?

Reframing Matrix and Four Ps: http://www.mindtools.com/ pages/article/newCT_05.htm. Look at the problem from different perspectives.

NOTES

1. Atul Gawande. 2008. The itch, *The New Yorker*, July 4: 58–65.

2. Michael Bar-Eli, Ofer H. Azar, Ilana Ritov, Yael Keidar-Levin, and Galit Schein. 2007. Action bias among elite soccer goalkeepers: The case of penalty kicks, *Journal of Economic Psychology*, 28 (5): 606–621.

3. Mike McIntire. 2009. Bailout is a windfall to banks, if not to borrowers, *The New York Times*, January 17 (http://www.nytimes .com/2009/01/18/business/18bank.html?_r=1).

4. Amos Tversky and Daniel Kahneman. 1986. Rational choice and the framing of decisions, *Journal of Business* 59 (S4): S251; Daniel Kahneman and Dale T. Miller. 1986. Norm theory: Comparing reality to its alternatives, *Psychological Review* 93 (2): 136–153.

5. The stories about the challenges of reducing petrified wood stealing have appeared in many different publications and on Internet sites. See, for example, http://www.arizona-leisure.com/ petrified-forest.html; Richard H. Thaler and Cass R. Sunstein. 2008. *Nudge*. New Haven, CT: Yale University Press: 66–67; Robert Cialdini, L. Demaine, D. Barrett, K. Rhoads, P. Winter, and B. Sagarin. 2006. Managing social norms for persuasive impact, *Social Influence* 1 (1): 3–15.

6. Jon Gertner. 2008. Positive deviance, *The New York Times: 8th Annual Year in Ideas*, December 8: 68; for information about the Positive Deviance Initiative, check the Web site: http://www.positiv edeviance.org/about_pdi/index.html.

7. Claudia La Rocco. 2008. A choreographer gives his dream an Idaho address, *The New York Times*, September 12: AR 31; in addition to LaRocco's article, several others have commented about the Trey McIntyre Project's business model and decision to move to Idaho. See, for example, Tresca Weinstein. 2009. A new beginning: Choreographer Trey McIntyre takes his company full-time, *Pointe Magazine*, February/March: 25–26; Curt Holman. 2009. "Speakeasy with John Michael Schert, *Creative Loafing* (http://atlanta.creativeloafing.com/ gyrobase/john_michael_schert/Content?oid=736111).

8. Mark Van De Walle. 2008. "Upside-down demolition," *New York Times: 8th Annual Year in Ideas*, December 8: 78.

Chapter 6

Seeing What's Not There

The unapparent connection is more powerful than the
apparent one.
           —Heraclitus, quoted in Hippolytus, Refutations[1]

During the late 1970s, I worked as a technical economics and business planning researcher for Battelle Memorial Institute, a contract
research organization, based in Columbus, Ohio. At the time,
Japanese firms were beginning to establish manufacturing sites in
the United States and Canada, and Nomura Research Institute
asked us to assess the image of Japanese business in North America.
Honda had built a car plant in Ohio, YKK Zippers had a facility
outside of Atlanta, and others were coming on stream. Even so,
the Japanese presence was low-key and few in North America
anticipated the *tsunami* that Japanese firms would become during
the 1980s.

I was the junior researcher on the project but did most of the
work. I traveled the United States and Canada, interviewed North
American government and business experts, and wrote most of
the final report. So when it came time for the final presentation,
the principal investigator sent me to Japan. When we telexed our
Japanese counterparts that I was coming, they sent back three
questions: (1) is she married; (2) how tall is she; and (3) what does
she eat? Those days of being an exotic professional woman working in Japan paid off years later in a book.[2]

On the flight from Chicago to Tokyo, I sat next to the Japanese
manager who headed the Chicago office for Sumitomo Metals in
the United States. We spent the ten-hour trip talking, and he gave

me a lift in his company car to my hotel in the center of Tokyo. Two days later, I delivered my talk to a lecture hall filled with a sea of businessmen clad in navy blue suits from 200 of Japan's bluest-chip firms. The bulk of my findings were that American business and government representatives had little impression—positive or negative—about the incoming Japanese firms and saw no threat. At the day-long conference, however, one Japanese academic predicted that the firms would eventually be seen as "invading" the United States and face enormous pushback. Indeed, by the end of the 1980s, his prophesy came true.

When I returned to Ohio, I wrote the Sumitomo executive that the presentation was a big success. He wrote back saying he was greatly relieved. Since I was young, female, and foreign, he had worried that the presentation would be a disaster because no Japanese men would take me seriously. I was only grateful he had not shared those misgivings with me on the way over.

We have remained friends for more than 30 years. He visited my family in Seattle, and I stayed at his home when I returned to Japan as a young professor doing research. As we rode into Tokyo on the train one morning, I asked him why traditional Japanese art seemed so spare: muted brown or black ink on a white background with a few bold strokes to convey a tree or mountain, and lots of white space. His answer surprised me, twice.

Ah yes, he said. I was just reading about Japanese art on the train into work the other day. That alone was a shock: How many American executives routinely read about art on their daily commute? But his next comment also surprised me, but then made good sense.

There is so much white space in the *Sumie* paintings, he said, because it lets us imagine what we wish. Also, Japanese are homogeneous people so we do not "need" to have the white part filled in with color or design because we know what the artist is saying without it. We can "read" what is not there because we think alike, so we fill in the gaps.

The importance of white space or what appears to foreigners as "nothing" is fundamental in Japan. As my friend suggested, the tribal, homogeneous nature of the Japanese give them some advantages over many Americans. Anyone who has negotiated or had a conversation with Japanese people knows how often long silences occur. Most Americans cannot endure silence for more than a few seconds and give away negotiating strength because of it. So the ability to see what is not there and to endure emptiness or white space helps the Japanese. By the late 1980s, I remembered the prediction about the Japanese firms being viewed as trying to conquer the United States: Ten years earlier, the professor had seen what was not there while American business and government experts had missed it. Along with putting odd pieces together and thinking in reverse, the notion of "seeing what is not there" can help spark aha moments. This chapter offers examples of how that skill can help eliminate confusion, solve problems, and be a strategy for action.

SEEING WHAT'S NOT THERE TO ELIMINATE CONFUSION

Lieutenant Aaron Shepherd is one of three jail commanders who oversee 200 of the jail staff, both uniform and nonuniform support staff, at the Ada County (Idaho) Sheriff's Office. He also oversees two teams of deputies in the Ada County jail cell blocks. The jailhouse teams of approximately 27 commissioned deputies work 12-hour shifts, four days on and four days off. According to Shepherd, a running joke has been that one of the teams "gets all the action; there's always something going on. In contrast, when the opposite team works, things are quiet and laid back and nothing ever happens." At the end of the shifts, the team with the action reported numerous incidents, like an argument between two inmates, a scuffle among inmates from different gang groups, or smuggled contraband. Its statistics in terms of number and severity of incidents far exceed that of the other team, which regularly had a relatively incident-free, "clean" report. Why would there be such a striking difference in the shift reports?

Shepherd's initial, and the obvious, conclusion was that the team where action took place must have been "stirring things up." Or, the team was unable to manage what was going on in the cell blocks, whereas the "quiet" team had the situation under better control. Indeed, the team leader and members of the "under control" team jived and teased the team that had all the "action."

But Shepherd felt there might be another story going on. As he reviewed the reports in more depth, he decided that what "wasn't there" might be the problem. As he said, when he started to look more carefully, it appeared that the laid-back team was not enforcing the rules, so they had no problems to report.

Jail deputies like Mike Zuberer talk about learning to see and feel that "something is going on" in a dorm, even when there may appear to be nothing happening. They develop a "sense" for seeing what's not there; perhaps that is what the "action team" was doing:

> A lot of times, if you sense something that's not right, then you take your gut instinct. If I'm working in a dorm and I go lock up an area and it's all sitting quiet, or something just doesn't seem right, then I'm going to take my gut feeling ... and the majority of the time ... that's right. There was something going on that you didn't know ... something that [the inmates] didn't want you to know about.

Shepherd sensed that the "under control" team members were not out in the cell blocks monitoring what was happening as closely as the other team. As a result, they were not finding and reporting as many incidents as the "action" team. That finding alone could generate an aha moment of understanding for the team leaders and members.

But even if the "under control" team was missing incidents it should have caught, Shepherd faced another dilemma. If he "found" the problem and offered it up to the teams, it became his to solve. Thus, Shepherd needed to encourage both teams' supervisors to examine the statistics to root out what was causing the very different results, without hinting that he thought the "under control" team might not be doing its job. Shepherd wanted to encourage the supervisors to experience their own aha moments to explain what appeared to be confusing, especially since the "under control" laid-back team's supervisor was convinced this group was performing better than the "action" team. So Shepherd's role became more one of encouraging communication between the two teams' supervisors so they could define, understand, and solve the problem.

Shepherd first met with the supervisor of the "laid-back" team to show him the comparison of statistics and help him see that there was a difference. Next, he brought the two supervisors together to talk about how they were running the shift teams and to decipher just what was going on. By taking the time to understand the statistics and by asking himself—and then the supervisors—what the differences might be, Shepherd realized that what was "missing" was the clue to identifying and explaining a bigger problem of how supervisors could manage shifts better.

The end result: Shepherd helped to generate insight in both supervisors and start them on a path of understanding how to manage their shifts better. In the process, he helped them move out of their shift "silos" and begin to look at the data and ask questions about what was going on. The shift supervisors began to communicate more frequently, and eventually were able to reach an aha moment of understanding: Not only were they part of a bigger team of supervisors, but they were in turn a part of the bigger team of the entire agency. In this case, by understanding the implications of what was "not there," Shepherd helped his subordinates begin to see their role in a larger way, a key element of insight thinking.

SEEING WHAT'S NOT THERE AS A WAY TO SOLVE PROBLEMS

> Opportunity is missed by most people because it is dressed in overalls and looks like work.
> —Thomas A. Edison (1847–1931), inventor[3]

Former ProClarity CEO Bob Lokken is a no-nonsense numbers guy who says more in three minutes than most people do in thirty and could easily take on Mr. Spock in left-brain target practice. Yet, Lokken can shift to right-brain insight thinking nearly without noticing it. While Daniel Pink, in his book, *A Whole New Mind*, may predict that right-brain people will rule the world, my bet is on people like Lokken who can use both logic and insight thinking with equal ease.[4]

When he started his most recent firm, WhiteCloud Analytics, Lokken wanted to create a new business venture, but went about it systematically and logically. Rather than waiting for frustration or chance to turn up an opportunity, he went looking for a "Big Problem" to solve, one that many people might miss, to paraphrase Edison, because it looks like work.

U.S. President Barack Obama has identified three Big Problems the country must tackle to maintain and thrive in a global economy—education, energy, and health care. By chance, Lokken had exposure to two of those Big Problems by the time he decided to start up another firm. While he was CEO of business intelligence analytics firm ProClarity, he helped start a statewide volunteer council of CEOs interested in improving K–12 education. As a potential employer of future software engineers, Lokken's focus was on strengthening high school math and science requirements. But the politics and molasses speed of government educational organizations frustrated him, making the possibility of a business venture in the area unappealing. His exposure to energy was based upon one of the co-founders of ProClarity, who left after they sold the firm to Microsoft to start up his own new firm, Inovus Solar, which focuses on solar-powered street lights for rural areas and developing countries.

Lokken turned to health care as a potential area for starting a new firm, partly out of personal interest and partly because he, like Obama and others, sees it as a Big Problem. He saturated himself, learning as much as he could about health care, all the while keeping his ears attuned for a problem that others were not seeing. He experienced a flash of insight during a conference for hospital CEOs in San Diego. Several presenters talked about the industry moving to a fixed reimbursement model, where patients arrive at a hospital for a knee replacement, for example, and the government says the hospital gets $5,000 to do the operation. If the hospital can do it for $4,000, it keeps the $1,000, a 20 percent margin. But if the hospital needs $10,000 to do the operation, they still keep $5,000 but have to absorb the additional 100 percent margin on that deal. As Lokken says, the hospitals have been forced

> from a price setter model to a price taker model, demanding efficiency ... I sat there and went "aha," they just had the industry flipped upside down on them.

Hospitals need help in finding best practices that are cost effective. Lokken's expertise is software that allows organizations like hospitals to aggregate and shape massive amounts of information into a visually accessible format that managers use in decision making. The missing ingredient that Lokken saw was finding a way to collect and disseminate information about best practices in a way that hospital managers, physicians, and others could use it. Lokken saw what hospital executives had not: The upside down industry shift, from a price setter to price taker, offered hospital executives an opportunity to form "insight clusters" of hospitals, in noncompeting regions, that could learn from each other about how to become more efficient.

Lokken systematically looked for and discovered a complex problem and, in so doing, saw what was not there as a trigger for a new business start-up. The skill of seeing what's not there is also especially useful for solving problems that are presented.

* * *

It is hard to imagine two people more different in their areas of focus and expertise than software entrepreneur Bob Lokken and Ada County Sheriff's Office Crime Scene Investigator Jaimie Barker. Barker is a big solid man who rocks forward in his chair when he gets excited. He is burly, yet there is a gentleness about him as he describes the way he walks around a crime scene, protecting evidence that is small, almost invisible. He is on call 24 hours a day, every day, and as you would want in a crime scene investigator, he is matter of fact when it comes to explaining his job: "Murder, rape, robbery, those kinds of things. Aggravated assault, burglaries and stuff like that." When a call comes, it is often about a suspicious death, and he bolts to the crime site. During a one-hour interview with him, his phone rang eight times. He checked it, turned off the sound, and refocused on our discussion. But I knew, if the wrong call came, he would be gone.

Barker's focus is physical forensic evidence. He does not interview suspects, victims, or witnesses or worry about why a crime happened; that is the job of the detectives, he says. Barker just lets the scene "tell me what it's telling me." But like Bob Lokken, Barker and other detectives know that what is "missing" may hold more information than what is in sight.

On May 10, 2007, Barker headed to the foothills near Boise, Idaho, after hikers reported finding a man, face down and dead, near a small campsite. In the 30 seconds it took Barker to walk from his car to the site, he let information rush into his mind.

> As I arrived at this scene, I notice police cars, tire tracks, and beer cans laying here . . . then a gate and a trail that goes up. . . . You go through a stream and then you start walking up this path. I saw that it's a well used path, and that there were tire tracks and shoe impressions. . . . I stay off the path as I walk in. I walk to the side of the path.

Because the initial patrol units had no reason to suspect foul play, they had walked up the main part of the path, their footprints joining those of the hikers. Barker takes that into account and begins to think about who might have been on the path or along the stream, making their mark. He is aware that anyone, including himself, can leave traces at the scene, and incorporates that into his observations, almost without noticing it. He initially tries to absorb the environment, to gain context for what he will encounter at the campsite. As he made his approach to the site, he stood off to the side, about 30 yards from the other officers, and just observed the area. He saw the hillside, where the hiking path continues, and a flat sandy stretch near the stream that he had crossed on his way in. He noticed a stream "kind of babbling along to the left of this initial scene," with thick overgrowth clustered nearby.

As he walks, Barker uses as many of his senses as possible— "what I saw, what I heard, what I smelled, all of that. We touch on the five senses here." The stream captures his attention, in particular. He listens to it, sees the "overgrowth" and wonders if something is hidden in it. He asks himself where the stream goes, if someone used it as a way to leave, as a place to discard something, or wash his hands.

As Barker approached the crime scene, he was building the mental database that helped him eventually create a theory of what happened. But then his antenna kicked in as he began to see what "wasn't there."

> First of all there *wasn't anybody else* lingering around. There *wasn't a tent* or anything that made me think that this was a permanent homestead or even a temporary sort of squatting place for a homeless person. So that tells me this is sort of transient in nature, sort of temporary, that he is a recent visitor, and that he isn't laying down roots there. Also, as I'm walking in, *I'm not seeing anything that's screaming at me that other people are involved*, it's just this guy right now.

His initial conclusion: There was no evidence (at first) of other people having been with the man, no evidence (at first) that this is a site where the man, or others, planned to stay. As he got closer to the crime site, he saw something unexpected. The sergeant on the case had told Barker there was a body by the stream, which is what he expected to find. What he did not expect was to see chairs, "a sort of formal campsite," with beer cans.

Then Barker reached "the dead guy," who was face down, "next to the rocks that form the ring around the fire, and . . . his head isn't shaved but it's really short hair. And I see on the back of his head what looked like three impacts . . . of a linear impact. So I can say decisively at that point, and I do tell the sergeant, this is a homicide."

The victim clearly could not have fallen, and then struck himself three times on the back of the head before dying.

The homicide investigators showed up and got to work, using Barker's observations to understand the context. They rely on him to point out "what I've seen and what's interesting to me." As the coroner and other investigators document the scene, take photos of the tops and bottoms of the victim's shoes, and put paper bags on his hands, Barker remains open to new information, including seeing what might not "be there." And he got it, as soon as the coroner turned the victim face up.

> And as we turned him over, we see . . . several little cuts . . . in his shirt. We thought that was interesting. . . . once we remove the clothing, we find that he has several stab wounds in his chest.

And again, Barker notices what is not there—no blood on the victim's shirt or chest. Given his knowledge of how people die, Barker knows knife wounds tell a story. Because the wounds did not bleed internally, which would cause blood on the shirt, he knows they are stab wounds and the victim was dead by the time someone else stabbed him. At this point, detectives begin to speculate about motivations of the killer or killers.

Perpetrators use different methods to kill for specific reasons, including availability of weapons and motivation. As Barker describes it, using a gun to shoot someone from 25 or 30 feet across a room signifies less personal involvement. There is a distance physically and mentally. In Barker's words, what is "dispatching the person is the bullet you're launching."

But this murder was emotional and personal, according to Barker:

> Somebody with the emotional drive to reach out and touch [the victim], not once or twice with a baseball bat, but three or four times, across the head . . . who does this guy [the victim] know

that would bring that level of savagery to that act? It's a very brutal act. And then ... to let him lay there and die and flip him over and stab him. Again, this brings a very personal edge to the act, very brutal.

Barker turned out to be right. Five days later, two women were arrested, one who had purchased a $.50 baseball bat murder weapon at a thrift store. She and another woman lured the victim to the campsite, talked and drank beer, and then struck him with the bat until it broke. The women were sentenced to life in prison, with 45 years fixed time. Neither has divulged a motive.[5]

Both Lokken and Barker have built up knowledge, experience, and skill to be able to look for what is missing, and that can lead to insights that help solve problems.

USING WHAT'S NOT THERE AS A STRATEGY FOR ACTION

Marty Schimpf is a chemistry professor and university administrator by profession, beer maker by avocation, and likely future bridge master if he gave up the other two. When he talks about university life, he is deliberate, slows down, and positions each word in the air in just the right spot. When he talks about bridge, though, his voice speeds up. You have the sense that he wants to reign in his enthusiasm and remain cool and controlled, as he does in a classroom and meeting of deans. But he really cannot. He acts like there is nearly no better way to spend his evenings than playing bridge.

Schimpf uses a term in bridge that a Japanese executive or a crime scene investigator would be unlikely to use, but is a concept each would recognize: "negative inference." Simply put, negative inference in the game of bridge is the notion that the cards that are *not* played may determine the outcome of the game, rather than the cards that *are* played. Some argue that it implies a weak hand, one with little that can be bid. Others claim that it may be a brilliant strategic move to outwit opponents. But most bridge players would admit that understanding and using negative inference separates the good players from the great ones.

Schimpf's bridge colleague, Katey Levihn, is an engineer and self-described novice player. While her analytical mind strengthens her play, she envies those who are savvy enough to use negative inference and see what's "not there."

What is not said or not played is as important, and sometimes more so, than what was stated or done. One has to be able to see both . . . what's stated triggers deductive reasoning and what's not stated . . . triggers inductive reasoning.

Levihn claims that a good bridge player analyzes the information available in her hand and on the table and makes positive inferences. By knowing "what's bid and what it means, what's played and what that means," she can assess the odds of certain cards appearing in future hands. But the better bridge player also triggers inductive reasoning, and that usually happens by using negative inferences, such as asking yourself the opposite questions: "what's not bid and what that means, what's not played and what that means." According to Levihn, all of this thinking may lead to a larger aha moment or insight for the profession as a whole, when someone develops a new bidding system or adds some component to the existing system that changes its nature.

Of course, the idea of white space, or seeing and using what is not there, can be a strategy in sports. Hockey star Wayne Gretzky reportedly once said that "A good hockey player plays where the puck is. A great hockey player plays where the puck is going to be."[6] He played well because he skated to "where the puck wasn't." More subtle perhaps is the player who appears to do nothing and yet has an astounding record for team performance. Houston Rockets basketball player Shane Battier has gained renown more for what he does not do than what he does. His statistics, by normal NBA measures, are abysmal: "He doesn't score

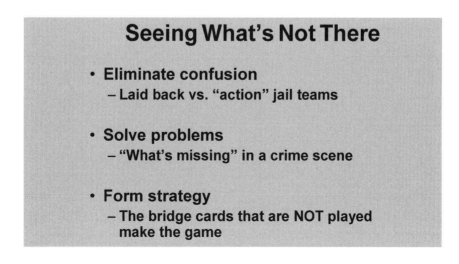

Seeing What's Not There

- **Eliminate confusion**
  - – Laid back vs. "action" jail teams

- **Solve problems**
  - – "What's missing" in a crime scene

- **Form strategy**
  - – The bridge cards that are NOT played make the game

many points, snag many rebounds, block many shots, steal many balls or dish out many assists."[7] Battier's invisible strengths, what you cannot see, are what make him and his team soar. When he is on the court, his team does much better and the other team does much worse. Battier gets the ball to teammates, he makes few mistakes, and he stymies his opponents. His coach claims that he "puts the pieces together" for the team, using intellect, not physical ability.

Jail sergeants, entrepreneurs, detectives, and bridge players each have an ability to see "what's not there." In a sense, they see void spaces and find ways to fill them, to find connections, whether purposefully or playfully, to generate possible ways the empty spaces make sense. They claim the ability is not difficult for them, and in fact they have honed the skill over time. But the first step is to ask "What isn't there? What is missing?"

The range of occupations and avocations suggest that these people are not unique, that it is possible to learn how to see and understand and use the white spaces. In the tips section, we will look at some of the ways.

INSIGHT TIPS: SEEING WHAT'S NOT THERE

Learning how to "see what's not there" is partly a matter of being able and willing to live "in the white space," or that area of ambiguity and unknown direction. But we may be more able to do this than we realize. Examples below look at the classic nine-dot puzzle, situations where we already "see" what's not there, and more to use as practice.

Nine-Dot Puzzle That Explodes the Borders

One way to start is by using puzzles that force us to move beyond the boundaries that we normally use. The classic nine-dot problem is one of the most notorious to make the point of moving "out of the box." It is a good example in part because there *is* no "box" but just our assumptions that the "lines" between dots create a box. We think we see boundaries, but of course we do not. The basic rules for the problem are to connect all of the dots using four lines without lifting your pencil from the page. But more advanced rules have developed: using three lines or using "one line." The solution for four and three lines

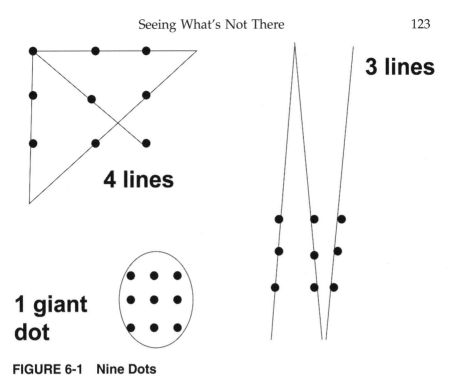

FIGURE 6-1   Nine Dots

appear above (Figure 6-1). The solution to "one line" includes two interpretation. In one, a person takes a pencil and draws through three dots, then imagines she "walks around the circumference of the earth," returning to the dots puzzle, runs her pencil through the middle three dots and then once again "walks" around the earth to return to the puzzle, and runs the pencil through the final three dots.

The last solution, to "just get a giant pencil and make a huge dot on top of all nine dots," is a solution that a 10-year-old came up with. The joy of uninhibited creativity!

Accepting That We Already "See What's Not There"

We often "see what's not there" but may not realize it. Viewing constellations, we rarely stop to think that we are "connecting dots" and seeing what does not exist in the pictures that we imagine as part of the stars. The hunter Orion, with his shoulders, belt, and sword, is just a cluster of stars, but for many of us, from childhood we have come to believe we see the man and his fighting gear (Figure 6-2).

WHAT DO YOU SEE?

FIGURE 6-2   Orion

Source: NASA and STScI

Seeing "More" Than What's There

The following example is a bit different in that we see "more than what's there." We read the instructions, then want to find the core word, and remove the letters around whatever it might be. The instructions themselves, though, are the solution so we are "not seeing what's there" rather than the reverse. (HINT: remove "six letters" is the clue.)

**Remove six letters, don't change the
sequence, and find a familiar word**

BSAINXLEATNTEARS

FIGURE 6-3   Seeing "More"

Solution: B (*S*) A (*I*) N (*X L E*) A (*T*) N (T E) A (R S) = BANANA

Seeing "Less" Than What's There

A final example illustrates how most people fail to see all that they could or should. Draw the following picture (rectangle with a squiggle in the center) on a white board and ask friends what they see. Most will zero in on the squiggle and "see" a bumble bee, a butterfly, a tangled fishing line, an airplane .... The point is they do not "see" the rest of the rectangle, the box that it forms, the border, or the open space around the squiggle. So by looking only at the one small spot in the center, we are not seeing the rest.

What do you see?

FIGURE 6-4   Seeing "Less"

NOTES

1. Jonathan Barnes. 2001. *Early Greek Philosophy*. London: Penguin Books: 51.

2. Nancy K. Napier and Sully Taylor. 1992. *Western Women Working in Japan*. Westport, CT: Greenwood Press.

3. John Cook, Steve Deger, and Leslie Ann Gibson. 2007. *The Book of Positive Quotations*. Minneapolis: Fairview Press: 594.

4. Daniel Pink. 2005. *A Whole New Mind*. New York: Riverhead Books.

5. Patrick Orr. 2007. Foothills murder plot took shape in text messages, *The Idaho Statesman*, May 18: A1.

6. Wayne Gretzky Quotes, The Quotations Page (http://www .quotationspage.com/quotes/Wayne_Gretzky/, last accessed July 23, 2009).

7. Michael Lewis. 2009. "The No-stats all star," *The New York Times Magazine*, February 19: 26–33, 56, 63–64.

Chapter 7

Hitting the Wall: Obstacles in the Path

> In the classroom, if I do hit that wall, I'm not opposed to restacking it . . . Some of my best aha moments happen when I run smack into a wall and I don't know what I'm going to do . . . And something . . . makes me [think], "That's what I meant to do! THAT's why I meant to go down this road."
>
> —Tom Willmorth,
> high school drama teacher and improv actor

Walls, obstacles, and constraints sound ominous on the aha journey but might just be one of the best sparks for successful organizations that want to nudge insight. Stories and research about insight frequently mention the importance of hitting an impasse that forces restructuring or "restacking," as Tom Willmorth says, a problem or way of thinking.[1]

Improv actors aggressively seek out obstacles and walls as a way to sharpen their performances and up the ante on the comedy and reactions they seek from audiences. Tom Willmorth and Joe Golden are theater teachers (high school and college), Equity actors who perform year round, and business partners in an improv comedy firm, called The Fool Squad. They have worked together doing Green Shows before the nightly summer Idaho Shakespeare Festival productions since 1993 and have had their improv firm since 1994. They finish each others' sentences, and sometimes it feels like they are in the middle of the next paragraph while the listener is still stuck mid-sentence ten feet behind. Their energy, wit, and attitudes about walls make sense not just for actors but for successful organizations. Rather than seeing obstacles as something to avoid, Golden relishes them as ways to spur him to try new ideas:

> I've always heard that the wall is a good thing. An actor wants obstacles and problems, because that's drama, that's conflict, that's interesting. If I get there too easy, it's a snooze. I want walls in my way, that I have to scale, knock down, paint a tunnel through . . .

Walls can help generate insight, sometimes without our realizing it. This chapter examines how organizations can deal with walls on the road toward insight. In fact, as Golden suggests, finding ways to "use" obstacles may help generate insight more than "fighting" them. This chapter includes five approaches to obstacles: pushing through a wall, tearing down a wall, going around a wall, painting a wall, and ignoring a wall. We start with an example that illustrates how "aha moments make all the difference" for a business college that smacked into several walls. The balance of the chapter explains the various approaches to walls in more depth.

FACING ALL THE WALLS

What chance does a brand-weak, geographically remote, resource poor business school have in a start-up venture for a highly visible executive program? To be blunt, none.

When Boise State University's College of Business and Economics investigated, under pressure from administrators, the possibility of developing and delivering an executive MBA (EMBA) program, the outlook was grim; the honest chances of success were not good.[2] The venture had many strikes against it, none of them minor. First, university administrators had given the college no choice about whether to do an EMBA program; it was simply imposed, thus forcing a team to come up with a program. Second, the university is remote, hundreds of miles from population areas of any significant size: five hours by car from Salt Lake City, seven from Portland, and nine from Seattle, thus severely limiting market potential (who would come to the program other than people within easy driving distance?). Third, name brand national EMBA competitors, like Wharton, Northwestern, Berkeley, and the University of Washington, had been luring locally based managers to San Francisco, Chicago, and Seattle for years. How could a start-up program with no reputation compete? In addition, even though the college was accredited by the most prestigious review group in the world, it lacked a clear brand image, and worse, its programs were viewed by potential customers in the area as being very similar to several lower quality programs in the region. Not to add any more pressure, given the college's lack of name to fall back on, it had only one chance to make any new program a success. Failure would not be acceptable.

It gets worse. The college had few internal assets—no executive education facility, no start-up funds, and few faculty members at a stage where they could likely be successful teaching an executive audience. Only one person in the 60-person faculty had ever taught in an executive MBA program anywhere. The possibilities for a start-up venture—in business or in education—with so many obstacles were daunting. Perhaps in part because of the location, though, the designers simply expected to find solutions and "make something happen."

Creative aha moments do happen, on long and successful journeys toward insight and success, even in university settings, one of the most conservative organizational arenas around. Given the edict to create a program, an EMBA team had no choice but to push on and come up with a program. A team that included highly creative to highly analytical members examined its many obstacles and tried to look at each in turn, using some of the techniques we have covered in earlier chapters: putting odd pieces together, reverse thinking, and seeing what is "not" there. And in the process, the team dealt with walls in many ways—pushing through, tearing down, using, bypassing, or ignoring them.

Over a two-year development period, the group found a way to deal with each wall. First, the remoteness disadvantage was reframed as an advantage. Being in a remote small state and city gave faculty members "relationship assets" in many different sectors—from arts and education to business and government,[3] and those relationships provided access to thought leaders across the state. Team members or senior administrators within the college had contacts, from the governor and U.S. congressional members, to CEOs of major companies, to leaders of city and county government, to nonprofit organizations. Being a lightly populated state and city also meant relative efficiency and ease of making things happen across sectors. Likewise, the college faculty members had connections from previous projects that had required buy-in and support from groups across the community and university that knew of the college's ability "to get things done."

Ultimately, the remoteness and unique ability to collaborate with the community were assets that outside big brand competitors could not easily replicate. The program was built on a consortium model, in which seven to nine organizations (none of them competing) became the core suppliers of participants and main partners of the program. The consortium members offered the use of their facilities, managers as speakers and co-teachers in the program, and strategic organizational problems for the students' final consulting projects. The college's ties to the local community generated learning experiences for EMBA participants that would be hard for competitors to emulate. So, instead of brand image in a traditional sense, the college had relationships that could, with a successful program, build a reputation that was quite different from what the existing competitors could offer. In a sense, it pursued the "blue ocean strategy" of creating a market and product where none like it had existed before.[4]

The program took two years to plan, ran the first cohort through in two years, and succeeded far beyond expectations: In a survey conducted by the top accreditation agency of all EMBA programs and of selected competitors (e.g., University of California–Irvine, University of Washington), the rookie program's graduates gave it better rankings than any of the others.[5]

The executive MBA example illustrates obstacles that many organizations encounter, and the team found ways to deal with walls it encountered. The team pushed through the wall of being forced to develop a program, tore down the wall of expectations from one "expert," and pursued ideas that "shouldn't work" in part because the team members did not know any different. The team also used remoteness by making it an advantage, rather than a disadvantage. Finally, it simply ignored the wall of no reputation, because there was simply nothing to be done until the program established one.

In this next section, we will examine in more depth each of the approaches to handling walls.

PUSH THROUGH THE WALL

> I think and think for months and years. Ninety-nine times the
> conclusion is false. The hundredth time I am right.
> —Attributed to Albert Einstein

As improv actor Joe Golden says, "We push through the wall and keep working until something finally breaks and we make forward progress." Einstein's "push" for his first major aha moment in 1905 came after two years of thinking and wrestling with the problem of light and velocity; his second major insight regarding gravity took eight years, which must have been very frustrating after his first experience. But even more exasperating would be his attempt to reach a final major insight, the universal theory, which never happened. Nevertheless, he continued to push through obstacles—the ideas that did not make sense, concepts that conflicted. Others do the same, albeit in different ways. A financial officer in a large western U.S. city was forced to look at a problem the city faced because "no one else would" and discovered new ways to solve it in the process. John Drake, director of business development and campaign planning at marketing/advertising firm Drake Cooper, talks of patience and being willing to study and think about a brand strategy for a long time.

> It could be 11 o'clock at night and I still might be here with the whiteboard playing with ideas . . . leaving [does not help], so I just keep working on it. . . .

It may not be enough to push through walls that arrive on their own. Sometimes, putting walls up for others to push through is a strategy in itself. Football coaches may present obstacles to players to help them to learn to push through on the road to improving or understanding. Several talk of simulating a stressful environment to see how a player reacts versus sitting in a meeting where the discussion is methodical.

The EMBA team pushed through walls, partly because it had no choice. After the first few weeks of euphoria at the idea of working on a new exciting (albeit required) project, the reality of the time, work, and discord among group members set in and the group defaulted to "pushing through the wall." Had the group known the development process would take two years, it might have disbanded. But by pushing through the walls, overcoming some obstacles, and achieving small aha moments, the inertia kept it going.

TEAR DOWN THE WALL

> Mr. Gorbachev, tear down this wall!
> —Ronald Reagan, U.S. President, June 12, 1987, Brandenburg
> Gate, Berlin, Germany[6]

The most dramatic tearing down of a wall in recent history is undoubtedly the fall of the Berlin Wall in November 1989, when West Germans hammered through the graffiti-plastered concrete structure into East Berlin. However, walls in organizations can often be structural or human. In some cases, demolishing the walls is like opening the opportunity for aha moments and insight.

Haeir, China's largest maker of appliances, has done just that, tearing down walls between functions and units to enhance collaboration and understanding. Every Saturday morning, the company's top executives meet for half a day to discuss problems and seek answers. The group divides into small teams of six to eight people, mixed by business functions, units, and provinces, to hear and give ideas about problems. By tearing down the silo walls, the executives gain diverse opinions, and, as *Financial Times* reporter Don Sull puts it, "ongoing exposure to the issues faced by different parts of the business helps executives to *connect the dots* to understand Haier's situation as a whole, rather than looking at the market through the window of their own silo."[7]

In the EMBA program's development, a person became a wall. Early on, the team deferred to the only member of the faculty of 60, and the only member of the EMBA team, with experience in teaching executive graduate programs. While the team had been told to think about a "blank slate," the member with past EMBA experience frequently nixed ideas—from online interaction with participants to weekend schedules, to offering a program that integrated disciplines, rather than teaching separate silos of courses in finance or marketing or operations.

After six weeks, the team hit a wall: The "expert" with experience in executive MBA programs had become an obstacle. Ultimately, the wall was torn down when that member left the team to take on a committee chair position in the college. Once the wall disappeared, the team's first aha moment exploded. The lack of expert knowledge in a particular area could be an advantage, rather than a disadvantage, because it allowed ideas to emerge that no one knew "could not work." Naïve (and inexperienced) as the remaining team members were, many ideas emerged and ultimately became core principles of the program. Tearing down a wall opened up the chance for creativity.

GO AROUND THE WALL

Improv actors Tom Willmorth and Joe Golden talk about walls like a skateboarder might—they take a run at them, jump over them, smash their heads against them, find a hole and walk through them, and sometimes, simply go around them, leaving the physical challenges behind. In his college classes, Joe Golden throws himself against a wall, moves a bit to the side, and does it again and again. Finally, he notices that the wall has an edge, an "end," and he simply walks around it. His point to the students is that trying to solve a problem using the same failing solution over and over will not work. So sometimes, it is best to find a way to walk around the wall.

Bob Lokken had to do the same when his start-up ProClarity faced a huge wall called Microsoft. ProClarity was, like the Boise State College of Business and Economics, a small, unknown firm in a remote location that lacked the resources of a giant like Microsoft. When Microsoft had a new piece of software, it simply put money behind the product and marketed it to millions of users and buyers worldwide. ProClarity, a comparative ant, had to find a way to deal with such a giant.

To explain how ProClarity bypassed the giant, Bob Lokken drew three concentric circles on a white board. The outer rim represented customers and users of software—a huge group. This was the group Microsoft could go after—the potential users of software who could request that their purchasing managers buy the software. The middle circle was the potential purchasers, the buyers within companies who made decisions about which software packages the users would be operating within firms. Microsoft could also market to this group, as could many other firms. ProClarity had little chance with either group, mainly because it lacked the resources to blanket the industry with advertising.

Instead, as Lokken recalled, his company had to find a way to "go around the wall." Bypassing the end users and purchasers, his firm targeted the innermost circle, which represented "thought leaders" of the industry, people who reviewed and wrote about new software and could influence potential organizational buyers. By going around the Microsoft wall, ProClarity played its own best game, zeroing in on a group others had left relatively open. Lokken's insight from that experience became useful for him in understanding the "value" of constraints.

PAINT THE WALL

> Sometimes we paint the wall . . . we paint a picture of a tunnel
> on it and then go through it, like Wile E. Coyote. If we hit a
> wall, we don't necessarily change our direction, we change
> the wall!
>
> —Joe Golden,
> improv actor and theater professor

When pushing, demolishing, and circumventing do not work,
sometimes it is possible to alter the wall to become an advantage.
This approach fits the "necessity as mother of invention" adage—
when the situation works against an organization or person, many
find ways to turn it to their advantage. The EMBA program did just
that by using remoteness and relationships as positive sellers
rather than as a lack of obvious resources and access to markets.

Some sports teams excel at "using the wall" as well. Piedmont
High School, a small suburban high school near San Francisco,
faces much bigger teams on a regular basis.[8] Its coaches use an
offense formation, A-11, that allows all 11 players to be potential
receivers, confusing the opposing teams' defensive players. The
play revives the so-called "single-wing formation" first used in
1907 and more recently revived as the "Wildhog" by the University
of Arkansas. Boise State University is in a similar position as
Piedmont at the college level: fewer resources and less well-
known (perhaps until recently). As a result, its recruiting efforts
pale in comparison to the Pac-10 schools, which can offer better
facilities, scholarships, and prestige. So, over the years, the coaches
have learned to "paint the wall" by developing creative ways to
carry out the program—from recruiting to training and practice,
to the plays they use on the field. By using the constraints they face,
such organizations are forced to look for new ways of achieving a
goal, and in the process, often gain aha moments along the way.

IGNORE THE WALL

> So maybe we move the wall into someone else's yard.
>
> —Joe Golden,
> improv actor and theater professor

If an impasse appears impossible to work through, around, or
use, the time may come to ignore the wall or move it elsewhere.
Instead of seeking to create a brand or reputation that would draw

candidates from programs like Northwestern's, the EMBA team focused on making the program unique and its first cohort's experience the best possible. Because there was nothing to be done about it, the team ignored the "lack of reputation" wall so it could create its own brand, rather than try to mimic other programs. The result was highly satisfied graduates and a brand that will emerge over time.

Likewise, the EMBA team's decision to focus courses on "topics, not disciplines" was an aha moment that reflected an attitude of moving the wall to someone else's yard. University education, especially business education, has a long history of function or discipline focused courses: economics, accounting, finance, marketing, human resources . . . if you have gone to business school, you know the list. Instead of fighting the normal political battles of "how much time each discipline should receive" in the program, the team moved the wall: The courses focused on "topics," rather than on disciplines. A course called "Creating Competitive Advantage" included elements of disciplines, but rather than being separate boxes, the sessions and professors integrated topic elements through common cases, joint teaching, and multidisciplinary projects.

* * *

Encountering walls or constraints is part of the aha experience. In fact, brain activity and the way we deal with walls supports that. When we hit a wall or impasse, the left hemisphere is simply overpowering the right hemisphere in what is called "solution coding."[9] The left hemisphere is very "loud" and dominates problem solving processes by more methodical step-by-step methods, which may impede the brain from finding an insight flash and ultimately a correct problem solution. Only after exhausting logical options—or hitting a wall—can the brain "restructure" a problem and allow for more of the right-hemisphere thinking to come into play.[10] Perhaps it is only when the left hemisphere slows or "quiets down" that we can "hear" and allow into consciousness the solution from the right hemisphere. Even then, we may still require some detours or stepping away from a problem to let new ideas come about, which is the focus of the next chapter.

If we take the improv actors' advice, and see walls as a positive way to generate more ideas and solutions, we might look for them, instead of complaining when they appear. By finding approaches that work for us, we can use obstacles as sparks for insight, rather than as dampeners.

INSIGHT TIPS: LESSONS FROM WILE E. COYOTE

When we face a messy problem, or try to learn a new complex topic, it is only normal to run into obstacles or walls. As we have seen in this chapter, walls can be thought of and handled in many ways. Drawing upon some of the ideas from improv comedy, try the following ideas.

Draw the Wall

Think of the most recent walls you have run into while trying to tackle a personal or work-related problem and think through what the "wall" is like:

1. Grab a pen and paper and "draw" the wall! What does it look like? How flimsy, how thick, and how high is it? Could it be "painted" to look different? Are there any benefits to the wall? How could you use it to spark new solutions?
2. Now look at where you "drew" the wall? Could you draw it somewhere else? Could it look different? Could you "move it" to another part of the paper, or to another side of the room? Can it be moved to "someone else's yard"?
3. If you must tear down the wall, should or can it be rebuilt or tweaked to become an advantage? One software development team found that a senior developer acted as a "wall" in terms of criticizing the team's work and demanding perfectionism (which was nearly impossible). Finally, one team member

used the attention (even negative) to his advantage and turned the senior manager into a mentor over time. As the relationship built, the team member was eventually able to circumvent the (senior manager) obstacle by "restacking" the bricks, working directly for the manager, and helping him see the benefits of the team's actions.

Remember, walls do not necessarily need to be broken down to reach a solution; they can be used to your advantage. Much like a comedian will take advantage of a disruption in a performance as a springboard into a new routine, via improvisation, so can we often take advantage of the very obstacles that stand in our way. Sometimes it just takes a bit of creative thinking, inspired by that pesky roadrunner.

NOTES

1. Karen Gasper. 2003. When necessity is the mother of invention: Mood and problem solving, *Journal of Experimental Social Psychology*, 39 (3): 248–262; M. Jung-Beeman, E. M. Bowden, J. Haberman, J. L. Frymiare, S. Arambel-Liu, R. Greenblatt, P. J. Reber, and J. Kounios. 2004. Neural activity when people solve verbal problems with insight, *PLoS Biology*, 2 (4): 500–510; E. M. Bowden and M. Jung-Beeman. 2003. Aha! Insight experience correlates with solution activation in the right hemisphere, *Psychonomic Bulletin & Review*, 10 (3): 730–737.

2. N. K. Napier, P. R. Bahnson, R. Glen, C. J. Maille, K. Smith, and H. White. 2009. When "aha moments" make all the difference, *Journal of Management Inquiry*, 18 (1): 64–76.

3. R. K. Srivastava, T. A. Shervani, and L. Fahey. 1998. Market-based assets and shareholder value: A framework for analysis, *Journal of Marketing* 62 (January): 2–18.

4. W. Chan Kim and Renee Mauborgne. 2005. *Blue Ocean Strategy*. Boston, MA: Harvard Business School Press.

5. See the survey results for 2006–2008 graduating cohorts: http://cobe.boisestate.edu/emba/files/2009/04/real-world-results-2.pdf.

6. In June 1987, at the 75th anniversary of the building of the Berlin Wall, Ronald Reagan made a speech at the Berlin Wall, calling on the leader of the Soviet Union, Mikhail Gorbachev, to remove the wall. Just over two years later, on November 9, 1989, it did fall, brought down by protests among people in several countries

throughout Eastern Europe. The wall's destruction led to the reunification of East and West Germany.

7. Don Sull. 2009. Developing general managers: The Haier case, Financial Times Blogs (http://blogs.ft.com/donsullblog/2009/05/17/developing-general-managers-the-haier-case/).

8. Richard Morgan. 2008. Spreading the offense, *The New York Times: 8th Annual Year in Ideas*, December 14: MM74.

9. E. Bowden and M. Jung-Beeman. 2003. Aha! Insight experience correlates with solution activation in the right hemisphere. *Psychonomic Bulletin & Review*, 10 (3): 730–737.

10. M. Ollinger, G. Jones, and G. Knoblich. 2008. Investigating the effect of mental set on insight problem solving, *Experimental Psychology*, 55 (4): 269–282.

Chapter 8

Making a Detour: Changing Activity in the Aha Journey

I began to study arithmetical questions *without any great apparent result*, and *without suspecting that they could have the least connection* with my previous researches. *Disgusted at my want of success*, I *went away* to spend a few days at the seaside, and *thought of entirely different things.* One day, *as I was walking* on the cliff, the idea came to me, again with the same characteristics of *conciseness, suddenness, and immediate certainty*, that arithmetical transformations of indefinite ternary quadratic forms are identical with those of non-Euclidian geometry. [Italics added]

—Henri Poincaré,
mathematician and philosopher (1854–1912)[1]

Poincaré's last phrases are ones only a mother, or, more likely, another mathematician, could love. His earlier comments about studying ideas "without suspecting that they could have the least connection . . ." make sense to anyone on the journey toward insight. In the process of moving toward aha moments, we may have collected and processed information, tried to view it in different ways, used various options to spark an aha moment, and even encountered and overcome walls and obstacles. But still, we may come up short.

Sometimes we can try too hard to find connections and reach aha moments. So, we need to step away, to take a detour, or to try a different activity. Few of us are as fortunate as Poincaré, able to "spend a few days at the seaside," but the notion of doing something different, changing activity, is one many people feel is part of insight.

TAKING A DETOUR TO REACH THE FLASH

A key assumption about aha moments is "they come out of nowhere." By now, we know that they arrive after effort and work. But often we need a break or change of activity to allow them to simmer. Few did that better than Nobel Prize winner James Watson, who was a master at changing activities just before he experienced a flash of insight. Here are a few of the many activities he engaged in just prior to reporting a flash of insight:[2]

- "on the bus to Oxford . . . "
- "In a conversation with . . . "
- "While daydreaming . . . "
- "I fell asleep . . . "
- "on our walks . . . " (with Crick)
- "spending most evenings at the films, vaguely dreaming that any moment the answer would suddenly hit me . . . "
- "doodling . . . "

He experienced quite a range of what some might call "non-work" activities before he bumped into a flash of insight. Far from goofing off, taking a break or detour during the aha journey has seemed necessary for many. In the preface to his poem "Kubla Khan," Samuel Taylor Coleridge noted that he furiously wrote the first 200–300 words after a three-hour nap (apparently fused in part by opium, although he is coy about that part). Playwright Neil Simon goes "into a state that is apart from reality"; Mozart found that his best ideas came when he was "traveling in a carriage, or walking after a good meal, or during the night when [he] cannot sleep."[3]

For years, researchers, scientists, artists, and other creative individuals have tried to understand what is going on in a break or change of activity prior to an insight flash.[4] Neuroscientist Nancy Andreasen debunks the notion that when brains "rest" they are "inactive."[5] She claims that the period when the brain is not actively working on a specific problem is a state of "free-floating and uncensored thought," in which multiple regions of the brain interact and thoughts are "self-organized" without our conscious awareness. In the process, the brain is "disorganizing" symbols or words and reorganizing them in ways that we had not conjured.

Sounds like a busy place.

Psychologists do not wholly agree on what happens during "incubation," or stepping away from directly confronting a problem. Based upon self-reports and anecdotal evidence over the years, many assumed that as we shift activities or take a "break," we are "unconsciously processing," that our brains are working even though we are not aware of "thinking" about a problem. Psychologists describe incubation in many ways:[6] as a "sweeping" of the mind, as "selective forgetting" that pushes unnecessary information or data aside, allowing ideas to emerge, as a "diversion" of the problem solver's attention to allow for "opportunistic assimilation" or chances for more connections to occur, and as a chance to "reorganize" information and try a new approach to the problem.[7] Still others couch the change of activity in terms of how we learn: Our brains learn better when we take a break, which allows assimilation of new information before additional input arrives.[8]

Perhaps we never do take a break, but just continue "creative worrying," where our minds repeatedly return to the problem, even for a few seconds, never pushing it entirely from our consciousness.[9] A creativity researcher from Temple University, Robert Weisberg, argues that we are conscious, but simply not focused on the particular problem at hand.[10] These last two approaches may help explain why not everyone claims to "need" a break or change of activity when they are faced with learning something new or solving a problem.

CHANGING ACTIVITY—WHAT PEOPLE DO?

Think about one of your own aha moments—what were you doing just beforehand? Napping? Taking a run or walking in the mountains? Listening to music? Standing in the shower? You are not alone. Regardless of what the experts may think is happening, many of the ordinary among us report that insight often seems to "come out of nowhere," following some activity that would appear unrelated to our problem.

Since aha moments seem universal, we sometimes assume the experiences that nudge them should likewise be universal or similar. Indeed, the types of experiences that people use are similar, but they vary by person, scale of the task, and other factors, like culture. Some people also report they have tried several different ways to change activity or take a break and "found what works" for them. For instance, one senior manager has learned that when he "sleeps on" a particularly thorny problem, about 80 percent of the time he generates a solution the next morning in the shower.

So what types of activities appear to help nudge insight? The range is narrower than you might think, with a few common methods that most people use, from being in water and nature, to sleeping or learning a new skill and being very bad at it.

Water

Becky Logue's eyes slope downward slightly, giving her a deceptively relaxed look. But she is anything but relaxed when it comes to rats, in her case "dental rats." Logue was a dental hygienist for years, work that requires repetitive action: working inside patients' mouths, then swiveling to a side desk to jot notes on a patient's chart. Switching between mouths and charts meant her hands were easily contaminated, forcing her to wash them often, slowing the teeth cleaning process. Computer technology allowed hygienists to input patient data directly, rather than writing it on a chart, but still required a shift from mouths to keyboards, so contamination remained.

Logue combined several factors—the multiple movements, constant contamination, and new technology—saw what "wasn't there," and developed the Dental R.A.T. (remote access terminal): a foot-operated mouse on the floor next to the patient's chair that would allow a (multidexterous) dental hygienist to enter data as she worked on the patient. There is no need to turn away from the patient, and no need to use her hands. All is done with the tilt and press of a foot. The idea for the product and its name, as well as several business model insights since its introduction, happened in a place she knows helps her generate aha moments.

> My husband and I sit in the hot tub and start talking about . . . what's going on, or how can I do something better? We're relaxed, our minds are open, and we just start brainstorming. That's when the Dental R.A.T. came about, and the name of calling it "the R.A.T." So we call them "hot tub moments."
>
> Becky Logue,
> CEO and founder, Dental R.A.T.

As many entrepreneurs know, coming up with an interesting new product idea is the easy part. Selling the new concept, in this case to dentists and hygienists, was anything but. Resistance stemmed from perceived cost, the learning curve, and "newness" of the idea. Logue tried for years to convince dentists to use the product, with slow adoption. So, she went back to the hot tub. One day, she and her husband created a new way to get the R.A.T. into dental offices—by using "reverse thinking." Instead of convincing dentists and hygienists already committed to existing data input systems, she is taking a step back in the "customer chain." Logue is now working with universities that have dental hygiene programs, exposing the Dental R.A.T. technology to the students. Younger, more open to new technology, and moving into a field where they can command good jobs, newly minted hygienists are Logue's potential ticket to getting her product into dental offices. As the young hygienists join dental practices, they have begun to ask their new bosses to purchase the Dental R.A.T. system. Slow inroads, but now the R.A.T. seems to be taking off with a vengeance, with over 600 percent increase in sales in the past year alone. And Logue swears by those hot tub moments.

Many people talk about insight flashes happening while they stand in the shower, which seems to have several advantages: Warm water relaxes us, perhaps making us more open to ideas, a shower stall is a contained safe space, and we do not have to "think" since washing is a routine we have doubtless perfected over the years. And for many, time in the shower is one of the few during the day without distractions or interruptions.

I cannot find a scientific survey of people correlating hot water and aha moments. In fact, one German study suggests that cold water stimulates cognitive ability in the elderly.[11] Yet, when it comes to encouraging aha moments, warm water dominates the anecdotes from the people I interviewed. Few people dispute the need to conserve electricity and water. But if we cut hot water use dramatically and took only cold showers, would we lower our collective aha moment generation, reducing the likelihood of new ideas, solutions, and inventions?

ZZZZZZZZ

What do Bill Clinton, Eleanor Roosevelt, and Albert Einstein have in common? They are all famous nappers.

Naps are making a comeback; even daydreaming is getting more press.[12] Until 2009, there was a National Siesta Day, but then some research found a possible link between napping and type 2 diabetes.[13] Rumor has it that Einstein napped with a pencil propped in his hand so he could "purposefully doze off" and awaken when it fell from his hand, long enough to joggle some ideas but not so long to put him completely asleep.[14]

Interestingly, some people claim that they have learned to use sleep as a near surefire way to solve a problem. Microsoft principal development manager Craig Boobar has learned, over the years, that he can count on an aha moment most mornings after he sleeps on a problem. As he says, stepping away from a problem, particularly by "sleeping on it over night," definitely helps. He frequently faces vexing engineering problems and finds that the next morning in the shower he knows how to frame the problem and how to solve it. And that surprised him. When he did not think he was "consciously thinking" about his problem, the solution came. That is why it feels like the flash of insight comes from nowhere.

Brain researcher Nancy Andreasen, mentioned earlier, studied brain activity during times when people were at "rest" and times when they were focused on trying to remember something.[15] She calls the resting period "random episodic silent thought" (REST) and the frustrating memory task "focused episodic memory." Like others, she found that when the mind is in a more "free and unencumbered fashion," in a sleep or near-sleep state, it accesses the more complex parts of the brain, which generate less linear, more creative thoughts and outcomes.

As firms become more systematic about trying to increase creativity and innovation, they are looking for any edge to help that happen, including ways to encourage napping. Companies like Cisco and Procter & Gamble have created space for nappers through meditation or "quiet" rooms, including using "Energy-Pod" recliners with what looks like a movable half egg shell covering a napper's head, blocking noise, light, and distractions.[16]

University of California–San Diego researcher Sara Mednick claims that there is a "right kind of nap" for problem solving— one that includes rapid eye movement (REM) and dreams.[17] In a research study, she compared performance of volunteers on a word-association test under different conditions of sleeping and not sleeping. Some volunteers took naps with REM/dream sleep, others took naps lacking in REM sleep, and still others simply stayed awake. According to Mednick, the REM sleepers performed

40 percent better at the task she gave them than the other groups. She thinks that REM or dream sleep allows the mind to connect ideas that would otherwise not have been and in the process generate better solutions. Her workshops and Web site offer a "nap wheel" to determine just the right time of day for that "perfect nap."

So, the message seems to be: When you have a problem, just sleep on it, but be sure it is the right kind of sleep!

Medium and Scale

In designing single family homes, office structures, and a few multi-unit housing buildings, architect Elizabeth Cooper already uses techniques to look at problems from different perspectives. Computerized design software allows her to devise various layouts, shift rooms and dimensions, and look at designs from different angles. But sometimes she gets stuck, unable to find a satisfying solution to her architectural problem. Instead of leaving her work task altogether, though, she changes the medium she is working in, moves away from the computer, and uses old-fashioned drafting or drawing by hand.

> The computer, for me, is much more technical . . . more repetitive; there's much less creativity involved. I never do any artistic expression on the computer. . . . So I've learned if I'm trying to get an aha moment on a technical problem, I [use] something I would normally do for creative problem solving [like drawing by hand].

Also, for Cooper, a problem's scale may dictate how much change she needs or how long the break needs to be. Essentially, Cooper uses different types of "breaks" depending upon how complex the problem is or how much "thinking space" she needs. Medium-sized problems require her to "go for lunch." When she comes back, she has a solution. Smaller problems may be just a matter of leaving the desk for five minutes, "to get a cup of coffee or talk to someone about something unrelated." Again, like Boobar, Cooper has learned over time what nudges aha moments for her and in the process, encourages them to come more systematically and less purely by chance.

Ryan Woodings, "Chief Geek" at a high-technology firm called MetaGeek, also relates problem complexity to scale of change in activity. For smaller problems, he and his colleague need breaks. It may be as simple as doing something else for an afternoon, or leaving the office and tackling a problem the next day. When one colleague hits a wall, he leaves the office and says, "When I come back tomorrow, it will click." And it does. For bigger problems, Woodings works on a problem, then "doodles" on it, and then sets it aside. And as Boobar reported, Woodings also has plenty of solutions "pop into my head in the shower in the morning."

Hot water again!

Creating "Brain Space" Through Physical Movement, Being in Nature

Irish mathematician and astronomer William Rowan Hamilton (1805–1865) wrestled with a problem that Henri Poincaré could appreciate: how to extend complex numbers to higher spatial dimensions. He is famous among his crowd because of his invention of "quarterions," which use four dimensions, and a formula, simple to remember but hard to understand (for nonmathematicians):

$$i^2 = j^2 = k^2 = ijk = -1.$$

But Hamilton may be best known among nonscientists for walking across a bridge.

On October 16, 1843, Hamilton and his wife strolled across the Broom Bridge in Dublin, where his flash of insight—the formula—hit him, mid-bridge. Fearing he would forget it, Hamilton etched the formula into a wooden pillar at the end of the bridge. While the etched formula has long worn away, the celebration of Rowan's insight has not. In 1989, the National University of Ireland mounted a stone carving commemorating Hamilton's stroll and aha moment. Annually, on October 16, mathematicians from around the world come with their sense of history and humor to honor Hamilton by walking to the bridge.

People often report that they walk, run, or spend time in nature as a change in activity. MetaGeek's Ryan Woodings runs because of the "mundaneness," far different from what he feels when he tries to solve a problem at the office. At his desk, the problem "won't go away," and he feels pressure to solve it there. That causes stress and he is even less apt to solve the problem. But running lets him think and not think.

Running's a good time for me because I can be thinking about [a problem], but I'm not totally thinking about it. I'm thinking about the problem, then the beautiful trees, then back to the problem, then to some rocks I have to watch out for. [It's a] time where you don't feel so pressured.

Angeli Weller, an ethics director, recently started a firm called Earthpaw, which sources and sells local and sustainable products for pets and their owners. Weller runs half marathons and hikes on a regular basis with Earthpaw co-founder Elvis the Boxer. But Weller hikes in the foothills near her home, rather than runs, to encourage aha moments. Both are exercise, but hiking lets her mind wander in a more relaxed manner. She is more likely to have an aha moment when she is hiking than running, because running for her is "work."

If I'm having to concentrate because I'm exercising and I'm trying to get a good workout, I would never have an aha moment, it just won't happen. But if you send me off into the hills to traipse around and walk ... that's more likely to be a trigger.

For Weller, hiking in the mountains with her dog is relaxing, like a mini-vacation. Away from the computer and work, she says she has "brain space" to generate ideas and make connections that lead to insight flashes.

Being "Really Bad" at Something

Craig Boobar is a software development manager who talks with gusto about performing poorly, not in his job but in learning to play the guitar. He has been a software engineer and manager for over a decade and he is very good at it, but when he started learning to play the guitar several years ago, he was taken aback by his inaptitude. Not only was it much harder than he expected, but even worse for an engineer used to seeing results, he saw almost no payoff for the time and energy he invested.

I was horrible. I was starting from the lowest of low. I was worse than I ever thought I would be, picking anything new up ... And that amazed me ... that the return and the investment ... aren't correlated over the short term. You [can't expect] to work really hard for a month, and ... be this much

better at it. So you're not going [to] see immediate returns all
the time.

Like many competent professionals, Boobar had forgotten what
it felt like to be a beginner and fail at something, especially when
he worked so hard at it. But he stayed with it, and he had an
"understanding aha," realizing again that others experience such
frustration, from his children learning math to customers wrestling
with a new software program. Learning to play guitar also reaf-
firmed for Boobar the importance of patience and persistence.
"That's so obvious," he would say, but an insight he needed to
relearn. He has also applied it at work, staying with a "messy problem," seeking more alternative solutions, rather than taking an easier solution. He found it took him a long time to learn to play the
guitar and that many times he was tempted to give up, especially
since his performance was far from what he felt his skills were.
But he forced himself into a position of learning, which opened
up ways of thinking and ideas he had not expected. He realized
how easy it can be, as we age, to "stay in the safe zones and not
look for new things to learn."

Even more useful for him, as Chapter 2 covered, he learned that
not all problems are what they appear at first blush. Playing the
guitar is not about finger coordination, it is more about rhythm,
"so it takes a long time [to learn] . . . but what you think is impossible actually becomes pretty easy after awhile."

Boobar uses a different type of "taking a break," where he con-
centrates his mind on something completely different from his
work.[18] He has applied that experience to work, using the notion
of diversion as a way to break from a problem and return to it later
with a different perspective. So too can problems in the workplace
morph—from a seemingly straightforward one to something quite
different.

Finally, some people argue that doing "mindless work" helps
generate creativity and insight.[19] In essence, for jobs that demand
high performance and creativity, some researchers claim that a
workday should be designed to alternate between hours of challenging, intellectual work and low pressure, low cognitively challenging work. So next time you play video games at your desk,
remind your boss that your "mindless work" is just the change of
activity you need to nudge an aha moment.

* * *

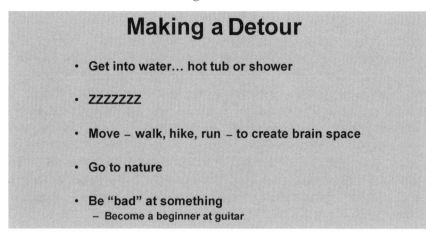

Making a Detour

- **Get into water... hot tub or shower**

- **ZZZZZZZ**

- **Move – walk, hike, run – to create brain space**

- **Go to nature**

- **Be "bad" at something**
  - **Become a beginner at guitar**

We tend to follow common patterns when we take breaks or change activities. We typically do so alone, rather than in groups. We often move locations, a few steps or something more dramatic. And often, the change is quite brief. Some researchers at Texas A&M University reviewed research studies on incubation time during simple insight problem experiments. They found that the more preparation people had done before changing activities, the more effective the benefits of the break. They also found that 30 minutes was an "optimal" break, while more than 24 hours began to lose its punch.[20]

But part of the key of learning to "use" our detours is knowing just when we need to take them.

INSIGHT TIPS: KNOW WHEN TO FOLD

How do you know when it is time to step away? Take a break? Change the activity you have been doing to solve a problem? Several people have learned "when to fold," and their approaches provide tips for the rest of us.

Talk About It

While he was writing *East of Eden*, the book he would claim was his best work, Nobel Prize winner John Steinbeck kept what he called a "journal."[21] His editor had given him a large leather-bound notebook. On the left-hand pages, Steinbeck wrote letters to his editor, which would not be read until after the novel was complete. On the right-hand pages, he drafted the novel itself. The letters to Pascal Covici ("Pat") were, for Steinbeck, mainly to "warm up" for the day's writing but also revealed much of his thought process during his 11 months of producing the novel. The letters are an inside, "real time" story of how one man worked through the creative challenge of building a novel. The ebb and flow of his energy, his ability to focus on the challenge of creating a scene or character, the amount of thinking that went into the process away from his writing table, the types of "detours" or changes in activity that he knew were useful for him, and the times when he had a "breakthrough" or moment of insight are all tracked in sometimes excruciating detail. The process is useful for others to read and may be a valuable exercise to do ourselves to identify those times when we need to step away from a challenge, as well as what types of activities work for us when we need that detour.

People like Steinbeck, Craig Boobar, and Ryan Woodings know themselves well enough to recognize when they need to take a break, and once they learned what works for them—hiking or sleeping or lounging in hot tubs—they have been able to use those techniques and wait for the payoffs. Confidence that insight will happen builds over time with experience and ultimately makes the aha moment less unpredictable and more "systematic." In a sense, they are developing insight muscle memory, a sort of skill for "aha on demand."

Next time you face a big problem or are struggling to learn about a new concept, write about it, talk to others about it, and try to "watch" yourself from a place in your mind that is apart from the problem solving itself.

Figure Out How Long You Need to "Bang Your Head"

Software development manager Craig Boobar has gotten good at knowing "when to fold," or take a break from a problem. When he was younger, he worked relentlessly on a problem, never giving up until he was exhausted. He would "bang his head against the wall" and could not understand why pieces of a problem did not gel for him. Now, as a wise man in his forties, he knows better. He learned, after many years of tracking his own process, that for a tough problem, he will struggle with it for up to three days, then he takes a break, giving "enough" concentration to a problem to plant "brain seeds," and then change what he is doing and wait for the flash. He comments that there is value to "letting yourself off the hook," and he is still "amazed" that quite predictably, he solves his problem in the shower after sleeping on it overnight. Now he has learned to have faith in himself and his confidence that knowing when to take a break will help him solve future problems.

When you work on a problem, try different lengths of time before you change the activity—see if you need one day or five, 2 hours or 12 before you need to step away. Several of the people I talked with felt that, as they understood their own approaches to solving problems, to encouraging aha moments, the time they needed before taking a break decreased. They felt that concentrating harder, stopping earlier, and then letting the unseen mind work made them more efficient in the longer term.

Find Your Best Detours

To learn when to take a step away and find what activities help encourage aha moments, we need to become more conscious, more aware, of the aha journey. Again, monitor yourself to find which detours work for you—whether walking, learning a new instrument, or standing in the shower.

When we become more mindful of when "to fold" or take a break and what types of activities help generate insight, we may be more likely to spark insight. Like Weller, some people need the mundaneness of walking or hiking rather than the "work" of running. Does water work for you? Perhaps several different changes in activity help for different types of problems.

Keep a small notebook at hand and jot down what you do during the time you wrestle with a problem and what you do when you take a break. Try to assess whether some activities appear to relate more readily to helping a solution emerge. Find the time of day that seems best for you to work on a problem and when is best for the change of activity.

NOTES

1. Henri Poincaré. 1952. *Science and Method*. New York City: Dover Publications, Inc.: 54. Translated from the original by Francis Maitland: Henri Poincaré. 1908. *Science et Methode*. Paris: E. Flammarion.

2. For each of the quotes, the source is James D. Watson. 1968. *The Double Helix*. New York: Mentor Books. Page numbers are in parentheses: "on the bus to Oxford . . ." (77); "In a conversation with . . ." (82); "While daydreaming . . ." (98); "I fell asleep . . ." (98); "on our walks . . ." (with Crick) (99); "spending most evenings

at the films, vaguely dreaming that any moment the answer would
suddenly hit me ... " (114); "doodling ... " (116).

3. See Nancy C. Andreasen. 2005. *The Creating Brain*. New York:
Dana Press: 75–77.

4. Graham Wallas. 1926. *The Art of Thought*. New York: Harcourt, Brace, and Co.; Robert W. Weisberg. 2006. *Creativity: Understanding Innovation in Problem Solving, Invention, and the Arts*.
Hoboken, NJ: John Wiley & Sons: 386–446.

5. See Nancy C. Andreasen. 2005. *The Creating Brain: The Neuroscience of Genius*. New York: Dana Press: 75–77.

6. Graham Wallas. 1926. *The Art of Thought*. New York: Harcourt, Brace, and Co.; Robert W. Weisberg. 2006. *Creativity: Understanding Innovation in Problem Solving, Invention, and the Arts*.
Hoboken, NJ: John Wiley & Sons: 434.

7. Eliaz Segal. 2004. Incubation in insight problem solving,
Creativity Research Journal, 16 (1): 141–148.

8. C. M. Seifert, D. E. Meyer, N. Davidson, A. L. Patalano, and
I. Yaniv. 1995. Demystification of cognitive insight: Opportunistic
assimilation and the prepared-mind perspective. In R. J. Sternberg
and J. E. Davidson (eds.), *The Nature of Insight*. Cambridge, MA:
MIT Press: 65–124; J. D. Mollon and Marina V. Danilova. 1996.
Three remarks on perceptual learning, *Spatial Vision*, 10 (1):
51–58.

9. Robert M. Olton. 1979. Experimental studies of incubation:
Searching for the elusive, *Journal of Creative Behavior*, 13 (1): 9–22.

10. Robert Weisberg's excellent book, *Creativity: Understanding
Innovation in Problem Solving, Invention, and the Arts*, offers great
reviews of the history of research into insight. See Robert W.
Weisberg. 2006. *Creativity: Understanding Innovation in Problem
Solving, Invention, and the Arts*. Hoboken, NJ: John Wiley & Sons:
432–433.

11. T. J. Doering, J. Thiel, B. Steuernagel, S. Johannes, A. Breulla,
C. Niederstadt, B. Schneider, and G. C. Fischer. 1999. Changes of
laboratory markers of cognitive brain function by thermostimuli
in the elderly, *Archives of Physical Medicine and Rehabilitation*, 80
(6): 702–705.

12. U. Wagner, S. Gais, H. Haider, R. Verleger, and J. Born. 2004.
Sleep inspires insight, *Nature*, January 22, 427 (6972): 304–305;
Robert Lee Hotz. 2009. A wandering mind heads straight toward
insight, *The Wall Street Journal*, June 19: A11.

13. See, for example, the Web site Siesta Awareness, which promoted (until 2009) National Siesta Day, because of a recent possible

link between napping and type 2 diabetes. The site nonetheless claims benefits to productivity, reduction of stress, and lower likelihood of workplace accidents. http://www.siestaawareness.org/pages/siesta-facts.php.

14. Walter Isaacson. 2007. *Einstein: His Life and Universe*. New York City: Simon & Schuster: 436.

15. Nancy C. Andreasen. 2005. *The Creating Brain*. New York: Dana Press: 72–73.

16. Leslie Berlin. 2008. We'll fill this space, but first a nap, *The New York Times*, September 28, BU4; http://www.metronaps.com/mn/the_metronaps_service/the_energypod.

17. Nicholas Bakalar. 2009. Behavior: Better performance after a dreaming nap, *The New York Times*, June 23: D6: taken from a study by Denise J. Cai, Sarnoff A. Mednick, Elizabeth M. Harrison, Jennifer Kanady, and Sara C. Mednick. 2009. REM, not incubation, improves creativity by priming associative networks, *Proceedings of the National Academy of Sciences*, June 8: http://www.saramednick.com/.

18. Eliaz Segal. 2004. Incubation in insight problem solving, *Creativity Research Journal*, 16 (1): 141–148.

19. Kimberly D. Elsbach and Andrew B. Hargadon. 2006. Enhancing Creativity through "mindless" work: A framework of workday design, *Organization Science*, 17 (4): 470–483.

20. A. Rebecca Dodds, Thomas B. Ward, and Steven M. Smith. 2004. A review of experimental research on incubation in problem solving and creativity. Working Paper from Texas A&M, College Station, TX.

21. John Steinbeck. 1969. *Journal of a Novel: The East of Eden Letters*. New York: The Viking Press.

Chapter 9

Aha! Reaching the Insight Summit

It feels like the *tipping point* . . . you get enough [information] in your head and then one additional factoid suddenly makes six things fall into place. [That] one piece of information falls into place as a mini-aha and that causes other collected pieces of information to fall into place from a chain reaction. That's when I know I've got something—I've just discovered *something that caused six other things to fit together in a new comprehensive model of depth.* [Italics added]

—Bob Lokken,
CEO and founder of WhiteCloud Analytics

Use this joke with some friends and watch the reaction:

QUESTION: How do you get down from an elephant?

Skip a beat before you give the punch line.

ANSWER: You don't get down from an elephant. You get down from a duck.

Huh?

A few seconds pass. Then, BOOM!

How long did it take your friends to "get it?"

Jokes are one of the most useful forms of teasers to experience an insight flash.[1] The elephant joke is a mini-problem. When we first hear it, we try to solve it and often cannot. Then, when we hear the answer, we're motionless for a few seconds, there's a delay, and then, BOOM! One additional "factoid" falls into place and it all becomes clear. The joke makes sense; we chuckle and relax. And the next time we hear that joke, we will remember the right answer faster.

In this chapter, we will talk about what happens at the "tipping point," as Bob Lokken refers to it: the aha moment in the seconds just before and after we experience insight. Humor and jokes encapsulate in a condensed way much of that experience and help explain what happens during insight.

Henry Gurr, retired physics professor at the University of South Carolina (Aiken), does not look like a rabble rouser. A photo of him from ten years ago shows a full head of white hair, parted on the left side and combed back and to the right. His eyebrows are black, the creases in his cheeks look like the pointed parentheses around <Enter> as he shows the start of a smile. But his writings are fervent and relentless about how to help students learn physics.[2] A big part of that is helping to inspire aha moments.

In years of teaching, Gurr has watched hundreds of students have insight flashes. In the process, he has identified specific characteristics and series of steps that we humans experience when we hit that aha moment. He uses humor to illustrate it. Go back to the elephant joke at the beginning of the chapter. When we hear the joke, we typically have visual images—perhaps a *mahout*, sitting on an elephant's back, feet just behind the ears, short stick in hand. We begin to imagine ways he can go from atop the elephant to the ground. As we are figuring out the answer, the punch line comes. We freeze, waiting to be enlightened. We are stumped, often tense, as we try to decipher the answer: "you don't get down from an elephant. You get down from a duck?" Since we have been thinking about "getting down" from atop an elephant, we are confused, because "getting down" from a duck makes no sense.

In a group, usually a few people see the point of the joke sooner than others and start laughing. We may still be puzzled and also perhaps embarrassed by now, and then suddenly, a flash—the solution and understanding of the joke arrive: Ahhhh, "down" from a duck, as in feathers. We relax, laugh, and the tension resolves.

* * *

Gurr claims that faces reflect what occurs in the brain as tension recedes and relief spreads. After watching so many student faces for years and studying the brain to understand more about insight, he thinks our facial expressions in particular convey what is happening. His ideas apply beyond students, of course, to anyone or any group trying to understand or solve a problem. Before insight, many people will show a face that has a "blank look," one that teachers, parents, or managers know well. He calls it a "lock up," a form of puzzlement that freezes the face and the body. Sometimes, a person may nod, but usually that means "I hear, keep going" not "I understand." Once the insight flash happens, tension flows away, and the body and face relax.

Tension may leave, but that is not the end of the insight flash. According to Gurr, we feel happiness and success at "seeing" the solution. Many of the people I talked to referred to the aha moment feeling as being quite emotional and often physical, as James Watson recounted when his pulse raced. Euphoria, relief, and joy come when we solve a problem or understand a new concept. The thrill can be powerful as we learn something or unravel a puzzle and we add that new information to our memories.

But before we add to those memories, Gurr stresses that the flash of insight requires that we have some knowledge before we can solve a problem. Sherlock Holmes would agree. Chapter 2 focused on problems and Holmes commented that a good detective needed the skills of deduction and observation but also knowledge.[3] While Dr. Watson could deduce and observe, he lacked the range of knowledge—about poisons and geography and chemistry and more—that Holmes had. Thus, to understand the "down from a duck" answer in the joke, we have to know that "down" is a type of feathers found on ducks. Young children or non-native speakers of English may think of "down" only as a movement (from up to down) and thus, lacking that knowledge, the aha moment is lost on them. So certain knowledge or experience allows us to "connect the dots" more quickly on problems that might require insight thinking as well as on problems that require more linear logic thinking. Thus, the knowledge gained from the joke's answer generates new memories from the aha moment experience, and that adds to the store of memories for the future. You remember the response to that joke faster or, when you hear it, you understand the point sooner.

Research confirms that memory is linked to aha moments: We tend to remember problem-solving experiences that invoked the feeling of "aha" better than ones that do not. From a neuroscience perspective, it may be a function of a part of the brain, called the hippocampus, and its evolutionary development. Scientists claim the hippocampus is a mechanism for storing powerful memories, such as those that come with an aha moment, which could have developed as a knack for piecing disparate ideas together.[4]

Gurr claims that when we understand how this flash of insight happens, and what its impact can be, we transfer the skills to other parts of our learning and problem-solving lives. By building more knowledge, adding more memories, and opening our perceptions, we have more chance of future insight.

CONNECTING THE DOTS: WHAT WE SAY HAPPENS AND WHAT GOES ON IN OUR BRAINS

How often have you said, after an aha moment, "it seems so obvious, why didn't I see it before?" As we have learned, insight occurs when we suddenly and clearly understand or see something we had missed earlier. We can describe conceptually what we perceive happens. First, we say that someone has "connected dots and sees the big picture." Second, the ability to see a bigger picture also suggests that we can apply the lessons from the aha moment to situations other than the specific case where it happened.

In addition, much occurs physiologically in our brains during this process—before, during, and after the flash. Neuroscience research from the past two decades increasingly offers knowledge about what physically occurs (e.g., connections of neurons, changes in brain waves, role of glial cells). We may know *where* activity happens, but we still need to understand more about why it occurs.

This section covers both what we perceive happens and what happens in our brains.

Step 1: Seeing the Big Picture

The BOOM of an insight flash comes about when we perceive two shifts taking place in our thinking and understanding: We see relationships among factors that we had not seen prior to the flash. This then allows us to "see the bigger picture" or the whole situation, when we had before seen only parts of it. When we "connect the dots," we recognize new (for us) links among factors. The factors may be ones that have existed all along, or they may include new "dots" or pieces of information that we had not known about. As Sherlock Holmes made clear, having lots of knowledge and experience helps connect dots, but sometimes, even with knowledge and experience, we may not see the connections right away. Likewise, the elephant joke at the beginning of the chapter shows that most of us had the "dots" of information about down being feathers, but we needed to put them together in a new way. An hourglass metaphor works here: We have all the pieces of information or sand in the hourglass, but not in the right position. By turning the glass upside down, or by shuffling the dots into new positions, we see the new solution.

Aside from poor communication skills, inability to "see the big picture" is one of the most frequent laments senior managers make about their employees' weaknesses. To help jail deputies learn that concept, Pat Calley tries to help them realize that the way they treat inmates may affect much more than themselves and that one other person. He knows that jail deputies' interactions with inmates' relatives, especially the younger inmates, may have long-term ramifications. So he models behavior that may have payoffs in ways he cannot predict. As he says, when adult children (over 18 years) get into trouble and are arrested, the police have no legal requirement to talk to the parent about the arrest or what has happened to the inmate. Calley has seen deputies follow that rule over and over; he knows it is "correct," but he also sees the situation in a broader perspective, from the view of the parents. So he tries to model behavior to his deputies so they will see that other viewpoint.

As Calley says, "every inmate has a mother and father." Those parents, especially if their child is facing a first arrest, are concerned and anxious about what is happening when the child/adult is arrested. So Calley talks with the parents, tells them what is going on with the child, and explains what the process of arrest involves. Calley calls it being human, when one "human cares for another."

But Calley has another "dot" in mind. The parents are also potential voters: "that's the person that's going to vote for your jail bond two years from now, because they're going to remember your contact." And, of course, if that parent's contact with the jail representative is positive, the future bond may have a better chance. His ability to see the relationships among several factors—the concern of parents for their arrested child as well as the role of those parents in a larger perspective—reflects an ability to "see the bigger picture." By modeling behavior that shows an understanding of many factors, Calley encourages deputies to take a bigger view and to look at their daily interactions as being part of an interconnected whole.

* * *

Professors can usually tell who the freshmen football players are during their first semester because their clothes seem too small. Shirts barely stay buttoned and T-shirts stretch wide across their chests and shoulder blades. I suspect they come to college with clothes they wore in high school or bought just before starting their university lives. But once they start intensive college football training, their clothes no longer fit right; they stretch and pull in odd places.

Ian Smart still has the build of a defensive back, the position he played as an undergraduate, but his clothes fit right. He is now a graduate student in accounting, but his memories of the early days of football at Boise State emphasize learning how to connect the dots. As all freshmen are, he was overwhelmed with information about plays, training, and his position. The information he got from the coaches' blackboard discussions or on play sheets "looked like Chinese." But as the weeks wore on, he focused on smaller parts of the game, on his training, and on his role on the field and put the pieces into a whole. As he became comfortable with his own position, he lifted his head and began to see and understand what others around him were doing, and he put himself into the context of the whole defensive lineup. As he said, "we came together as a defense and could see the whole picture."

For Smart and his defensive teammates, understanding the whole picture is critical for knowing where to move so they can execute a play successfully. In other fields, like the fast-paced software industry, keeping up on information in and out of the field and seeing a bigger picture may be useful for solving problems. MetaGeek troubleshoots Wi-Fi problems for home and office computers by identifying the source of Wi-Fi interference in a building, whether it is the microwave or cordless phone. Founder Ryan Woodings insists that employees keep up to date with competitor software programs, ideas, and methods in their own slices of the industry because it develops their ability to understand the "big picture" of the problems they deal with. He claims further that keeping up with industry trends, and beyond, makes it easier to encourage aha moments. As he says, awareness of what others in the industry are doing gives employees more information that they can mesh together with what they already know to solve a problem. That integration or "mesh," according to Woodings, often is the aha moment.

From novice athletes and students to sophisticated high-tech engineers and managers, "seeing the big picture" is a key component to the insight journey. Being able to see relationships among factors, and implications of those connections, helps spark the aha moments.

Step 2: Shifting to Conceptual Thinking

New Yorker staff writer and physician Atul Gawande, who wrote about the woman plagued by horrific itching (Chapter 5), found new mischief when he discovered one of America's most expensive health-care centers in McAllen, Texas.[5] In McAllen, Medicare spends $15,000/person, twice as much as it does anywhere else in the United States, except Miami. He went to McAllen to find out why health-care costs average $3,000 more per year than the annual average income of McAllen's inhabitants. Community members shrugged it off. Of course health-care costs are high here, they told Gawande, because people are unhealthy. McAllen's poverty, drinking, and obesity rates are among the country's worst. But on many measures, citizens had better health than many parts of the country—fewer heart problems and lower rates of smoking, HIV, cancer, and infant mortality. Gawande investigated further and was surprised to find that, in a town with profound poverty and low incomes, the nearest hospital housed technology that would rival that at The Mayo Clinic or Stanford University. Were costs so high because the health care was so good? Not so. Medicare ranks McAllen's two hospitals among the worst on measures of care. The dots were not connecting.

As he searched for answers from the local medical community, Gawande found that several physicians offered explanations that ultimately did not hold up. Some people suggested that perhaps McAllen residents received better service (others disagreed); some argued that malpractice fees were higher (although they acknowledged that lawsuits were nearly zero). Finally, one surgeon came clean: Doctors ordered more tests and procedures so they could generate more charges, benefitting their incomes. McAllen doctors had simply learned better than others how to scam the system.

The article evoked astounding reaction and interest, and even mention from the U.S. president in a speech he gave on health care within a few weeks after the article appeared. Gawande saw a situation in one town, connected the "dots" of information, and had an aha of understanding that he could eventually extrapolate beyond this single case. The McAllen story made sense in a bigger picture of health care, where individual physician self-interest drives costs beyond reason. He was able to unravel and define the problem; next comes the difficult road toward finding a solution.

The article offers a good example of one of the most critical steps in the aha journey—gaining the ability to take what we have learned from an experience and apply it beyond the current situation or problem. That ability to think more conceptually—transfer of skills, knowledge, and ways of thinking—builds our mental muscle strength to be able to generate more aha moments in the future. According to WhiteCloud founder Bob Lokken, it represents movement up the insight curve from an aha moment to being able to "abstract a problem," or make it more conceptual, by applying the insight to another industry or situation. In Lokken's case, his new firm could take the understanding aha he gained from Gawande's findings to generate a "creative aha" that turned into his new firm idea.

John Michael Schert, executive director of the Trey McIntyre Project, expects the company's dancers to be able to make an equivalent step beyond dance. In Chapter 3, Schert explained that when dancers learn a new step or set of movements from a choreographer, they memorize and practice until it becomes "their own," with the goal of making it "bigger" than what it was when they received it from the choreographer. In other words, they fit the steps and movements into something that exhibits the creativity they also bring to the experience and makes the dance piece that much better. When he wears his director of the organization hat, he says he wants to see the same thing happen when dancers think about the organization. As he says, "I expect them to process information like they do as dancers," which means they should be able to take the insights they have—in understanding or problem solving—and use them for improving other aspects of the organization.

A final example from football happens when coaches know that players have reached a flash of insight. Former Boise State defensive coordinator Justin Wilcox says football players "get it" when they understand plays, their positions, and the overall program's system in a conceptual way, rather than "just memorizing" it:

> The guys that hit the aha moments are much more conceptual ... this player could ... tell me on our defensive call *why* we're doing this, *why* he's doing his move, and *how it affects* other people.

The players who do not experience that same insight may make the moves and do what they are told, but "they don't know why."

BUSY BRAINS

Right at the point of a flash of insight, our brains are active, even when we may not be conscious of it. As Chapter 8 made clear, neuroscience research suggests that our brains have a way of "priming the pump," or working on a problem even when we are unaware of it.[6] Often, that "priming" works better after we have failed to reach a valid solution, which supports the notion of trying and failing. As we begin to tackle a problem, the left hemisphere of the brain takes a key component of a problem, like the idea in the joke of "getting down" from an elephant, and searches for what are called "strong associations." These strong associations are concepts and ideas that link to other closely related components. In the joke case, it would include thinking of ideas related to "coming down from" a high place—a rooftop, building, diving board—to reach an answer for the joke. With such "closely related" dots, the process is a more linear, step-by-step approach to an outcome. But for insight problems, which the elephant joke is, such linear, strong association approaches fail.

Since aha moments rarely come out of such linear thinking, the brain then lets the right hemisphere pick up the heavy lifting. It takes the key component of the problem (i.e., "getting down") and searches for so-called "weak associations" or links to distantly related ideas or ways of viewing the phrase or concept. Linking distant "dots" or ideas is more difficult and requires the "leap of imagination" of insight thinking that the left hemisphere is less able to achieve.[7] In this, the right hemisphere excels, and in reaching for those weak associations, the aha moment often occurs.

In the elephant joke, the left hemisphere seeks what makes sense and is easy to access or consider first: getting down from atop an elephant's back. When it fails to find a solution, effort shifts to the right hemisphere for less obvious solutions, as in "getting" or "collecting" down or feathers. In essence, because the right hemisphere is more sensitive to weakly related concepts and potential connections, it also is more receptive to breaking "mental set" and using different perspectives to solve a problem in less obvious and familiar ways.[8]

Perhaps the most interesting hallmark of an insight flash is its suddenness, the sense that it comes out of nowhere. In fact, researchers have discovered distinct mental patterns of preparation when we consider insight-based solutions,[9] what some call the "unseen mind." In other words, the brain's neuron connections continue to happen, even though we may be unaware of the activity, so when the aha moment occurs, the correct connections have been made, even when we may believe nothing is happening.

Chapter 8 talked about taking a detour or break from thinking about a problem just before the BOOM! experience, and relaxing is part of the process. Biofeedback experiments on people who thought about relaxation or were relaxed found that there was more activity in a part of the brain[10] that allows the brain to switch to focus on insight thinking.[11] So even *intending* to relax, let alone being relaxed by sleeping or hiking, helps the brain wipe clean the slate of irrelevant ideas to allow the right hemisphere to start fresh.

Thus, while we may think we are not working on a problem, the right hemisphere has already activated a solution search in the unseen mind. A solution sits below some threshold of awareness, waiting to crack the surface. This is the phenomenon of "it came out of nowhere." In fact, the flash was probably destined to emerge eventually; it is a matter of time and connection before it reaches our awareness.

In essence, the aha moment results from quieting the "louder" processes of the left hemisphere so that "quiet" insight-based solutions can emerge. The brain shows that such a transition or shift happens in other ways, such as the various waves that alter just before a flash of insight. Three types of waves activate just before an aha moment explodes. First, alpha waves spike, which "quiet" the activity in the left hemisphere.[12] Next, a burst of theta waves indicates a search across memory space for possible more creative solutions.[13] Finally, gamma band waves take off, and those are thought to signal the sudden transition of the solution processing from an unconscious state to a conscious one.[14]

* * *

The actual flash of insight will continue to fascinate neuroscientists. But as they narrow in on where and how the aha moment occurs in the brain, we still need to understand better how to spark it. Even with the techniques from Chapters 4–8, we need to use and practice them to generate more "muscle memory" and the ability to use insight thinking. Some people seem to have learned to do it already.

Several people who have made big realizations about their organizations and how to change them say they have *fewer* aha moments than they used to. Two reasons seem to be behind their comments. First, people like Sheriff Gary Raney, CEO Bob Lokken, and Coach Chris Petersen seem to have incorporated insight thinking techniques into their general way of approaching problems. They do not stop, ask themselves explicitly how to connect odd pieces of information, look for what is not there, or determine how to "use a wall." They seem to do those activities almost without recognizing that they do. As a result, perhaps, all three (and others) say they do not really notice aha moments much any more; they just solve problems in ways that tend to be creative.

Second, they each tend to be good "anticipators" and "forward thinkers." Raney, in particular, has talked about thinking forward, trying to anticipate potential problems and prevent them from even arising. If we are able to learn and use the aha journey as a matter of regular routine, perhaps we will be less likely to find aha moments so dramatic because they will be part of a normal pattern of events.

Even as we reach the "summit" of the aha moment experience, we still have more work, but it is easy to pass over that part of the formula. In John F. Kennedy's famous "moon speech" in 1961, his goal for the space program was to send a man to the moon, which is what many remember most. The second part of his charge, though, was equally important: to return that man safely back to earth. The aha journey is incomplete if we stop at the specific moment of "click!" There is more work, as Part III shows, to check its validity and to see whether it can be done more than once and whether we can make it routine.

Aha! Reaching the Summit!

- **See the big picture**
  - Connecting the puzzle pieces

- **Shift to conceptual thinking**
  - Using what you learned in a different situation

- **Let those brains stay busy**
  - Keep pushing beyond the comfortable

NOTES

1. John Cooley. 2004. *The Joke Model of Creative Thinking*, July: http://www.mediate.com/articles/cooley3.cfm.

2. Henry Gurr. 1999. The flash of insight in teaching and tutoring. ... AHA, Eureka, it dawned on me, light bulb, bolt of lightning, zeus, epiphany, American Physical Society, 66th Annual Meeting of the Southeastern Section of the American Physical Society, November 7–9.

3. Sir Arthur Conan Doyle. 1930. *The Complete Sherlock Holmes.* Garden City, NY: Doubleday & Company, Inc.: 91.

4. J. Luo and K. Niki. 2003. Function of Hippocampus in "insight" of problem solving, *Hippocampus*, 13 (3): 316–323.

5. Atul Gawande. 2009. The cost conundrum: Annals of medicine, *The New Yorker*, June 1: 36.

6. E. M. Bowden and M. Jung-Beeman. 2003. Aha! Insight experience correlates with solution activation in the right hemisphere, *Psychonomic Bulletin & Review*, 10 (3): 730–737.

7. The ideas are part of the "Graded Salience Hypothesis," which suggests the left hemisphere seeks what makes sense and is "easy to access" first, and then shifts to the right hemisphere to reach for less obvious solutions. E. M. Bowden and M. Jung-Beeman. 2003. Aha! Insight experience correlates with solution activation in the right hemisphere, *Psychonomic Bulletin & Review*, 10 (3): 730–737.

8. M. Oellinger, G. Jones, and G. Knoblich. 2008. Investigation of the effect of mental set on insight problem solving, *Experimental Psychology*, 55 (4): 269–282.

9. J. Kounios, J. L. Frymiare, E. M. Bowden, J. I. Fleck, K. Subramaniam, T. B. Parrish, and M. J. Jung-Beeman. 2006. The prepared mind: Neural activity prior to problem presentation predicts subsequent solution by sudden insight, *Psychological Science*, 17 (10): 882–890.

10. The brain area is called the anterior cingulate cortices (ACC).

11. H. Critchley, R. N. Melmed, E. Featherstone, C. J. Mathias, and R. J. Dolan. 2001. Brain activity during biofeedback relaxation: A functional neuroimaging investigation, *Brain*, 124 (5): 1003–1012.

12. J. Kounios, J. L. Frymiare, E. M. Bowden, J. I. Fleck, K. Subramaniam, T. B. Parrish, and M. J. Jung-Beeman. 2006. The prepared mind: Neural activity prior to problem presentation predicts subsequent solution by sudden insight, *Psychological Science*, 17 (10): 882–890.

13. M. Oellinger, G. Jones, and G. Knoblich. 2008. Investigation of the effect of mental set on insight problem solving, *Experimental Psychology*, 55 (4): 269–282.

14. M. Jung-Beeman, E. M. Bowden, J. Haberman, J. L. Frymiare, S. Arambel-Liu, R. Greenblatt, P. J. Reber, and J. Kounios. 2004. Neural activity when people solve verbal problems with insight, *PLoS Biology*, 2 (4): 500–510.

Part III

Can We Do It Again?

Before enlightenment, chop wood and carry water.
After enlightenment, chop wood and carry water.

—Zen proverb

Lucius Annaeus Seneca (4 B.C.–A.D. 65) was a busy man. Roman philosopher, statesman, playwright, and tutor for Nero, as well as an exile to Corsica for awhile, Seneca also carried on a long and robust correspondence (124 letters) about moral philosophy with a young student. In his XXIII letter to Lucilius, who later became governor of Sicily, Seneca comments that "Real joy, believe me, is a stern matter."[1] So too is a flash of insight a "stern matter."

As we have seen in previous chapters, for insight thinking to occur, it takes work, as the Zen proverb suggests—"chop wood and carry water." Then, when an aha moment happens, it is tempting to relax and feel real joy. Many people report euphoria, relief, and excitement at "the" moment of insight. But, Seneca's advice in life applies as well for aha moments: Real joy is a stern matter, with more work to be done. More wood to chop, more water to carry.

Aha moments are catalysts, integrators of information and knowledge that can be of tremendous value if used well. In some ways, they kick off the final part of the journey, to verify the aha moment and find its long-term value.

Insight, when it synthesizes our knowledge and generates a solution or better understanding, can have real joy and real value for an individual and for an organization. Part III seeks to finish

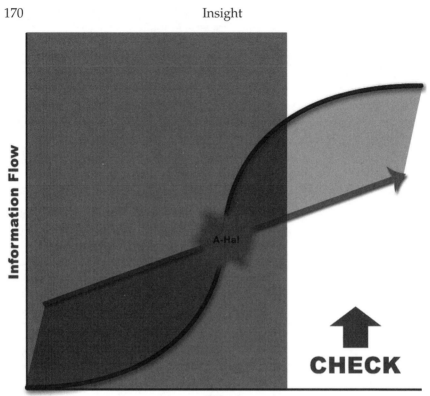

Checking the Insight

the work of the aha journey and shifts again to more linear, logical approaches. For insight thinking to have merit, it needs to be tested against discerning audiences—theories and people alike—which is the focus of Chapter 10. Finally, even the most creative insight-filled persons or organizations will wither unless they have the characteristics and environment that encourages those efforts. Chapter 11 will outline those critical elements, and Chapter 12 offers a summary of key ideas.

NOTES

1. Lucius Annaeus Seneca. 1917. *Seneca, IV, Epistles 1–65*. Translated by Richard M. Gummere. The Loeb Classical Library, Vol. I. Cambridge, MA: Harvard University.

Chapter 10

Did the Journey Work?
When Aha Moments Go Public

My scheme was torn to shreds by the following noon.
—James Watson, *The Double Helix*[1]

Never neglect to ratify your deductions.
—Dr. Joseph Bell[2]

Two social scientists with new ideas about how disease spreads found out what happens after they experienced creative insight: the reactions from "regular people" and their peers ranged from "that's so obvious" to "that's crazy."

After five years of studying relationships between social networks and health, Nicholas Christakis from Harvard and James Fowler from the University of California–San Diego came up with a conclusion that seemed too simple. Christakis's wife was nervous when she heard that her husband and his colleague had applied for $11 million of U.S. taxpayer money to do more research on a question that seemed to have such a clear answer: Do friends influence friends? What is controversial about that? How could it be otherwise? But the worry was misdirected, because as word got out on the researchers' initial findings, many of their peers thought they were nuts. They could not accept that obesity and other health problems "spread" among friends.[3]

Christakis and Fowler have shaken the sociology and health research worlds with their findings that seek to explain links between social relationships and health. They claim that just about everything relating to health, except our eye color and birth order, may be influenced by our friends. That means that the likelihood of obesity, smoking, even acne, height, and headaches could be related to whom we spend time with.

The two researchers came to their "obvious question" from very different backgrounds. When Christakis worked with hospice patients, he learned about the so-called "widower's effect," an observation first written about in 1858.[4] Now commonly accepted, and increasingly supported by research, the notion is that following the death of a long-married spouse, very often the second spouse will die within a year. William Buckley and Richard Nixon, for instance, each died within a year after their wives.[5] Fowler did his doctoral dissertation at Harvard on how social interactions might influence the ways voters choose candidates. When the two met at Harvard, they clicked and built a bicoastal research relationship, leading them to set up video links between their home bases across the country.

In 2003, the researchers sought $25 million to study how social relationships and networks might affect health. The staggering amount of money was considered too much by funders and the study seemed destined for the dustbin. But these entrepreneurial social scientists got lucky when Christakis raised a question about why a small town in Massachusetts was able to retain so many of its inhabitants while so many other towns were losing population. He talked with a woman who had been conducting a long-term study on heart disease of inhabitants in Framingham, Massachusetts. She had data going back to 1948 on almost 15,000 participants from the town. The original study data, on green sheets of paper, included health information about participants as well as a seemingly innocuous request at the bottom of the form: "Name a close friend who can find you in case we can't." For the two social scientists, this 30-year data set on social relationships and health was better than what they had sought with their failed $25 million grant proposal.

Using the Framingham study data, they were able to track obesity in the participants and their friends over 30 years. In 2009, they published their results[6] based upon data from 1971–2003 on some of the original cohort, as well as offspring and others mentioned in the study (friends). The result threw the health research community for a loop: People who became obese were much more likely to have friends who became obese in the same time frame. In other words, the conclusion so obvious to Christakis's wife— that friends influence friends—shook the research world because it applied that notion of social networks to *noninfectious* disease.

Essentially, Christakis and Fowler said that "person-to-person spread" of noninfectious disease could occur in areas from smoking to alcoholism to depression. Bottom line: We do what our friends do. They created a new theory, challenging much of their peers' accepted thinking, and yet, "it seems so obvious" to people outside the medical and health fields.

DOES IT MAKE SENSE?

The sudden complete clarity of an aha moment is powerful, but to experience real joy, as Seneca says, we need to pursue the stern matter of checking whether it holds under scrutiny. This is the stage in the aha journey where the still tender idea goes public so others beyond a small circle can assess its validity. If the creative or understanding aha experience is meant to change thinking or behavior in the long run, it needs to have value and verification beyond a specific case or situation,[7] which demands more logical and left-hemisphere thinking. As Chapter 9 suggested, aha moments happen when dots connect, when the bigger picture is clear, and when the lesson becomes more conceptual than specific. But at that point, if the aha moment result still holds, its value becomes evident and sustainable.

Christakis and Fowler's story illustrates not only how a creative aha moment came about—putting together "odd pieces" of information and "seeing what's not there"—but also what happens when it goes public. The insight must face scrutiny if it is to have value beyond the single incident. This is the stage in the aha journey curve where we ask "can you prove it?"

On the road to understanding the structure of DNA, James Watson repeatedly experienced complete joy and clarity and then despair.

> As the clock went past midnight I was becoming more and more pleased ... to my delight and amazement, the answer was turning out to be profoundly interesting. For over two hours I happily lay awake with pairs of adenine residues whirling in front of my closed eyes. Only for brief moments did the fear shoot through me that an idea this good could be wrong.[8]

Less than 12 hours later the idea was "torn to shreds." The thrill of a flash of insight can be shattered in an instant. So it becomes critical to check for validity, review, and eventually take the idea to wider audiences. Watson and the two health-social network researchers sought to check their insights, checking for proof of their ahas—looking to see if they work, have validity, and can stand up to scrutiny. When a creative aha generates new knowledge or "dots" or combines "dots" in new ways, it may shatter or expand the way people behave and think about something that has existed for some time.

FOUR WAYS TO CHECK

To get there, at least four approaches appear common in this "check it" stage. First, ideas may be checked against some existing theory. Einstein's general theory ideas were eventually tested by Arthur Stanley Eddington, secretary of the British Royal Astronomical Society, in South Africa, May 1919. But this fits in normal work as well: A football player "tests" his aha moments on game day; a detective evaluates evidence against a theory about how and who was involved in a crime.

A second approach is somewhat similar to checking against theory but focuses more on gaining reaction of knowledgeable peers. Einstein had his colleague Michele Besso and many others, with whom he talked about his ideas. Organizational leaders have a board of directors; academics have peers in their field. Expanding beyond a single person, having a sounding board, makes an idea public and forces more scrutiny.

A third check is that of simplicity. Can we explain our aha moments and what we have learned or solved to someone who has no expertise or knowledge of the field? Christakis's wife felt his conclusion that "friends influence friends" was so obvious she could not understand why he needed millions of dollars to research the question. The idea was simple (although not simplistic) and it "made sense" to her, although no other researchers prior to Christakis and Fowler had made the connection that noninfectious disease spreads among friends.

Finally, some people test the validity of their insights "in the rearview mirror." When they look back at what their organizations have done, do they realize something about them that they had not seen before? They may have learned or solved problems using insight thinking but just not realized it fully until they reflected back. We will look at each in turn.

Check Against Theory

Creating a new theory is not like destroying an old barn and erecting a skyscraper in its place. It is rather like climbing a mountain, gaining new and wider views, discovering unexpected connections between our starting points and its rich environment. But the point from which we started out still exists and can be seen, although it appears smaller and forms a tiny part of our broad view gained by the mastery of the obstacles on our adventurous way up.

—Albert Einstein (*Evolution of Physics*)[9]

Captain Linda Scown was promoted to run the Ada County jail after 26 years with the agency. She has the energy to rival her nearly 300 subordinates, even after nine years as a detective and five as an investigation supervisor. Over the years, she has had several aha moments of understanding, especially when it comes to solving violent crimes, and she has had to test those moments against early-forming theories to see how they hold up.

On March 10, 2008, a co-worker went to the house of 45-year-old Dennis Lewis, when he did not show for work, and found him dead in his bedroom, sitting in a chair. When Scown later entered the house through its back door, she walked through the mudroom. It seemed in disarray with Band-Aids on the floor, which seemed "out of place" compared with the tidiness of the rest of the house. She "filed away" her observation but did not see a connection to other evidence, at least initially.

No obvious evidence of blood was in the bedroom, where the victim was found. Also, because of the man's large size and position in the chair, detectives did not realize at first that he had been shot in the back of the head by a small caliber weapon. Scown began to sort through evidence, building a possible theory that the man had been killed elsewhere and then brought to his bedroom. Three evidence sources—the crime scene, the victim, and the suspect—became critical in this case and ultimately helped generate an initial theory of what may have happened.

The crime scene. Luminol is a chemical that reacts to the protein in blood. When the team sprayed it thoughout the house, it confirmed that the father had been killed in the mudroom, and then dragged to the bedroom, where the killing was staged. The house had been cleaned, so there was little evidence of just how awful the crime had been but also explained the discontinuity between the messy mudroom and the tidy rest of the house. As Scown said, "when you spray luminol on it, it is a horrific crime scene."

The victim. A second piece of the puzzle came from the victim, which detectives evaluated in terms of factors like risky behavior or other habits. The detective team learned from neighbors and work colleagues that the father was "very dedicated, a single parent, very strict, and recently had to discipline his son." The recent disciplining of the son was a trigger that made Scown think the son could be a suspect.

The suspect. Scown sought as much information about the son as she could get before detectives interviewed him. From other sources, she learned the son "had anger issues," the father and son had not been getting along, and the father had recently had to discipline his son. Finally, the son (and his father's truck) had disappeared over the weekend, leading Scown and the other detectives to begin thinking that perhaps the son had been involved in what was by then clearly a homicide.

Reported as a runaway teen on Monday, two days after his father died on Saturday evening, 17-year-old Derek Lewis was arrested in western Oregon later that day after a police chase by car and on foot. That added more fuel to Scown's budding theory, but she still lacked direct evidence—a witness, the murder weapon, a confession—to test the theory that the son had murdered his father. When the son returned to Idaho, the detectives still had no concrete evidence though, so when they talked with him, it was delicate:

> When we sat down and talked with him, we had nothing. We had no ammunition. . . . It's important to understand as much as you can about the circumstances before you interview the suspect, because the suspect will lie to you. So it's a mental game, to walk through the lies. . . . One of the theories . . . was the son. The other theory, you would certainly think, was this may be a random case.

In her case, though, an "aha moment of understanding" that pulled the puzzle pieces together came from a discussion with one of the son's friends, in which he said Derek had talked about killing his father. Because the father was a precise and punctual man, his son knew he would walk in the door of their home at 6 o'clock. The son threw a box of Band-Aids on the mudroom floor, knowing the father would be irritated at the mess and lean over to pick them up. According to the son's friend, that is when the boy planned to shoot his father in the back of the head. Now the messy mudroom made sense. As Scown said, "the aha moment came [when] a student friend [gave us] that one piece of the puzzle we didn't know about—that preplanned, premeditated piece." That put more weight to the theory.

In this case, the theory held. The insight made sense, even when tested in the broader public. Derek Lewis is serving a life sentence.

Check Against Peers: What Would Besso Say?

Albert Einstein credits Michele Besso with helping him have his aha moment of understanding the murky question of time and space. The walks and talks meant a lot to Einstein, and he made that clear in his first "Miracle Year" paper, which includes no references but does acknowledge Besso.[10]

Besso and the many colleagues after him helped Einstein assess whether the aha moments he experienced had value beyond his initial thrill. As sounding boards, these people challenged or helped refine Einstein's emerging theories. In Besso's case, we have the sense that he played more of the role of a listener, truly a "sounding board," rather than a vocal challenger to Einstein's comments and commentary. In a letter written in August 1918,[11] Besso claimed that Einstein had overestimated the meaningfulness of his observations. He felt his statement was "inadvertent" and he did not see the consequences of what he had said, whereas Einstein was able to take and use it. He said that he thought of Einstein as an eagle, while he was a sparrow. "Under the eagle's wing, the sparrow had been able to fly higher than it would have alone."[12]

Nevertheless, Besso represents the kind of sounding board we need when we check insight thinking—someone who is trustworthy and who knows enough about the topic to challenge ideas if they are clearly untenable. One of my sounding boards is a person I refer to as "the meanest guy I know." His ability to think logically and use insight are remarkable; when I go to him with a far-fetched idea, I trust that he will challenge the idea and not judge me. He has held up his end of the bargain and helped validate an insight or "tear it to shreds," as James Watson so often experienced. In the process, the ideas get stronger when I am able to address his withering questions.

But when reactions from peers may not be so supportive, the way we deal with those reactions may influence what happens with insight moments.

* * *

Checking ideas against peers like Besso is closely related, in some fields, to testing against theories. If peers have developed theories and the results of a creative aha moment challenge those theories, a rough ride may be in store. Steve Lekson is an archaeologist from the University of Colorado with a theory not many people want to buy. He stands apart from the rest of his field in arguing that early Anasazi people, who were in New Mexico from about A.D. 900 to A.D. 1150, migrated north and south, along the 108th meridian, stretching over 400 miles from Sacred Ridge in Colorado, to Aztec Ruins and Chaco Canyon in New Mexico, south across the border to Paquime, Mexico. He points to common architectural features, ball courts, and effigy shapes in the wide-ranging sites as evidence for his claim. His latest book, *Chaco Meridian*,[13] starts out with an intriguing warning, unlike any in a textbook or most books for the lay reader: "This book is not for the faint of heart, or for neophytes. If you are a practicing Southwestern archaeologist with hypertension problems, stop. Read something safe."

It is not easy to be a Don Quixote, charging at ideas and theories that have firm foundations and wide acceptance. Lekson says he is seeking to "connect the dots" and create a new theory of how and why early people migrated. He argues that his field of Southwestern archaeology has used an approach of examining Pueblo societies "like cultures in laboratory petri dishes." Instead of the long-accepted approach of separate unlinked sites, he argues for "appreciation of the unquantifiable" understanding of the "grand sweep" of history—connecting the dots. By looking at the parts, instead of what he would argue is the "whole picture," the questions that archaeologists ask could well be wrong, or worse, "pointless."

> Steve [Lekson] is possibly the best writer in Southwest archaeology. Our academic writing has this inherent gift of taking something interesting and making it dull and boring. And Steve doesn't have that problem. He thinks outside the box, and the rest of us comb through his ideas. . . . Having said all that, I personally think that [Lekson's idea of] the Chaco meridian is a crock.[14]
>
> David Phillips, curator of archaeology,
> Maxwell Museum of Anthropology at the University of
> New Mexico

Lekson's critics like Dr. Phillips, who calls the ideas "a crock," disagree vehemently with how Lekson has put his dots together. Traditionally, science moves forward by testing and challenging any assumption or hypothesis. Proving hypotheses wrong, step by step, eliminates possible alternative solutions, moving toward a more likely theory. Lekson takes a different route, making it harder to prove his ideas have merit. So in some cases, checking with peers is treacherous, but as Lekson would likely say, his thinking becomes sharper in having to defend them.

* * *

Testing an idea against someone equivalent to Besso is not always as contentious as Lekson's experience. A sounding board—one or a few trusted but honest advisors—can be critical in understanding the implications of an idea. Newspaper editor and merchant Joshua Speed acted as Abraham Lincoln's sounding board and long-time friend.[15] Charles Darwin's friend Joseph Hooker, a botanist, was able to challenge and help sharpen Darwin's thinking on evolution.[16] Apparently, Hooker also recognized early on the controversial nature and implications of Darwin's ideas, saying that he felt "simply believing in evolution seemed like confessing to a murder."

Barack Obama may owe his term in the Senate, let alone the presidency, to a group he met with in late 2002 when he raised the possibility of going for a top job. As a rookie state senator, he called together friends and colleagues to talk through a potential run for the U.S. Senate. According to reports in *BusinessWeek* and *The New York Times*,[17] his advisors initially tried to talk him *out* of a Senate run. After losing a race for U.S. Representative, his funds and reputation sagged. Campaigning would mean more time away from his young family, and none of his friends thought he could win.

But Obama presented his plan for why he thought it was worth a try to run for Senate. His first "semi-public" airing of the idea, according to his friend and advisor Valerie Jarrett, was thorough. He had gained support of a key state senator, which he lacked during the U.S. Representative run. He had thought through the financial challenges and wanted the one person with deep business experience (Jarrett) to handle raising and managing money. Finally, he promised his wife that if he lost, he would take a "normal" job in the private sector and never run for office again. The group talked through his arguments, the pros and cons, and eventually agreed he should run. The key to the group, though, was its willingness to be frank, to challenge and question the premise, a task as critical for Besso as for a politician's advisors.

As we check our aha moments, sounding boards—close and further away—become crucial in determining whether the idea is likely to become a catalyst for action. Even when the insight faces major challenges, like Lekson's 108th meridian idea, by putting the idea in public and addressing the challenges, it may become stronger (or die altogether, as Watson experienced). Yet another test is to see just how understandable the idea really is.

Check with a Barmaid

History shows that the best solutions to scientific problems are simple and elegant . . . the ultimate conceptual framework is generally simple.

—Jeff Hawkins[18]

The wireless telegraph is not difficult to understand. The ordinary telegraph is like a very long cat. You pull the tail in New York, and it meows in Los Angeles. The wireless is the same, only without the cat.

—Attributed to Albert Einstein[19]

One of the most exclusive meetings in the United States is the annual TED (Technology, Entertainment and Design)[20] conference, held in Long Beach, California, and selected sites outside the United States (Oxford, United Kingdom, and India). Attendance at the four-day conference is by invitation only, and the more than 1,000 participants hear talks from some of the most creative and provocative thought leaders in the world. Each of the presenters attends without compensation, each has no more than 18 minutes to present, and many of the best presentations become classics on YouTube. The talks encompass a wide range of topics, from neuroscience to aquatic ape theory, from art that "looks back at you" to the mind of a killer. All are given by experts who have spent their lives researching, teaching, and writing about their fields, accumulating hours and years of work. And they have less than 20 minutes to create insight and offer wisdom that will shake up the thinking of the attendees. Einstein, one of the world's best simplifiers, would love it.

Many people have claimed that Einstein was a stickler for simple explanations of complex ideas. His quote explaining the "wireless" telegraph, a major innovation in its day, is an example. Indeed, one of Einstein's close colleagues and friends, Ernest Rutherford, said that an "alleged scientific discovery has no merit unless it can be explained to a barmaid,"[21] a comment frequently and falsely attributed to Einstein. But in essence, that is what Einstein has done and the TED presenters do: make complex ideas simple, but not simplistic—easy to say, hard to do.[22] Industrial designers and product developers would agree as well. Some of the products that have had the most impact are the easiest to explain to the nonexpert. We may not understand (or want to understand) how the products work, but we certainly "get" what they do: the Polaroid camera (instant photographs); the Walkman (personal portable music player); GPS system (personal direction provider); gravity (holds me to the ground); X-ray, CAT scan, and MRIs (photographs of the inside of my body); and many others. As WhiteCloud CEO Bob Lokken says, "You don't make complex things simple by explaining them better; you make them simple by explaining them less."

Lokken's experience with software engineers taught him that rarely do firms and engineers produce products that are truly accessible for the user. Instead, they expose what he calls the "inner guts of the software" to users, often completely overwhelming and confusing them. His approach mirrors Einstein's—to make software's purpose and use something a barmaid could appreciate. Software programs, in his view, would be more effective if the designers simply showed the user how the data will look in a chart, rather than showing the user how the chart is built. Fewer options, with less to assimilate, "so the customer immediately 'gets it' in context . . . eighteen steps and collapsed it to one."

That ability to explain a concept so others can understand it— from Harvard researcher Christakis's wife, to a barmaid, to a software user—often separates insights that will prove long lasting from those that fizzle. One final example of a complex idea made simple comes from one of the best companies in the world at doing just that.

In February 2008, a high-tech firm applied for a patent (serial no. 069352).[23] The patent application's abstract reads:

Systems, methods, computer-readable media, and other means are described for utilizing touch-based input components that provide localized haptic feedback to a user. The touch-based input components can be used and/or integrated into any type of electronic device, including laptop computers, cellular telephones, and portable media devices. The touch-based input components can use, for example, a grid of piezoelectric actuators to provide vibrational feedback to a user, while the user scrolls around a click wheel, slides across a trackpad, or touches a multi-touch display screen.

Short, fairly simple, but the title for the patent is even better: "Multi-touch display screen with localized tactile feedback."

The patent led to the Apple iPhone. Even a smart barmaid could understand it and Einstein would have applauded it.

A theory is the more impressive the greater the simplicity of its premises, the more different kinds of things it relates and the more extended its area of applicability.

Albert Einstein[24]

Check in the Rearview Mirror

You can't connect the dots looking forward; you can only connect them looking backwards.

—Steve Jobs[25]

Boise State University head football coach Chris Petersen is not a man who excites easily. In the most pressured game situations, he paces in short steps with his head tilted forward. His mouth is horizontal with lips pressed together, but his eyes, gestures, and shoulders show no signs of whether he is frustrated or worried. His expression changes only slightly when something good happens on the field: He crosses his arms, barely nods his head, and tilts his body back just a bit. Extremely thoughtful and rational, he does not take to kooky ideas, at least not until they have proven themselves. So when I first talked to him several years ago about the idea that creativity might play a role in what the Boise State football program did, he was too polite to tell me outright that I was crazy. "I'm not a creative guy," he said, "there's nothing new in football."

Over the years, we have continued to talk. I show up perhaps twice a year, and he says he never "quite knows" what I will ask him about, but we settle into a routine. I ask a lot of questions; he takes them seriously and answers, or asks me something else. I learn, he learns.

As I mentioned earlier, every year, I invite Petersen and several of his coaches to meet with other creative organizations in the community—The Gang organizations are top performers in their respective fields (measured objectively); all are known by outsiders to be creative and innovative; and all happen to be based in Boise, Idaho. Then coaches and dancers, software engineers and law enforcement administrators, actors and health information providers compare notes on creativity and innovation, organizational culture, and leadership.

One year, I asked the leaders of each group to talk about a "major aha moment" they had had in the past year and why it was important. Petersen's answer astounded me. His aha moment was realizing that much of his program's actions and approaches are indeed creative, from the way coaches recruit (e.g., looking at whether the player will fit the culture, what the potential might be), to training and practice approaches, which have become off limits to outsider viewers in recent years, and even to game execution. He had reached an "understanding aha" that gave him the confidence to generate more innovative approaches and instill a sense of "how do we improve" throughout the program.

Indeed, in my conversations with the coaches, that sense of looking for innovative ways to improve was striking. When they talked about some technique, several would say "keep that to yourself." (Since I understand next to nothing about the technical side of the game, their secrets are definitely safe.) The changes they have made over the years makes Petersen's comment that sparked this book—that it took players 2–2.5 years to "get it" in the program—obsolete. It happens much faster now. And creativity seems to be increasingly a reason for the change. In fact, following the team's most recent success in the January 2010 Fiesta Bowl, against Texas Christian University, Petersen commented publicly that "I just like creativity . . . I don't like plays everybody else does."[26]

As Steve Jobs said, "you connect the dots backward." Petersen's aha moment came from looking in the "rearview mirror," which is another way that some people check the validity of their insight experience. Despite his skepticism about applying creativity and innovation to football when we first began to talk, he was open and willing to listen to a kooky idea.

I started realizing that we were doing things differently from other programs, that we were finding new ways to improve in all sorts of areas of the program. That got me thinking that perhaps there is creativity in what we do.

At a conference for college coaches not long ago, Petersen talked up ideas of innovation in football. Now *he* knows how it feels when someone looks at you like you are crazy.

* * *

Sometimes, the rearview mirror assessment of the aha journey can be discomforting. The recent economic crisis has raised questions about the fundamentals of economic theory, long "settled" for many around the world. *The Economist* magazine's cover story on July 16, 2009, was "What Went Wrong with Economics?" The *Financial Times* ran a series of editorials and features about "The End of Capitalism." Even members of the venerable University of Chicago, home of Milton Friedman, are questioning the prevailing theories as they look backward.[27]

Efficient market economics theory first felt chinks when behavioral economists in the 1970s challenged the idea of strictly rational decision making in the stock market.[28] Jeremy Grantham, one of the most prominent critics, goes so far as to say that the efficient market hypothesis is largely responsible for the financial crisis. Because government and financial leaders believed in the efficient market theory, he argues, they ignored the signals of how fragile the system had become.

Aha journeys through the rearview mirror may happen also when the insights are so embedded and part of the organization, they become routine. Vince Martino, former chief operating officer of marketing firm Balihoo, had just such an "understanding aha": Many insights existed in his firm without him recognizing them, until he looked in the rearview mirror. In his blog, Martino mused that like many people, he first thought aha moments had to be big, "like when Lowe's came to the realization that women made 80% of the buying decisions for home improvements, but home improvement stores didn't cater to women. . . . Or when Starbucks realized it's not just about the coffee, but about the customer connection."[29] But Martino realized he had never clearly identified or captured the "ahas" that were embedded already in his firm. He claims they are not huge, but nonetheless provide his firm new ways to think about business, "or simply corroborate what you already know."

In Martino's case, the insights were "understanding ahas." He realized that core values of a firm should be aspirational, rather than simply voicing what already exists. He recognized the importance of a recruiting policy of "hire slowly, fire quickly," critical in

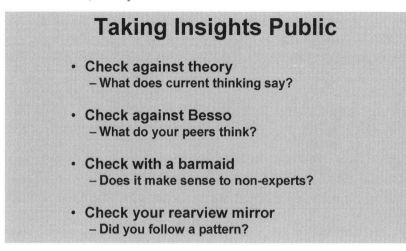

Taking Insights Public

- **Check against theory**
  - What does current thinking say?

- **Check against Besso**
  - What do your peers think?

- **Check with a barmaid**
  - Does it make sense to non-experts?

- **Check your rearview mirror**
  - Did you follow a pattern?

start-up firms because of the large costs associated with hiring people who do not fit the culture. Finally, Martino felt the firm's managers and employees understood the danger of focusing on too many things. When that happens in a start-up firm, it ends up focused on nothing. Like Petersen's rearview mirror aha journey, Martino's after-the-fact insights also gave him the confidence to know that his firm could have more.

* * *

The aha journey does not end. Once we have a flash of insight and verify its usefulness, the process cannot stop. To continue to understand and innovate, the process may start over. By being aware of the journey, though, and techniques we might use to sort information, to spark aha moments, to deal with obstacles and detours, and to verify them, we can encourage aha moments and perhaps make them more systematic. The journey is only part of the puzzle, however. For insight thinking to stand a chance for long-lasting impact, the context in which it (may) occur is critical. For all the techniques and practices we might learn, if the individuals and organizations do not have key characteristics to nurture the journey, little will come of it.

NOTES

1. James D. Watson. 1968. *The Double Helix*. New York: A Mentor Book: 120.

2. Ely Liebow. 2007. *Dr. Joe Bell: Model for Sherlock Holmes*. Madison, WI: Popular Press: 132; Dr. Harold E. Jones. 1904. The Original of Sherlock Holmes, *Colliers*, January 9, 32 (5): 14.

3. Jennifer Couzin. 2009. Friendship as a health factor, *Science*, 323 (5913): 454–457; Nicholas A. Christakis and James Fowler. 2009. *Connected: The Surprising Power of Social Networks and How They Shape Our Lives*. New York City: Little, Brown and Company.

4. Christakis and Paul Allison of the University of Pennsylvania Sociology Department used Medicare records to track the health of 518,240 couples over age 65 for nine years, from 1993 to 2002. During that time, 383,480 husbands and 347,269 wives were hospitalized, and 252,557 husbands and 156,004 wives died; Nicholas A. Christakis and Paul D. Allison. 2006. Mortality after the hospitalization of a spouse, *New England Journal of Medicine*, 354 (7): 719–730.

5. See, for example, Christopher Buckley. 2009. *Losing Mum and Pup: A memoir*. New York City: Hachette Book Group, Inc.

6. Nicholas A. Christakis and James Fowler. 2009. *Connected: The Surprising Power of Social Networks and How They Shape Our Lives*. New York City: Little, Brown and Company.

7. Graham Wallas. 1926. *The Art of Thought*. New York: Harcourt, Brace, and Co.

8. James D. Watson. 1968. *The Double Helix*. New York: A Mentor Book: 118.

9. Anna Beck (translator) and Peter Havas (consultant). 1989. *The Collected Papers of Albert Einstein: Volume 2, The Swiss Years: Writings, 1900–1909*. Princeton, NJ: Princeton University Press: 171.

10. Michel Janssen. 2002. The Einstein-Besso manuscript: A glimpse behind the curtain of the wizard, *Freshman Colloquium, Introduction to the Arts and Sciences*. From Michel Janssen and Gérard Lhéritier. 2003. *Le manuscrit Einstein-Besso: de la relativité restreinte a la relativité générale; [la pensée de deux génies de la physique décryptée] = The Einstein-Besso Manuscript*. Paris: Scriptura-Aristophil.

11. Ann Hentschel (translator) and Klaus Hentschel (consultant). 2006. Vol. 8, 607a. From Michele Besso, in *The Collected Papers of Albert Einstein, Volume 10*. Princeton, NJ: Princeton University Press: 108–110.

12. Michel Janssen. 2002. The Einstein-Besso manuscript: A glimpse behind the curtain of the wizard, *Freshman Colloquium, Introduction to the Arts and Sciences*: 3; From Michel Janssen and Gérard Lhéritier. 2003. *Le manuscrit Einstein-Besso: de la relativité restreinte a la relativité générale; [la pensée de deux génies de la physique décryptée] = The Einstein-Besso Manuscript*. Paris: Scriptura-Aristophil.

13. Stephen H. Lekson. 1999. *The Chaco Meridian: Centers of Political Power in the Ancient Southwest*. Walnut Creek, CA: AltaMira Press.

14. Quote from David Phillips, curator of archaeology, Maxwell Museum of Anthropology at the University of New Mexico, in George Johnson. 2009. Scientist tries to connect migration dots of ancient Southwest, *The New York Times*, June 30: D1, D7.

15. David Herbert Donald. 2003. *"We Are Lincoln Men": Abraham Lincoln and His Friends*. New York City: Simon & Schuster.

16. Charles Darwin and Joseph Carroll. 2003. *On the Origin of Species by Means of Natural Selection*. Peterborough, Ontario: Broadview Press: 36; For Hooker's quotation, see Randy Moore. 2002. *Evolution in the Courtroom: A Reference Guide*. Santa Barbara, CA: ABC-CLIO: 157.

17. Roger O. Crockett. 2008. Obama's executive sounding board, *BusinessWeek*, May 19. http://www.businessweek.com/bwdaily/dnflash/content/may2008/db20080518_242310.htm; Robert Draper. 2009. Obama's BFF, *The New York Times Magazine*, July 26: 30–37, 46–47. http://www.nytimes.com/2009/07/26/magazine/26jarrett-t.html.

18. Jeff Hawkins and Sandra Blakeslee. 2004. *On Intelligence*. New York City: Times Books.

19. Scott Thorpe. 2000. *How to Think like Einstein: Simple Ways to Break the Rules and Discover Your Hidden Genius*. Naperville, IL: Sourcebooks: 61.

20. TED: Ideas worth spreading (http://www.ted.com).

21. Royal Society (Great Britain). 1955. *Biographical Memoirs of Fellows of the Royal Society, v. 1*. London: Royal Society: 54; W. Bennett Lewis. 1972. Some recollections and reflections on Rutherford, *Notes and Records of the Royal Society of London*, 27 (1), August: 61; G. J. Whitrow, 1973. *Einstein: The Man and His Achievement*. Mineola, NY: Dover Publications.

22. Jeffrey Kluger. 2008. *Simplexity*. New York: Hyperion.

23. ———. 2009. (WO/2009/085060) Multi-touch display screen with localized tactile feedback, World Intellectual Property Organization (http://www.wipo.int/pctdb/en/wo.jsp?WO=2009085060, last accessed August 7, 2009). Serial number is 085060.

24. Alice Calaprice (Ed.). 2005. Princeton, NJ: Princeton University Press: 246, taken from Paul Schlipp (editor and translator). 1979. *Albert Einstein: Autobiographical Notes*. La Salle, IL: Open Court: 33.

25. Steve Jobs. 2005. *Commencement Address at Stanford University*, June 12, Palo Alto, CA.

26. Following the January 1, 2007, football game, in particular, several newswriters and TV commentators began to mention "creativity" in relation to Boise State football. See, for example, http://bleacherreport.com/articles/116073-boise-state-football-coach-chris-petersen-in-the-mold-of-alonzo-stagg; Brian Murphy. 2008. Is the grass greener away from the blue turf? *Idaho Statesman*, December 19. http://www.idahostatesman.com/murphy/story/608878.html. Even Idaho's U.S. Senator Mike Crapo got into the act: http://crapo.senate.gov/media/newsreleases/release_full.cfm?id=267180: "Earlier in 2006, Boise was named the 8th most inventive city in the nation. That creativity and innovation was certainly the Spirit of Idaho at its best on the field of play at crunch time and made this dreamed Bronco victory a reality." Petersen's comment appeared in Chadd Cripe. 2010. Trick Ponies. *Idaho Statesman*, January 10: B1.

27. Joe Nocera. 2009. Poking holes in a theory on markets, *The New York Times*, June 5: B1, 5.

28. Richard Thaler of the University of Chicago is one of the early and most noteworthy of the behavioral economists. His latest book is Richard H. Thaler and Cass R. Sunstein. 2008. *Nudge*. New Haven, CT: Yale University Press.

29. Vince Martino. 2008. Blog: Little Aha's, April 4. http://blog.balihoo.com/index.php/category/balihooers/vince/page/3/.

Chapter 11

Making the Aha Journey Routine

> The worst pain a man can suffer: to have insight into much and power over nothing.
> —Herodotus (484 B.C.–425 B.C.)[1]

For many individuals and organizations, Herodotus's words apply all too often nearly 2,500 years after he wrote them. The exhilaration of an aha moment, without support or "power" from an environment and people who appreciate it, can wither in a flash. When that happens, employees *and* their organizations lose. Given the complex and messy problems facing both individuals and organizations now and in the near future, why not do everything possible to capture and use the flashes of insight that spark improvement and understanding?

Chapters 2–10 focused on ways to encourage and validate aha moments. But for organizations to reap value from such experiences, several characteristics are critical—in both individuals and organizations. This chapter puts the aha journey into that larger context, examining attributes that empower insight as a catalyst for change.

During interviews with people in several organizations, five key characteristics emerged repeatedly (Figure 11-1):

- "Enough" experience to be able to recognize an aha moment
- Motivation to *want* to learn or solve a complex problem
- Openness to the aha journey and insight
- Confidence that an aha moment will come
- Ability to make the aha journey a habit

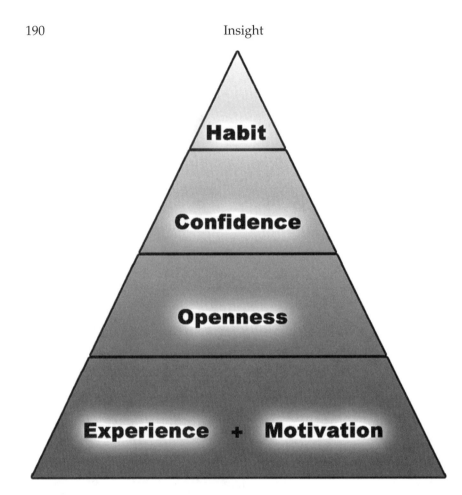

FIGURE 11-1   AHA! Foundations

"ENOUGH" EXPERIENCE AND KNOWLEDGE

Aha moments happen when we have enough experience and knowledge to understand when pieces of a puzzle can come together and that their connections can become something of value.[2] Without knowledge of physics, Einstein would have failed to recognize (and perhaps to reach) the *Aha Erlebnis* (Aha Experience) that he experienced with Besso and set him on the Miracle Year of the special theory of relativity, as well as later. Without burying himself for months in articles and discussion with health care experts, Bob Lokken would not have seen the connection between the changing price model and data analytics. Football player George Iloka needed the experience playing (and not having the chance to play) football in high school so he could recognize the flashes of insight when they hit him.

Also, experience includes the history or patterns that employees see within an organization—how leaders react to new ideas and risk taking and how they convey their values to employees. Over time, an organization that values creativity and innovation will build a culture that welcomes insight flashes, encourages people to evaluate *ideas*, not to judge the people who generate them, and finds a way to use aha moments. The patterns that organizations show with regard to their cultures can also spill into how much trust employees have in the leaders and the organization in other aspects. The 2005 Ada County jail escape triggered in Chad Sarmento an aha moment of understanding—realizing that he wanted to work in an organization with a culture that realized mistakes happen but can be vehicles for improvement, not punishment and blame passing. The specific spark for Sarmento came in a press conference three days after the escape, when Sheriff Gary Raney admitted mistakes had occurred that led to the escape, took responsibility for them, and asked the community for help in recapturing Harlan Hale. Sarmento watched Raney on TV "over and over again," flabbergasted that Raney would admit to the public that "we messed up." For Sarmento, that aha experience led him to switch jobs and take a major step down in his position. That shift in his career signaled the importance he attached to the organization's culture of being willing to try, question, and learn.

MOTIVATION: WHAT'S IN IT FOR ME?

To make insight thinking, learning, and change happen, people in organizations have to want it. That means buying the notion of taking action and doing work that supports a larger picture beyond their self-interest alone. In organizations where the measures of success are clear and frequent—football game scores, sales or quarterly earnings reports—some managers feel it is easier to encourage organization members to see themselves as part of a bigger system because the payoffs come more quickly and appear clearer. But in nonprofits or public sector service organizations, external measures and results are hard to see or may take years to achieve. How does an organization like Healthwise *know* that it is "helping people make better health decisions?" How does a law enforcement organization measure whether a community is "safer" from one year to the next?

Such challenges make leaders realize the importance of instilling a sense of being part of a larger picture and, as Sheriff Gary Raney says, finding a way to answer the WIIFM ("what's in it for me") question. In the public sector, where financial incentives and clear "scores" do not exist, the importance of building in pride of belonging to a high-performing, "winning team" becomes key. Years ago, Raney said he would like his organization to become "the agency of choice" within the county for any type of law enforcement need. If a community member needed help, he wanted that person to think first about his agency, rather than local police or private emergency help, for instance. In addition, the phrase implies that his organization has the best practices of any competitor. As the phrase spread and practices have indeed improved, he senses pride among employees; most now want to be part of "the best" such agency in the region, which helps them understand the role their own jobs play in a bigger picture.

OPENNESS

A third characteristic that supports insight thinking and creativity is openness to ideas, ways of thinking, and different perspectives. In the many examples throughout the book, openness has been key: Einstein's presumed willingness to consider so many ways to look at time; Raney's openness to examining the jail escape beyond its security implications; Iloka's ability to "keep his mind open," even when he was an angry young man denied the glory of a football position he wanted.

For openness to succeed, it also means that two subfactors must be present—curiosity and humility. Curiosity and motivation are connected in that we need to want to learn, to solve a problem, and find ways to accomplish that. To do so requires the energy and curiosity to keep pushing to spark aha moments, and then the courage and curiosity to check their validity and value. Humility is simply being prepared to accept that there is much to learn from others, that no single individual or organization has "all the answers." When The Gang meets, the openness to ideas—even far from their own fields, or perhaps especially those far from their own disciplines—is palpable. That the leaders and members of those organizations *want* to meet says that, at least to date, they are humble enough to know both the value of learning from others and the need to constantly push to find new and better ways to operate. In all cases, the organizations are successful enough that they could, if they are not careful, succumb to the pattern Jim Collins describes in his book, *How the Mighty Fall*, and assume that past success means they know what to do in the future. By reaching outside their fields and their zones of comfort, they may also spark insight and creativity.

Ensuring openness demands continuous monitoring and work. Jamie Cooper, chief executive officer of Drake Cooper, an award-winning marketing and advertising firm, hires with the expectations of having different "voices and views" in his firm. He also encourages employees to achieve the organization's vision by taking "different paths," including the ways they pursue the aha journey. Some people naturally take more direct routes, relying on logic and "straightforward" paths to reach the vision in the shortest manner possible. Others, though, may amble, taking detours, looking at ideas that others may miss, and deliberately seeking out and using insight thinking. Cooper wants the organization to appreciate and value those different approaches and make full use of people who pursue the vision using different journey approaches.

Of course, building and maintaining a culture and context that values risk taking and is open to different perspectives is extremely difficult. Even in organizations where openness is a value, where senior leaders discuss it often and try to model it, some employees may not "believe." In one highly successful, very focused organization that prides itself on a culture of innovation at all levels, employees question whether the openness to ideas truly exists. A senior leader hearing these comments in a meeting was shocked and asked for examples of why employees would question the commitment to openness and innovation. Several (brave) employees said they see it in the way senior managers can squash the enthusiasm for a new idea, even when those managers are unaware of what they are doing. The actions can be small—"a grimace, silence, or even outright comment about an idea's value." If such actions happen even infrequently, employees "get the message" and begin to question whether it is worth the discomfort to put forward new ideas or talk about aha moments.

Constant vigilance and repeated examples of "walking the talk" seem to help instill belief in the value of openness. Sometimes it means hiring an "outsider" who has enough credibility and respect to be able to ask questions that others would not or do not think to ask. Other times, it may mean stacking a group task force with such different personalities and ways of thinking that members are forced to look at issues they might not have; those outside the group seeing such behavior then learn that being open to different approaches is acceptable. When the leaders themselves exemplify such attitudes, it further cements the value of openness. Gary Raney and Ron Freeman, the top two leaders at the Ada County Sheriff's Office, point to themselves: neither came from a military background, which is unusual in law enforcement. As a result, they feel their less traditional backgrounds have allowed them to look at ways of managing that differ from paramilitary models. By doing so, and questioning how to improve, by drawing ideas from business, they open the door for others in the organization to experience their own aha journeys.

CONFIDENCE

Before I officially talked to any football program members about this project, I informally asked Boise State University running backs coach Keith Bhonapha what the most important factor was in generating aha moments for football players. Without skipping a beat, he said, "Confidence, in themselves and in us." Bhonapha's response rang true for individuals and leaders of other organizations as well. In fact, several commented that "confidence" was the "X factor" that helped employees make the leap to aha moments. Believing in the likelihood of experiencing insight, finding that those aha moments are valued, and then realizing it is possible to generate them to learn and solve problems build confidence.

Part of confidence, especially for people trying to encourage aha moments in others, is trust. And when there is trust, people are willing to test budding ideas and what they may be learning. To build trust, of course, the culture and expectations and outcomes of performance need to be very clear.

Boise State University football coaches talk frequently about the importance of trust among players. Twenty years ago, older players tended to use hazing when the younger players arrived, making them "prove themselves." The Boise State program coaches have since convinced the older players to trust the coaches to bring in the "right guys," removing the need for younger players to "prove themselves" to the older players. That, in turns, speeds up the process of building a team and helping the younger players learn the system and become effective. As one coach says, "without trust, we've got nothing."

To build trust among players, the coaches also have simplified the information they deliver and made clear the key values of what is most important about the program. One of those is being open to risk taking and trying out plays or making decisions that may fail.

The most recent example of such trust appeared in the January 4, 2010, Fiesta Bowl game between Boise State and Texas Christian University (TCU). Neither team had much offensive success during most of the game, and the scoreboard showed—for these teams— uncharacteristically low scores in the final quarter (10–10). At a fourth down and 9 yards in the fourth quarter, the Boise State's special teams group jogged onto the field. But instead of punting, the kicker passed the ball 29 yards, which set up the team to go in for the final and winning touchdown.

Even though the special teams coach called the fake punt, one player had the final say on whether to do it or not. Being on the field, he could better read the opposing team than the coach. The player responsible for the final call decision saw the opportunity for the surprise play and called it. The fake completely flummoxed the TCU side. That the coaches generally put much responsibility and trust into their players is a result of the confidence on both sides.[3]

Because the coaches model behavior that instills trust and confidence, and show that mistakes are opportunities for improvement, the players do the same, trusting themselves and others.

One other way that trust emerges is through communication and interaction. Some employees at consumer health information provider Healthwise claim the organization is "meeting happy," but the importance of so much interpersonal interaction is its ability to build trust among employees. That trust is part of what helps a group find its "humming" tempo, working well and moving toward aha experiences. By asking others to "tell me how this works" and "walk me through what you're thinking," they are able to process information, remain impersonal about ideas, and try out aha moments before committing. In the process, lacking the fear of being judged, many people find that they become more confident about trying out insight with others.

HABIT: MAKING THE AHA JOURNEY ROUTINE

How many authors hope their books become obsolete? If this book has helped people embed insight thinking into their daily routines as a habit, then it has done its job and becomes unnecessary. I doubt, though, that will happen right away. Habits are tough to acquire—and to lose—even when we approach them systematically, as Benjamin Franklin tried to do over 200 years ago.

In 1793, a year after he died, Benjamin Franklin's autobiography hit the publishing scene. Originally titled *The Private Life of the Late*

Benjamin Franklin, LL.D. Originally Written By Himself, And Now Translated From The French, it is a fun and remarkable read about the long life of a statesman, inventor, writer, and much more. As a young man, he began his "bold and arduous Project of arriving at moral Perfection," by trying to instill 13 "virtues" into his ongoing behavior. The virtues ranged from frugality to temperance, chastity to humility. Although he later acknowledged that "perfection" is unattainable, his approach to making virtues into habit is worth the price of the book.

Franklin concentrated each week on a single virtue. If it became habit within that week and he did not stray from it, he moved on to the next virtue. His goal was to incorporate one virtue per week, then run through the entire process (focusing on one per week) throughout one year. If he executed the plan perfectly, that would allow him to nearly go through all virtues four times. He failed, since it took more than a week to focus on some virtues. But his notion of building habits is similar to other experts, like William James, who estimated it takes most of us about three weeks to create or eliminate some habit.

Habits take time, and learning to spark aha moments on a regular basis and use insight thinking will definitely demand effort for most of us. Yet, several people I talked to over the years felt it was feasible. Software manager Craig Boobar says that "80% of the time" he has an aha moment in the shower, after he wrestles with and then "sleeps on" a problem. Football player George Iloka's repeated experiences of insight flashes—from both good and bad triggers—give him confidence that they will happen again in the future. Insight thinking, like creativity and innovation, happens when a structure exists to encourage them and repetition and habit set in.

* * *

As people talked about these five characteristics, it became clear that not all exist at the start of every aha journey. In fact, they appear to "build on themselves." In other words, those at the bottom of the pyramid—experience and motivation—appear fundamental; without them, openness, confidence, and habit seem unlikely to emerge. If those characteristics do exist, and openness leads to an aha moment, confidence can build and the journey can repeat. When that happens, and with repeated insight flashes, several people commented that they felt they could count on finding a solution to a messy problem or learning some new concept. Rather than panic, many said it was just a "matter of time." So rather than all five characteristics being necessary at the beginning of the aha journey, they seemed to build and progress as individuals gained more experience with insight thinking.

Also, at least initially, I assumed the five factors applied only to individuals, in terms of the characteristics they needed to generate aha moments. But as Herodotus's comment suggests, having (the ability to generate) insight but no power to use it may lead people to forego even trying to spark aha moments. For insight flashes to occur, an organization's leaders and culture need to nurture the characteristics and the journey. The closing example suggests the power of a leader, even in a context that seems unlikely to generate an aha experience.

UNEXPECTED COLLECTIVE AHA MOMENT

In the United States during World War II, young men from all backgrounds—education, income level, and ethnicity—clamored to join the war effort. Some of the most fervent were American citizens of Japanese descent, who formed one of the most celebrated battalions in the war. The renowned 442nd Infantry Regiment, whose members were Japanese American soldiers, became one of the most decorated units in the war and one with among the highest casualty rates of any equivalent-sized unit in the war.[4] The regiment's renown has grown over the years through a 1951 movie called *Go for Broke*, as well as for its rescue of the so-called "Lost Battalion" of several hundred men surrounded by the Germans in 1944. A war memorial dedicated in 2000 in Washington, D.C., several memoirs and books, as well as research theses have examined different aspects and experiences of the group.

But in the summer of 1943, the celebrated 442nd nearly disbanded before it had a chance to fight in the war. After the invasion of Pearl Harbor on December 7, 1941, the United States had no choice but to enter the ongoing World War II. Shortly after, the Japanese army and navy dominated the Pacific theater and eligible men throughout the United States enlisted in the war effort. In May 1942, partly to recruit more men, but partly to keep an "eye on" the Japanese Americans from Hawaii, the army established a small Hawaiian provisional battalion, later named the 100th Infantry Battalion. During its initial training in Wisconsin, the group received among the highest training ratings in the army.

In the spring of 1943, the battalion transferred to Camp Shelby, Mississippi, for advanced training. There the army renamed the battalion, created the 442nd regiment, and recruited more members. The army intended to build a regiment of some 1,500 volunteers from Hawaii and 3,000 from the mainland, but missed those goals. The anticipated numbers and the actual response by volunteers may have (or at least should have) been an "aha moment" for some army officials. Instead of the hoped-for 1,500 from Hawaii, some 10,000 Hawaiian *Nisei* (second-generation Japanese American young men) volunteered, far beyond what the recruiters had anticipated. The army accepted about 2,600 and sent them to Camp Shelby in May 1943. On the mainland, the recruiting scenario was the reverse from what happened in Hawaii. The army wanted 3,000 Japanese American recruits, which meant it needed many more volunteers to start with. Although there were 23,000 Japanese American men of draftable age on the mainland, only about 1,200 volunteered, 5 percent of the possible volunteers. Of those, 800 were accepted, far fewer than what the army had expected.[5]

The Japanese American soldiers all converged on Camp Shelby, near Hattiesburg, Mississippi, for training. The mainland volunteers arrived in February 1943, followed by the Hawaiians later in the spring. The frustration and anger at the Japanese for bombing Pearl Harbor was, at the time, vented by Caucasians around the country on Asians generally. The resentment in the camp reflected the anger felt throughout the country. Caucasian soldiers taunted and antagonized anyone who looked Asian, including the Japanese Americans from the newly formed 442nd. The fights between the Japanese Americans and Caucasians were frequent and serious, but the tensions between the two groups of Japanese Americans were far worse.

Conflict between the mainland and Hawaiian volunteers was vicious. Each group saw the other as alien. The outnumbered "Mainland Boys" called the Hawaiians "Buddha heads." This was a play on the Japanese word "buta," meaning "pig." They saw the Hawaiians as backward, from a primitive island, with little sophistication or knowledge about life in the "real" United States. The group of volunteers from Hawaii, including Daniel Inouye, who became a U.S. Senator in 1963 and still serves, had an equally dismal view of the "Mainland Boys." They had a derogatory nickname as well, and referred to their unfriendly, aloof counterparts as "kotonks," which is Japanese for "stone head" and is the sound an empty coconut makes when it hits the ground, reflecting what the Hawaiians thought of the mainlanders: empty-headed.

Because the mainland group had arrived at the camp earlier, they held more senior positions and were expected to train the "Hawaii Boys." The Hawaiian volunteers had among the highest IQ scores in the army and were thus frustrated at taking orders from those they perceived to be less intelligent "kotonks." Fights became so frequent that the army talked of disbanding the unit altogether.

Instead, Camp Shelby's commanding officer, Colonel Charles Pence, sent the Hawaiians to visit two nearby concentration camps, which the government called "war relocation camps." During the course of World War II, some 100,000 Japanese Americans lived in those camps, scattered across the United States. Essentially, they were U.S. citizens held captive by their own government. The Hawaiians knew that their mainland counterparts had volunteered for the army out of the internment camps, but had little idea of the conditions in the camps. Katsugo Miho was one of the Hawaiians to visit the camps at Jerome and Rohwer, Arkansas. At one of the camps, he ran into a former teacher.[6]

As Miho recalled, when the bus stopped at the Jerome camp, the rifle-wielding guards frisked the uniformed Hawaiian soldiers, which irritated them. As Miho and others entered the camp, they noticed the "ten-foot-tall barbed-wire fence bordering the encampment," and the four corners with machine gun posts "like a stockade." The whole time the soldiers were in the camp, and after they left, the guards' machine guns pointed toward the Japanese American civilians—old men, women, and children—inside the camp.

The Japanese American civilians were essentially prisoners. They had work assignments in the schools, the infirmary, and the cafeteria, making what Miho called "unreasonable, atrocious wages..." Despite the conditions, however, the civilians in the camps "put up a cheerful front" for the Hawaiian soldiers.

Camp commander Colonel Pence's inspired decision to expose the Hawaiians to the internment camps spurred a collective aha moment, quelling friction between the two groups. Because the mainland soldiers had rarely spoken about where they lived before joining the army, the Hawaiians had little knowledge of the internment camps. Visiting Jerome and Rohwer was the first time they had seen and thought about the conditions in which their mainland counterparts and families lived during the war. To realize their counterparts had volunteered for a country that put its Japanese American citizens into prisons was eye—and mind—opening.

After the Hawaiians returned to Camp Shelby, the fighting stopped and the group coalesced.

The example illustrates that aha moments can occur, even when the surrounding conditions seem destined to prevent them. The members of the regiment did not use the term "collective aha moment," but some of the memoirs seem to suggest that is what happened when the Hawaiians went to the camps. Miho's shock at the conditions, at the wages, and at finding one of his own former teachers in the camps suggests the experience led him to a leap in understanding about the mainland soldiers. So while we have no specific records mentioning "flashes of insight," some clues may suggest that aha moments happened. Also, it appears that several of the characteristics—experience, motivation, openness, confidence, and habit—critical to encourage aha moments in individuals and organizations also existed.

First, the Hawaiians had *enough experience* to recognize discrimination. In the 100th and later 442nd battalions, no Japanese Americans were officers, only Caucasians, which irritated the Japanese Americans. They had heard Caucasians use the phrase "A Jap's a Jap," since they blurred all Asians, lumping Asians of Chinese or Japanese descent into one hated cluster. But the humiliation, anger, and discrimination that really shocked them apparently came when they saw the stark setting of the camps. Those visits became a trigger for insight.

Second, the *motivation* of both groups of Japanese Americans to fight in the war was strong. The unexpectedly high numbers of recruits from Hawaii emphasized the strong commitment to be part of the war effort. The lower number of mainland soldiers may have disappointed some officers, but given the circumstances under which those recruits joined (out of the internment camps), their motivation was also very high. Finally, the trigger from the camp commander, who said essentially "get along or get out" also likely motivated the two groups to fuse and become more committed to each other and to the war.

The camp commander's decision to send the Hawaiians to see their counterparts' "homes" was a way to force their minds and perspectives to open. By seeing the conditions, their curiosity also likely increased. To think that 23,000 mainland Japanese Americans *could* have volunteered but only 1,200 did begged the question, Why did *they*? How could they rationalize fighting for a country that so devastated their families? In that instance, many of the

Hawaiians perhaps also realized they had much to learn from their fellow mainland soldiers.

Colonel Pence appeared to have *confidence* that the Hawaiians could "get it" and that both groups would make a good fighting unit, if only they could get beyond their surface-level divisions. Other clues about some of Colonel Pence's action suggest he was determined to create a culture of tolerance within Camp Shelby and build confidence among the men of the 442nd. In June 1943, for example, he organized a dance for the 442nd men and Japanese American women from the two internment camps; he supposedly chastised, in a visible way, one of his key associates for derogatory language about the Japanese Americans. So perhaps Pence's openness and confidence in the group helped generate the aha moments that the Japanese Americans, and perhaps other Caucasians, needed to bring the 442nd infantry regiment to life.[7]

So in a sense, Pence created an environment to encourage the aha experience, and when the Hawaiians reached that collective aha experience, they realized they could view their counterparts in a new light, which is critical in any aha journey. Setting the tone and environment for that remarkable change in perception shows the power of aha moments.

Finally, the regiment's subsequent performance on the battlefield in Italy, France, and Germany, overcoming many odds in several battles, perhaps also built the soldiers' confidence in problem solving and understanding new situations, which may have led to more of a *habit* of finding creative solutions.

* * *

Making the aha journey routine or habitual is similar to having a structure that makes creativity and innovation systematic parts of

Creating an Aha Moment Habit

- *Experience* to recognize insight

- *Motivation* to want to learn or solve

- *Openness* to ideas that are unexpected

- *Confidence* that insight can happen again

- *Habit* through practice, practice, practice

an organization's activities. While it sounds like a paradox, creativity and innovation do in fact require a disciplined process if they are to occur reliably and regularly. Otherwise, they are left to chance.[8] Likewise, to build "insight muscle memory," organizations and individuals need to use and practice the techniques we have discussed throughout the book.

NOTES

1. Herodotus 484 B.C.–c. 425 B.C.

2. Dorothy Leonard and Walter Swap. 2005. *Deep Smarts: How to Cultivate and Transfer Enduring Business Wisdom*. Boston, MA: Harvard Business School Press: 33.

3. Chad Cripe. 2010. Boise State tops TCU for Fiesta Bowl title, *The Idaho Statesman*, January 5, http://www.idahostatesman.com/newsupdates/story/1030070.html; Pete Thamel. 2010. Boise State cracks open close game with surprise encore of trickery, *The New York Times*, January 5, http://www.nytimes.com/2010/01/05/sports/ncaafootball/05fiesta.html.

4. Several excellent reports describe the famed 442nd battalion of Japanese American (*Nisei*) soldiers during World War II. As a unit, they were the most decorated, but they also suffered among the highest percentage of casualties. Perhaps less known is that when various groups of the soldiers, from Hawaii and the mainland, came together in Camp Shelby, there was almost as much hostility between the groups as between the Japanese and Caucasian troops. See, for example, Katsugo Miho's essay, The Hawai'i Nisei story: Americans of Japanese ancestry during World War II, *The Hawaii Nisei Project*, 2006 (http://nisei.hawaii.edu/object/io_1206615020484.html).

5. The mainland *Nisei* eligible to volunteer were in the internment camps, most likely unenthused about joining an army that had imprisoned the some 100,000 American citizens who were "relocated."

6. Katsugo Miho's essay, The Hawai'i Nisei story: Americans of Japanese ancestry during World War II (http://nisei.hawaii.edu/object/io_1206615020484.html).

7. Pence led the regiment throughout the war as they fought in much of Europe until he was injured in the spring of 1945.

8. Nancy K. Napier and Mikael Nilsson. 2008. *The Creative Discipline: Mastering the Art and Science of Innovation*. Westport, CT: Praeger.

Chapter 12

Connecting the Final Dots

The mind can proceed only so far upon what it knows and can prove. There comes a point where the mind takes a higher plane of knowledge, but can never prove how it got there. All great discoveries have involved such a leap.

—Albert Einstein[1]

The aha journey's goal is to help us "leap" to a higher plane, to reach for insight to understand a complex issue, or to solve a messy problem. To paraphrase Einstein, we may not know just how we got there, but we can certainly nudge the process along, be aware of and use techniques that encourage insight thinking, and create environments that support it.

In the earlier chapters, we have deconstructed the aha journey to understand how it happens and how we can have some control over the process. We may know our goal at the start of the journey—to learn something or solve a problem—but it may change en route, as a result of unexpected opportunities and obstacles. We prepare for the journey by collecting information and equipment, but again, we may find much of it is extraneous and not quite what we need. As we move further along the path, we encounter, sift, and make sense of what we experience. Yet, we can be systematic and have a structure to each stage, whether looking at a problem in new ways, finding alternatives to deal with walls, or taking detours or breaks that fit our own personalities and situations. In this final chapter, we will review key points of the book and talk more about where it may be most helpful for managers.

REVIEWING WHAT WE TALK ABOUT WHEN WE TALK ABOUT AHA MOMENTS

Early on, I proposed several assumptions of what many people think they know about aha moments and then offered revised assumptions. Throughout the book, we examined stages in the aha journey that supported the revised assumptions about aha moments. Let us review some of the most important points.

We Can Encourage Aha Moments

Rather than "coming from nowhere," rather than assuming we have no control over whether or how they may happen, it appears that we can encourage aha moments. To do so, of course, requires work, time, and effort. That work includes defining a problem, sorting information, and using techniques and approaches to thinking that are unfamiliar and uncomfortable for many of us. Several techniques—from putting together odd pieces of information to looking for what is missing—can help individuals or groups of people experience insight, but it means shifting from reaching for "strong associations" in logical, left-side thinking to "weak associations" in right-side thinking. Most people resist such thinking. But by slowing down and consciously trying to use techniques to encourage that shift, we can learn how to think more creatively. With practice, it may even become "habit."

Second, while many people report dramatic and memorable flashes of insight, some report smaller "mini-aha moments" that build to larger ones. The leaps we experience in such cases may be smaller steps, with clarity at each stage of thinking through a problem, building up to a larger solution. Einstein's comment to Besso about having complete clarity on what the problem was came after much thought and effort, and likely some smaller revelations. In finding opportunities to practice insight thinking on smaller problems, we may become better able to generate bigger flashes of insight later.

Next, it seems feasible to nudge aha moments in ourselves and in others. Learning how to encourage aha moments in others is critical for managers, coaches, parents, or anyone trying to help another person "get it" or solve problems more effectively. Presenting the right information, in the right format, at the right time helps move that process along.

Structure Helps

Albert Einstein is famous for his "quirks": routinely wearing the same "uniform"—white shirt, dark trousers, shoes without socks, suspenders, and hat—or taking the same walks to and from work. Such "quirks" provided structure and routine in his life so that his mind was free from mundane decisions and he could focus on his creative work.

So too is this true with creative organizations. Insight thinking, like creativity and innovation, does not just "happen," but rather can be nudged along within a structured process and systemic approach. Many of the individuals I talked with followed the aha journey, almost without realizing it. Others recognized that they used parts of the process but may have "skipped" some stages of it. Once they learned the various phases, they recognized that they could seek to be more conscious in trying to build in the "spark" phase or would use questions more deliberately in trying to define a problem.

It seems paradoxical, but creativity and innovation need structure and discipline if they are to happen regularly. Likewise, for insight thinking to flourish, people need awareness of, attention to, and practice with the aha journey to generate the leaps of imagination that messy problems require. Theater directors, coaches, and managers in creative successful organizations often mention the value of structure or process to their creativity: The structure provides stability within which creativity can thrive. They also report that no structure can *guarantee* creativity or insight will occur; the goal is to increase the likelihood and increase the chances that a leap of imagination and thinking may happen.

Recognizing that insight thinking follows a general path helps us move from confusion to clarity to bringing an idea or solution to public view. The three broad stages—sort, spark, and check—provide some structure to know what general types of activities happen during the aha journey (Figures 12-1 and 12-2). Not all may happen (e.g., some people say they do not need to take a detour), but to understand that there is a common pattern may help us push through to insight flashes more easily.

Context Is Critical

Finally, aha moments happen when conditions support them—when individuals and organizations exhibit experience and motivation to learn or solve a problem, when they are open to new ideas and ways of thinking, and when they have confidence that they

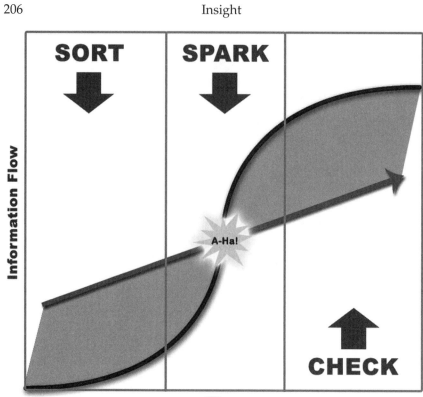

FIGURE 12-1   The AHA Journey

will be able to think using insight. The creative organizations used as examples throughout the book are relentless about pursuing and preserving cultures that encourage risk taking, creativity, and aha moments. Their leaders understand the importance of modeling those behaviors and strive to encourage them in others.

Culture plays a role in organizations, but also emerges in geographic contexts as well. Some of The Gang members that have a choice of location (e.g., Trey McIntyre Project, WhiteCloud Analytics) have decided to move to or remain in Boise, Idaho, in part because of the community's entrepreneurial risk-taking spirit. Such cultural drivers may well have quite different impacts in other parts of the United States and world. In Germany, for example, technology, engineering, and logical thinking dominate much of the business world; risk taking and entrepreneurship—especially start-ups that fail—are not routinely embraced as positive. Avoiding risk could translate into avoiding insight thinking and creativity

SORT

- **Collecting Information:**
  what we look for, what comes to us
- **Organizing Information:**
  chunk it, rank it
- **Processing Information:**
  try it out, reshuffle, talk it out,
  use time, fuzzy framework

SPARK

- **Combining 'Odd' Pieces of Information**
- **Thinking in 'Reverse'**
- **Seeing What's NOT There**
- **Hitting a Wall**
- **Taking a Detour**
  ...AHA!

CHECK

- **Testing Against Theory**
- **Testing with 'Besso'**
- **Testing on a 'Barmaid'**
- **Looking in the Rearview Mirror**

FIGURE 12-2   Stages of the Insight Process

as well. In Vietnam, Confucian tenets have long been part of the culture, and some could well affect how much aha moments could be encouraged in others. Hierarchy is generally very structured, which could limit the flow of information, especially from bottom to top, and the use of questions (because that might show lack of knowledge, which a manager cannot) or encouragement of risk taking. If such conditions of culture in places like Germany or Vietnam do exist, how likely will insight thinking be? In global organizations that operate in diverse cultures, managers need to be aware that encouraging aha moments (at all) may be a bigger challenge in settings that do not encourage insight thinking.

WHAT IS NEXT?

For managers and others to get the most value from understanding and using the aha journey process, they face more work, alas! First, the process of having insights must continue and the results must be of higher quality. Second, if the insight thinking process is something that can be learned and practiced, can we then speed up learning and problem solving? Finally, does this framework really work in all types of settings? We will look at each in turn.

Making the Aha Journey a Continuous Process

One of the most important points of the book is that the aha journey can be repeated and eventually become habit. Indeed, the value gained from one or a cluster of aha moments fades over time, as it becomes part of a person's ongoing experience and behavior. Boise State University football player George Iloka had an initial insight flash in high school when he realized he could influence his destiny in terms of how he played football, once he had the chance. He used that realization as a matter of course in his college career and then boosted it up a notch with another aha moment: the comment from the coaches that he needed to act more like a leader, with new behaviors and ways of thinking about himself and of others. The coaches experienced leaps themselves, in understanding and creating an environment and culture that models and supports behaviors that inspire risk taking and confidence. ProClarity co-founder Bob Lokken recognized the links between the brain and Internet browser use; he has capitalized on that with other business ideas and moved beyond in the latest venture (WhiteCloud Analytics) to come up with creative aha moments to help hospitals improve practices. Finally, Albert Einstein also had insights that built upon one another—about problems relating to time and light and gravity.

As each flash of insight becomes part of a person or organization, then others build on top of it. In some cases, the aha experience brings us into deeper understanding of our experience and knowledge. In other cases, it builds upon previous aha moments to generate new ideas and solutions to problems.

Going Deeper

During the American War in Vietnam (early 1960s to 1975), the Vietnamese living in the south built entire villages underground. The 75-mile network of the Cu Chi Tunnels, about 160 miles from Saigon, were invisible from above ground, except for an entry hole that often held sharpened bamboo trunks to impale unsuspecting American soldiers who happened upon them. The tunnels were about a yard wide and tall enough for a ten-year-old child to stand up in, and they went deeper and deeper underground, built like an ant farm. Scores of Vietnamese hid and worked in the tunnels; life went on as children were born and the elderly died.

Foreigners who worked in Vietnam during the 1990s often used the Cu Chi tunnels as a metaphor for trying to understand the situations we were involved in, the decisions that Vietnamese people made, or actions that organizations took, which fit no framework we knew. Even as we built an understanding of the culture and the way things worked, we were blindsided over and over.

In my more than 15 years of working in Vietnam, I have often thought I reached a level of deep understanding of the culture, the people, and their behaviors, only to discover I could not explain some experience, based on what I knew before: Another deeper layer or level of culture, more subtle than the others, was at play. Just as we reach an aha moment of understanding or resolution of a problem, we face another situation that requires us yet again to reorient our thinking and plunge down another level, like the tunnels.

Building upon Previous Aha Moments

Another way to explain the continuing aha journey is that subsequent insight flashes may build upon prior ones in a continuous process. Once we have an aha experience and generate value because of it, the benefit often seems to lose its power over time. For Gary Raney to realize that the inmate escape was a symptom of complacency in his organization, he used that insight to generate some major changes in the way he managed the sheriff's office. But he did not stop with that insight; he went further to see other means to improve, to learn, and ultimately to build upon the insight experience.

In a sense, the process of repeatedly better and stronger aha experiences looks like upward waves, continuing S curves or insight curves that build on each other (Figure 12-3). Presumably, with each new insight experience, we use that to build upon it, as Iloka, Raney, and Lokken did in improving their abilities to play, manage, and discover new business ventures. By repeating the aha journey, we practice it, and with practice, we embed the process and techniques and, eventually, make it habit. And that is key to the next step—speeding up the process of learning and problem solving through the aha journey.

Can We Speed Up Learning and Problem Solving?

As I mentioned in the beginning of the book, when I first began to interview people about aha moments, most had very firm assumptions. One of the biggest was that aha moments happened by chance and were not something they could encourage. And yet, as we talked, some slowly realized that they had—without being conscious of it—in fact developed methods for encouraging aha moments: They had learned how to absorb lots of information, they found techniques that helped them shift to insight thinking, and many tested their ideas—by talking or other means. So, they

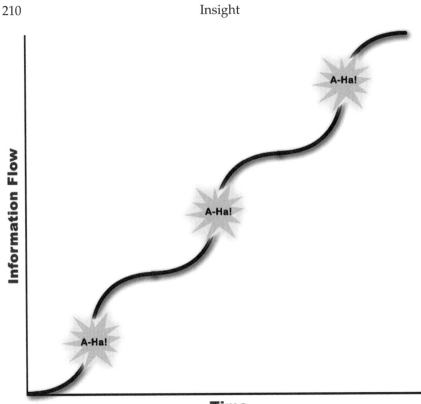

FIGURE 12-3   A Continuous Process

in fact had developed the "habit" of the insight experience, even if
they did not explicitly notice.

As the discussion about habit in Chapter 11 suggests, we can
learn and embed behaviors and ways of thinking with time and
effort. And with that habit—whether how to tackle a receiver in
football, how to start a new business, or how to swing a golf club
—many people begin to "speed up" learning and problem solving.
In essence, we learn to jump to the "spark" phase more quickly,
allowing us to "shift" the insight curve to the left, shortening the
time it may take for some problem or challenge (Figure 12-4).

Interestingly, the football group may be one of the best tests
for whether the learning and aha experience can speed up. Several
of the Boise State University football coaches commented,
unprompted, that players (now) take about 18 months to "get it,"
to understand their own positions but also the program's system,
including culture and way of operating. This contrasts with the
comment that Head Coach Chris Petersen made several years ago

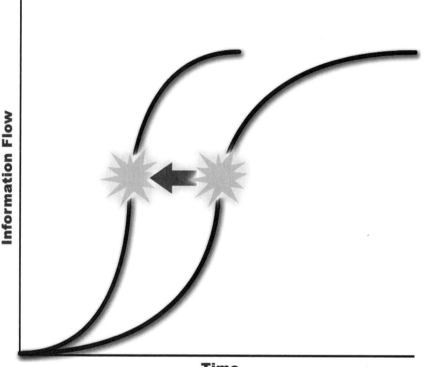

FIGURE 12-4   Speeding the Process

that many players needed 2 to 2.5 years to "get it." So perhaps the coaches and the players are finding ways to learn and speed up the aha experience.

Now, of course, this may not always hold, as Einstein made clear when he took *more* time on his subsequent aha experiences than he did in 1905. His challenges and the problems he tackled later were much more difficult, some would say impossible, than the earlier ones. Yet even for those of us who may not be in Einstein's universe, it appears that we can learn how to encourage the aha experience, and in essence, speed up the process of learning or problem solving.

Does the Aha Experience Work Across All Settings?

Part of the reason I looked at so many different organizations during this project was to see whether the aha experience phases made sense across various fields. Toward the end of the project, I returned to The Gang organizations to check the validity of the framework. It generally made sense to the group members, but each group offered critical observations that strengthened the framework and made it applicable for different types of situations—for people involved in physical movement (e.g., dancers and football players), in settings that were heavily analytical (e.g., software engineering), or in more emotional areas (e.g., art and theater).

The focus in this book has been on the aha journey largely as a way to learn/understand and as a way to solve problems, and primarily in organizations based in the United States. A next step is to see whether the framework applies in new environments and on new types of questions. First, for the framework to have value for organizations that operate globally, the process should hold in other cultural settings. At present, that is an open question. While I have talked to colleagues in Europe—the United Kingdom, Denmark, and Italy—and they find it logical, I have less understanding about whether it will work in Vietnam or Ghana or Mexico. Trying out and refining this aha journey framework—and perhaps changing it in unexpected ways—is a future challenge that could have real benefits to managers in global organizations or anyone who works with diverse groups of people.

In addition, if the model works, it should be applicable to other types of situations, including problem finding, not just solving. Many of the people I spoke with on this project—from Gary Raney to Bob Lokken or even to student George Iloka—said outright or implied that finding the correct problem to solve was sometimes "bigger" than the solution. For Raney, it meant moving beyond the escape and security. For Lokken, it was understanding that a software product should be driven by the users' thinking processes, not by the intriguing technological questions that so captivate software developers. For Iloka, it was that his running skills were not the issue as much as his attitude and persistence, as well as discovering that he could change the course of his athletic and academic career, not others. Once they identified the correct problem, the solutions seemed almost to fall into place. Thus, if the aha moment process is useful in helping us define the many messy problems we will face in coming years, maybe then we can speed up their solutions as well.

As we started the book, let us close with Einstein, who has the last word and gets it right.

The years of anxious searching in the dark for a truth that one feels but cannot express, the intense desire and the alternations of confidence and misgiving until one achieves clarity and understanding, can be understood only by those who have experienced them.[2]

NOTES

1. Ronald W. Clark. 2001. *Einstein: The Life and Times*. New York: Avon (paperback).

2. From a lecture at the University of Glasgow, June 20, 1933. Published in *The Origins of the Theory of Relativity*, reprinted in *Mein Weltbild*, 138, and *Ideas and Opinions*, 289–290. In Alice Calaprice. 2000. *The Expanded Quotable Einstein*. Princeton, NJ: Princeton University Press.

Index

About the Author

Nancy K. Napier (Ph.D., The Ohio State University) is Professor of International Business and Executive Director of the Centre for Creativity and Innovation at Boise State University. She managed Boise State's nine-year involvement in an $8.5 million capacity building project at the National Economics University in Hanoi, Vietnam, funded by the Swedish International Cooperation Development Agency and USAID. Her most recent books are *Insight: Encouraging Aha! Moments for Organizational Success* and *The Creative Discipline: Mastering the Art and Science of Innovation.* Her articles appear in such journals as *Creativity and Innovation Management, Journal of Management Psychology, International Journal of Cross-Cultural Management, Journal of Management Inquiry, Human Resource Management Journal, Academy of Management Review, Journal of Management Studies,* and *Journal of International Business Studies.* She is also co-creator and host of *Idaho Business Matters,* a weekday radio program on NPR News 91.